The Journey of James Boswell and Samuel Johnson Through Scotland, August–November, 1773

T
H
S
E
A
D

Whisky, Kilts, and the Loch Ness Monster

Elgin Cathedral

Whisky, Kilts, and the Loch Ness Monster

Traveling through Scotland with Boswell and Johnson

William W. Starr

The University of South Carolina Press

© 2011 University of South Carolina

Published by the University of South Carolina Press
Columbia, South Carolina 29208

www.sc.edu/uscpress

Manufactured in the United States of America

20 19 18 17 16 15 14 13 12 11
10 9 8 7 6 5 4 3 2 1

Library of Congress Cataloging-in-Publication Data
Starr, William W., 1940–
Whisky, kilts, and the Loch Ness Monster : traveling through
Scotland with Boswell and Johnson / William W. Starr.
p. cm.
Includes bibliographical references and index.
ISBN 978-1-57003-948-5 (cloth : alk. paper)
1. Starr, William W., 1940– —Travel—Scotland.
2. Scotland—Description and travel. 3. Starr, William W.,
1940– —Travel--Scotland—Hebrides. 4. Johnson, Samuel,
1709–1784—Travel—Scotland—Hebrides. 5. Boswell, James,
1740–1795—Travel--Scotland—Hebrides. I. Title.
DA867.5.S73 2010
914.1104'73—dc22
2010020165

This book was printed on Glatfelter Natures,
a recycled paper with 30 percent postconsumer waste content.

Contents

Acknowledgments

Many people contributed in many ways toward making this book a pleasure to research and write. I'm grateful to each, including those few who said they'd prefer not to be mentioned.

Since I've been employed full-time—and gratefully so—throughout the time it took to undertake my trip to Scotland and subsequent writing and research, I want to thank my boss, Darro Willey, director of the DeKalb County Public Library. He was a consistent supporter and somehow managed to find the ways to make it possible for me to get the time I desperately needed over a period of several years. My thanks also go to the entire staff at the DeKalb Library, many of whom responded kindly and quickly to my numerous questions. Rob Jenkins and Jack Riggs at the Writers Institute at Georgia Perimeter College generously supplied space and encouragement during the early stages of writing. The friends who helped me secure a cottage in the western North Carolina mountains for an extended period of writing furthered my work more than they could have imagined. Peter, Phil, Terry, Tom (both of you), Jack, George, and Pat all offered cheering words when I needed them.

There were many people in Scotland who enlightened me in so many aspects of Scottish culture and who made my journey a joy and an inspiration. I still miss their company: Kenny, Frances, and Roger in Stirling; Helen in Inverary; John in Fionnphort; Philip and Debra on Skye; David on Raasay; Susan and Ronnie on Lewis; Angus, Alistair, and Anna in Ullapool; Martin in Durness; Paul and Elaine in Thurso; Greg and Lesley on the Orkneys; Liz and Peter at Inverness; Lady Russell at Ballindolloch Castle; Jim in Pitlochry; Loris in Arbroath; Maureen at Auchinleck; and John in Edinburgh. There are others, including some helpful librarians, and I am most appreciative for your assistance. I happily absolve all of the above for any responsibility for my errors.

To the people of Scotland, for whom I have discovered a deep and abiding affection, my thanks for accepting me during the too-brief time I visited. A stranger asking nonstop questions about Boswell and Johnson couldn't have been high on their welcoming list, but the truth is I never felt anything less than welcome.

And to the staff at the University of South Carolina Press, long my favorites, I thank you for your careful work on my manuscript. I am grateful for your professionalism and friendship.

I am happy and grateful to acknowledge the remarkable generosity shown me by the talented staff at Lenz Marketing in Decatur, Georgia. My special thanks go to Richard Lenz for his unstinting support and to the gifted artist Matt Tinsley, who planned and created the delightful jacket for this book as well as the helpful chapter heading maps. Matt was a pleasure to work with—full of terrific ideas and rich imagination—and he possessed the artistry to make them happen.

Finally, thanks go to my extended family, past and present. Your love, acceptance, or toleration has been valued more than you could possibly imagine.

Introduction

The plane eased through the silver sky toward the sun-swept runway at Edinburgh International Airport. "Looks like we caught a good trade-off this morning," said the flight attendant as she herded the last group of empty peanut wrappers into her portable depository. "We're three hours late, but it's usually pouring rain when we get here. Not bad, huh?" No, not at all. A first-time visitor to Scotland might assume the appearance of the sun to be perfectly ordinary, but then you remember the joke—at least it's supposed to be a joke—that the Scots offer this greeting to visitors: "Hello; sorry about the weather." And then there are the words of Edmund Burt, as true today as when they were written in 1720: "In these northern parts, the year is composed of nine months winter and three months bad weather." Or Edward Topham, who wrote in 1774 that "the winds reign in all their violence, and seem indeed to claim the country as their own." Of course, anyone who reads a travel guide should know to expect the worst, for this is a country that embraces magnificent climatological legends. All true and all understated.

They begin with rain followed by showers, followed by a heavy rain, drenching rain, a bit of rain, light showers, a soft rain, lightening showers, driving rain, a forcing rain, easing showers, a touch of dampness, pouring rain, horizontal rain, sleety rain, rainy sleet. And did I mention the wind? Howling, screeching, relentless, hurricanelike, a hard blow, a light blow, pushing breezes, gusts, gentle gusts, hard gusts, moderate gusts, intense gusts, and, one of my favorites, blowing gusts. Winter gales start in September and can last until the end of April, when they become only intermittent, says one American who has lived for a dozen years in the Outer Hebrides. Wester Ross is the wettest place in all of the United Kingdom and gets more than two hundred inches of rain each year. And everywhere in the Highlands and Islands gets not only rain but that seemingly never-ending wind as well.

Everyone writes about it, everyone talks about it, visitor and native alike. "Motor vehicles are regularly pushed off the roads or flipped over by the wind; debris flies through the air as if in some hurricane-hit shanty town," wrote one observer seventy years ago. And nearly 250 years ago, another Scottish visitor wrote this amazing passage: "Not many days ago an Officer, whom I have the honour of being acquainted with, a man of six feet high, and, one would imagine, by no means calculated to become the sport of winds, was, however, in following another gentleman out of [Edinburgh] Castle, lifted up by their violence from the ground, carried over his companion's head, and thrown at some distance on the stones." Scots find their doors blown open, their homes blown down. One gentleman walking through Edinburgh on one windy eighteenth-century afternoon found a lady's petticoats blown over her head; as he attempted to "conceal her charms from public view," another gentleman not so oblivious concentrated so hard on the view that he failed to hold on to his hat and wig, which gustily blew him bald.

And no one is spared. In Queen Victoria's *Highland Journals* in 1860, she observed it was "a misty, rainy morning" followed by, "It became cold and windy with occasional rain," and later by "a thoroughly wet day." There was a photo in the newspaper the other day of Sean Connery carrying an umbrella. "Braveheart" probably had one, too. In Scotland pleasant weather can be as rare as a single malt served on ice.

But in fact the sun was shining, quite gloriously, and when I stepped out of the terminal after reclaiming my baggage and passed by a smiling, courteous customs officer, it was time to put on dark glasses and take off the hefty-weight sweater I prudently wore in expectation of the worst Scotland could throw at me. The lovely day was both harbinger and deceiver for what was ahead, for I had no idea I would be traveling through the wildest, most isolated parts of the Highlands and Islands in the spring months in what would turn out to be Scotland's warmest, sunniest months in nearly a century. But that is getting ahead of myself.

I had come to Scotland 234 years after James Boswell and Samuel Johnson made their celebrated journey through the Highlands in 1773 at the apogee of the Scottish Enlightenment. Theirs was an amazing adventure, a trip almost unimaginable today, through many poorly marked or uncharted landscapes, with only a few servants and friends of Boswell they met occasionally along the way. They encountered travel calamities of the most daunting sort of which those of us in the early twenty-first century could hardly conceive. Boswell was thirty-three, Johnson almost twice his age at sixty-three when he began the journey. Lacking planes, trains, cars, paved roads, and sometimes roads of any type, they made their way by horse, on foot, and by ship through a wild, remote, strange, and rugged landscape known to only a handful of the occupants of the eighteenth-century world.

Their journey occurred well before the age of tourism, certainly long before visitors had any thoughts of a fun trip to Scotland for a taste of castles, tartans, and "Braveheart." The eighteenth-century novelist Tobias Smollett wrote that "The English knew as little of Scotland as of Japan." In his 1771 novel *Humphrey Clinkr* Smollett has one character imagine that "she could not go to Scotland but by sea." Most travelers who departed England in the eighteenth century never imagined touring Scotland; instead they hotfooted it to the Continent to partake of what was called The Grand Tour. Edinburgh was a destination city at the time, a center of education and commerce. But its natives were openly disbelieving when a traveler showed up in November 1774 solely for the purpose of visiting. It was much as if a modern-day American had ventured to Kabul "just to enjoy a little vacation time."

Johnson, the preeminent man of letters in eighteenth-century England, and Boswell, a literary figure whose stature would only increase with his books about Johnson, left us two remarkable accounts of their epic adventure: Johnson's *Journey to the Western Isles of Scotland,* published in 1775, and Boswell's *Journal of a Tour to the Hebrides,* published in 1785. Johnson's book focused mostly on his thoughts about the people and places he saw; Boswell wrote mostly about Johnson. Even with their different approaches, both books wound up as monuments of English literature and travel writing. Simply put, they are classics, entertaining readers over the ages and giving them a remarkably vivid portrait of the two men and their times.

And yet—Boswell and Johnson and their accomplishments seem to be little remembered outside the well-kept fields of academe these days. I did a modest, unscientific survey of about two dozen librarians and high school teachers recently, asking them to identify Boswell and Johnson in some way, *any* way. The results were not encouraging. Only eight got it right, or close; one was sure I meant Ben Jonson, the seventeenth-century English dramatist. Only six could identify the correct century. Only two had read Boswell's magisterial biography, *The Life of Samuel Johnson, LL.D.* No one had read Boswell's *Journal* or Johnson's *Journey.* At least no one was proud of their ignorance. I figured their students would be even worse off. And adults in general, at least the ones who read, probably wouldn't fare much better in my little quiz, I reasoned.

That was discouraging, to say the least. But it also seemed to open some opportunities for me. Boswell and Johnson, after all, are two of the most intriguing figures in all of the history of England and Scotland, and the books they wrote are among the finest in all of English literature. Their journey to Scotland in 1773 was an extraordinary event by every measure—it received almost celebrity newspaper coverage and comment at the time—that helped awaken and change public attitudes about that nation; even so, it seems to be among the least remembered of their achievements by so many readers today.

But putting aside all the history and literature for a moment, consider that their jaunt through Scotland was packed with amusing scenes, eventful moments, revealing insights into the two travelers and the places they went and the people they met. What they wrote is, more than two centuries after their books appeared in print, still lively fun to read. And reading Boswell and Johnson is not and should not be an academic exercise; with a little background and updating, where they went and what they did should be savored by today's readers no less deliciously than the writings were devoured by Boswell's and Johnson's contemporaries. There were no rock stars or television personalities for public adoration in the eighteenth century, but an educated public lionized literary figures, and Johnson especially and Boswell to a lesser extent were at the top, the equivalent—sort of—of Madonna or Bono today.

And so, I resolved to try to fill the gap, as it were: to bring Boswell and Johnson and their world into ours. Not by writing a biography of the two; there are plenty of good existing biographies to satisfy all tastes. Nor did I want to provide a travel guide for someone headed to Scotland; they also exist in plentiful numbers. My goal was much simpler in design: to find Boswell and Johnson in 1773, to hear again their experiences in their words, and to write about what they saw with a latter-day perspective. There are, I feel confident, too many curious readers who are not familiar with or who may have forgotten the memorable 1773 journey, though the 2009 observance of the tercentenary of Johnson's birth may have caught their attention with its proliferation of books about Dr. Johnson and his life and world.

Boswell and Johnson were the reason why I flew three thousand miles to Scotland—and would add 2,789 additional miles in the country before my trip ended—in an effort to retrace their journey, as much as possible so many years later. I knew their words would be perfect traveling companions for me, refreshing my mind and my eye. I would miss conversing with those two wonderful conversationalists, of course. They were dead, and nothing's to be done about that. But their writings about the trip are so informative, so chatty, so opinionated, and so lively that I would be unfailingly entertained on my own journey. And they would be my brilliant companions, my keen guides, my wise and witty inspirations, my mean angels.

I also believed that following Boswell and Johnson was too important and too much fun to be left solely in the hands of scholars. As a longtime newspaper book editor and critic, I came to admire and respect the outstanding historians who could also write. I did come to understand that there were not a lot of them, at least when it came to producing books accessible to a general readership. In nearly thirty-five years as a critic, I thought I had earned a Ph.D. in reading incomprehensibly written histories. So my approach, I vowed, would be closer to that of a good student rather than a teacher, someone constantly curious, always open to the new or unusual, alert to nuance and detail, and someone who loved a good story. It didn't have to be absolutely true, either. Scotland, after all, is a nation all about myths, as we will see. I wanted to understand all of Scotland better with the hope of enriching and enlarging my experiences, and not in just the places Boswell and Johnson visited. At the least, I wanted to begin with no agendas or prejudices beyond a shameless affection for Boswell and Johnson. And I hoped my approach would have something less than the sour tone of the English journalist Charles Jennings, who described Scotland as "the dour granitic wedge atop the British Isles." Without all the baggage an Englishman brings to the subject, I thought I might be able to keep a more open mind.

Having read about the lives of both Boswell and Johnson for well over two decades, I knew I had made some assumptions that not all readers would be aware of or share. So it seems appropriate to offer a little background on the two men and why their journey mattered then, and now, two centuries later.

Johnson was the best-known literary figure in England in the mid- and latter parts of the eighteenth century, largely because of his *Dictionary of the English Language* (1755), a work he spent nine years completing and which went into five editions just during his lifetime. It is no less breathtaking an achievement now than it was then, even though it wasn't the first dictionary of the English language, nor the most comprehensive, nor even the most accurate. But it was an amazingly faithful record of the language as it was in his age, and it showed a unifying, incisive intelligence at work on every page. It also was—and is—the only dictionary that remains a great work of literature. Its authority extended well into the nineteenth century when it was basically superseded by the *Oxford English Dictionary,* which itself lifted more than 1,700 definitions directly from Johnson. Johnson acknowledged that he did his work well, but he also admitted that it was flawed. He wrote, with modesty, "Dictionaries are like watches, the worst is better than none, and the best cannot be expected to go quite true."

He produced many highly regarded works, among them *Rasselas* and the poem "The Vanity of Human Wishes." His *Lives of the Poets* remains an indispensable biographical commentary. His writings on Shakespeare's plays are among the most perceptive observations we have on that canon. His numerous essays for *The Idler* and *The Rambler* are incisive and instructive. He wrote poems, prayers, sermons, and commentaries on a variety of topics. And there is, of course, his *Journey to the Western Islands of Scotland.* His pen and his tongue could both inspire and diminish. He enjoyed a well-deserved reputation as the brightest mind and sharpest tongue of his time. His conversation was elevated, pithy, and cranky and frightened lesser wits with its slashing barbs.

His many curmudgeonly comments on Scotland readily attest to what his contemporaries had to put up with and why many Scots feared his coming. To wit: "Much may be made of a Scotchman, if he be caught young." And, "Sir, the noblest prospect which a Scotchman ever sees is the high road that leads him to England." And about his hostess at one stop on the Scottish tour: "The woman would sink a ninety gun ship, she is so dull, so heavy." You get the idea. Brilliant. Clever. Amusing. And he could be a trial.

Johnson was English-born, 1709, in Litchfield, and left his native country only twice—the first time when he joined Boswell in Scotland—before his death in 1784. He married once, in 1735, but his marriage may not have been a happy one, and his wife died rather early on, leaving Johnson's sexual feelings undiminished, possibly adding layers of guilt to his existence, and certainly providing fodder for biographers two centuries later. Physically he was an imposing man, and not always for good reason. Boswell sketched him at an older age in the opening of his *Journal of a Tour to the Hebrides,* and his description offers us a revealing, close-up view of Johnson. He was tall—about six feet—large, robust, "approaching to the gigantic, and grown unwieldy from corpulency," in Boswell's words. With a pockmarked face, he could be seen as almost repellent, and indeed some small children were frightened by him. He was affected by a palsy that set his head and arms often in motion and made him seem awkward and either terrifying or comical when he walked. He suffered from bad knees, bouts of gout, hearing loss, and a crushing depression. "Poised dangerously between control and madness, between doubt, fear and faith, tormented by the dread of loneliness and death and lacerated by physical as well as mental sickness, he often feared he would fall into madness," writes one of his most recent biographers, the Anglo-American writer Peter Martin. Johnson was a mess, physically and sometimes emotionally.

And he was full of contradictions. In spite of a deep and profound faith that colored his life, he worried that his place in heaven would be denied. Near death, he experienced acute guilt that he had not lived up to God's expectations. In spite of tremendously successful literary endeavors throughout his life, he feared the sin of sloth, which he despised. And remember, at an age when most men were sedentary if not close to the grave, he willingly undertook a physically testing journey to Scotland, and he did so in high spirits, more cheerful and positive through the experience than anyone could have anticipated.

Through all of his struggles and his ailments, mental and physical, Johnson survived to the age of seventy-six, and when he died he was more than a scholar and well-known writer: he was a celebrity, at least in the eighteenth-century sense. "I believe there is hardly a day which there is not something about me in the newspapers," he told Boswell. The press reported on his every move, his visits and his visitors, and there was concern expressed over every turn of his health and, ultimately, over his passing.

Today Johnson's reputation is formidable, and he is not merely admired but also honored and even venerated. The tercentenary generated at least three lengthy, new biographies and dozens of shorter studies. There are exceptions, of course. The author Bill Bryson, in his otherwise cheerful book *Notes from a Small Island* (1996), labeled Dr. Johnson "a tedious old git." But in spite of that, and some occasional scholarly quibbles mostly over style, Johnson's legacy seems assured. There are Johnson societies all over the globe, and his cultural impact may be gauged by the impressive number of appearances his words make in the *Oxford Dictionary of Quotations*. Academic studies flourish. New books and new admirers flourish, and a huge collected edition of his works, now more than seventeen volumes, is under way from the Yale University Press.

James Boswell is a bit of a different story. His monumental book, *The Life of Samuel Johnson, LL.D.*, published in 1791, is by just about any measure the finest biography ever written in the English language and one of the great books of our civilization. It was a "Bible" for Robert Louis Stevenson, who said "I mean to read him now until the day I die." *The Life*, despite its limitations, gives us a warts-included portrait of Johnson as a great man and is packed with unforgettable scenes of the man and the age. It also shows us the depth and humanity of Dr. Johnson and his unquenchable, relentless zest for life. It is fun to read, too.

So it should not be astonishing to realize that *The Life* has never gone out of print. It became a best-seller in London on the day of its publication, and it went through an astounding forty-one editions during the nineteenth century alone. New editions appeared constantly in the twentieth century, and a new one already has been published in the first decade of the twenty-first. Boswell wrote many essays and short pieces along with two other books that brought him a measure of literary fame during his lifetime: *An Account of Corsica* (1768), largely unknown these days, and his *Journal of a Tour to the Hebrides*. Of those two books, Boswell's latest biographer, Peter Martin, writes, "They are like silvery minnows swimming around a majestic whale." Smaller by comparison to *The Life* it is, but Boswell's *Journal* is a majestic work on its own considerable merits. In Johnson, Boswell had "a character as good as was ever invented by a novelist," and in writing about him Boswell's artistry and imagination leapt. But the Hebridean book is a first-rate travel account, and Boswell was a first-rate traveler, physically tough and resilient, curious and eager and showing good humor even in some occasionally poisonous situations. His is a book that entertains and instructs.

Boswell was a Lowland Scot, born in 1740 in Edinburgh, who spent much of his later life in his native country. He traveled over the Continent widely as a young man, from Amsterdam to Germany to Switzerland, Italy, Corsica, and France. He did that to establish his creative reputation, partly to avoid becoming a soldier and partly to elude the clutches of his stern, often overbearing Calvinistic father, a judge who wanted his son to follow him into the legal profession. If it had not been for Johnson, Boswell might have emerged as the best-known depressive of his day. He suffered from melancholia, a fairly common eighteenth-century malady that at times for him meant a debilitating depression that could stop him in his tracks. He regularly experienced profound, dispiritingly low periods followed by times when his spirits were high and exuberant. These contradictory periods, however, induced in him a restlessness that was a key part of his personality reflected in his frequent erratic behavior. He was well-educated, and did in fact become a lawyer, honest, sensitive to a fault, and possessing a strong and curious mind. His writing gifts were substantial and gave him abundant confidence.

He was at once a good husband, a loving father, a violently uncontrollable man, an alcoholic, and a sex addict who, to put it pleasantly, took his delights (and subsequent sexually transmitted diseases) from a succession of prostitutes throughout his life. Remarkably he kept diaries and journals in which he courageously—or foolishly—recorded his behavior as well as his repeated vows of repentance and renewal. Alas, he too frequently seemed to fall off the wagon and right on top of one of the lower-class of women. His contemporaries were largely aware of these propensities—and so was his wife, increasingly through their relationship—but the eighteenth century didn't frown on them in the same way that more moralistic societies before and since have done. His wife, however, did. The venereal diseases he contracted throughout his life, along with the recurring melancholia, might seem to have diminished his geniality, yet by all accounts he remained publicly the most convivial and open of men. Vigor he possessed in abundance. A ribald love of life never deserted him. Few enjoyed a party as much as Boswell, almost to the end. And Johnson loved his younger friend.

Boswell's wife died in 1789, and he was a widower until his death in 1795 at the age of fifty-five. His papers disappeared from public view, most likely because one of his executors was quite conservative and found Boswell's accounts too shocking to consider for publication or even for private eyes. Some papers may have been destroyed. Boswell's personal reputation, after all, was dismal, and there was little call for the journals and other materials, whatever they might be. So while Boswell's *Life of Johnson* endured and flourished, biographers cast Boswell as a "sot" and a "buffoon" who was struck by lightning and given a moment of genius to write his book before sinking back into a bog of misbehavior. Charitable scholars called him a "child" who never grew up.

A scattering of Boswell's papers appeared as early as the 1830s, but it was really in the 1920s with the incredible story of the discoveries of his journals in Ireland that the rehabilitation of his image began in earnest. That great adventure story has been well told by the great Boswell scholar Dr. Frederick A. Pottle and others. The results of the finds—they continue to this day—have enabled scholars to see Boswell in a different light and his work as anything but undisciplined. Boswell was, we now know, a careful student, an industrious researcher, and a thoughtful writer and editor (who had help and encouragement from a friend and Shakespearean scholar, Edmond Malone). His personal life—for all its manifold shortcomings—exposed a complex humanity that marked him, to my mind, as the most fascinating figure of the eighteenth century, more so even than his celebrated biographical subject.

Hundreds of books by and about Boswell, reassessing his life and work, have appeared over the last sixty years, including multivolume sets of his journals, letters, and other materials. Many have been published by Yale University Press in an ongoing series that is now nearly fifty years in the making. His *Journal of a Tour to the Hebrides* has undergone a bit of a tangled publishing history that readers may find interesting. The first edition in 1785 was heavily edited to obscure potentially upsetting passages, and those editions that followed in Boswell's lifetime had also been cut and words and phrases had been censored. Modern versions, however—those published under Pottle's editorship in 1936 and later and the most recent one edited by Ronald Black, for instance—give us what Boswell actually wrote in 1773 while he was on the tour with Johnson. Those modern versions are much more intimate and detailed, and they give us much clearer views of Boswell's heart and mind as well as of Johnson's language.

So how did Johnson and Boswell happen to get together in Scotland? Boswell was the promoter and planner, to be sure, but it was a trip that seemed inevitable almost from their first meeting in 1763 in London. Boswell had long been an admirer of Johnson's literary efforts, especially his essays and the *Dictionary of the English Language*. Typical of Boswell, he had been seeking ways of effectively ingratiating himself into Johnson's circle of friends. This he accomplished; Boswell truly was good at these sorts of things. Some thought him a sycophant, though hardly anyone who knew him could resist his boyish charm and energy. The proximity to Johnson, of course, provided the underpinning for what eventually would become *The Life of Johnson*. It turns out that Johnson found the younger man quite engaging if occasionally a trial. And though he disapproved of Boswell's misbehaviors, he accepted them, which is our strongest evidence of Johnson's qualities of grace and tolerance.

From the beginning both men evinced a fascination with the most isolated regions of Scotland. Johnson began his *Journey* with this statement: "I had desired to visit the Hebrides, or Western Islands of Scotland, so long, that I scarcely remember how the wish was originally excited; and was in the Autumn of the year 1773 induced to undertake the journey, by finding in Mr. Boswell a companion, whose acuteness would help my inquiry, and whose gaiety of conversation and civility of manners are sufficient to counteract the inconveniences of travel, in countries less hospitable than we have passed."

In the opening pages of his *Journal of a Tour to the Hebrides* Boswell recalled that Johnson as a younger man had read and been intrigued by Scottish explorer Martin Martin's 1703 book, *A Description of the Western Islands of Scotland*. Boswell wrote, "Dr. Johnson had for many years given me hopes that we should go together and visit the Hebrides. Martin's Account of those islands had impressed us with a notion that we might there contemplate a system of life almost totally different from what we had been accustomed to see; and to find simplicity and wildness, and all the circumstances of remote time or place, so near to our native great island, was an object within the reach of reasonable curiosity."

Boswell and Johnson discussed the prospect of the trip on a number of occasions from 1763 to 1773. The Johnson scholar Pat Rogers suggests Johnson had some other motives, too, including making "an autumn journey which was meant to prepare Johnson for the winter of his days" and a curiosity both philosophical and physical about the country to his north. The journey is best considered as a "fugue," Rogers declares, "an act of willful self-withdrawal" that permitted Johnson to have the time and focus to meditate on the largest issues of history and culture.

But other things were at work no less. Johnson earlier had been open about his feelings against Scotland; one of his close friends referred to it as "hatred." In that he would not have been alone; Scotland and England had warred less than thirty years before, and hard feelings remained alive on both sides, especially for the Scots, who lost. A devout Anglican, Johnson had little affection for Whigs and Presbyterianism, and so the anticipation of Johnson's visit, stoked by Boswell, met with some hostile reactions in Scotland, some silly, some genuine. Some believed he would arrive in order to make fun of the Scots' education and attire. One newspaper suggested that Johnson was coming in order to propagate the growth of potatoes in the Highlands, and others saw in his visit secret political motives. Such was Johnson's reputation that his work, whether perceived as good or bad, preceded him and made his arrival one of the most commented upon in Scottish history, rivaled since only by the coming of Queen Victoria and of the Beatles.

The genesis of my own journey occurred more than twenty years ago when I read an abridged edition of Boswell's *Life of Johnson* and became so enthralled that I promptly polished off the more satisfying and much longer unabridged version. That led one friend to comment that I seemed to have too much spare time, but it also opened the pathway to the Boswell and Johnson accounts of the trip to the Scotland, and that in turn led to a gradual absorption into the journals, diaries, and letters of the two men and into books written about them. They have since become something of an obsession—though I hasten to point out I have no pets named Bozzy or Dr. Johnson—because they seem forever fresh, forever inviting—and because I find myself laughing and moved to tears countless times throughout their works.

I've lived with both long enough to count them among my most valued friends and to be envious and admiring at accounts of their time together and apart. Because their work must be read to be appreciated, I have liberally stocked this book with their words, mostly from their accounts of the trip to the Highlands and Islands, but also from time to time with additions taken from letters, diaries, and other sources that I hope will further illuminate a point in the journey. Still, there can be no substitute for reading Boswell and Johnson directly, and if this book might persuade some to do so, then I will have succeeded beyond my wildest dreams. In a perfect world, this book would contain all of their entries along with my own comments and observations, making clear why these two eighteenth-century explorers still live so passionately in our minds and hearts. Practically speaking, that is a luxury neither I nor my publisher could afford.

Like Boswell, I had planned the trip to Scotland in my head for many years; I memorized enough maps to make the journey without the need for a GPS, which is a good thing since I wound up forgetting to bring mine. In any event it turned out not to be necessary; there was usually only one road in the Highlands and Islands, or there was a ferry. Either way, it was hard to make a wrong turn. I did a little walking on my trip but never got near a horse; there is such a thing as getting too close to your sources, I believe, and the prospect of climbing on a horse to trail Johnson and Boswell in the pursuit of authenticity was about as appealing as falling off one, which I have done enough of already.

After a frenzy of planning and arrangements, the stars seemed in place for a trip in 2007, 234 years after B & J. I would go in late winter and early spring for a total of seventy-two days. (Boswell and Johnson were together for 101 days, but their travel was much slower than mine.) The time of year would mean I would likely encounter some challenging weather as they did; they went in the late summer and fall, and they found the rain and wind as unpredictable as I would. But it also meant I would miss the bus-herds of tourists and legions of midges (more on them soon). It was a good plan, and for the most part it worked out satisfactorily. I got a rental car, though no one seemed to believe I wanted it for more than a week or two much less that I planned to drive it into the Highlands—and beyond. I had no friends to call on, as Boswell did in so many places along the way, nor did I have any limitations on what I could do, beyond the obvious climatological sanctions. Much more on them later.

I beg your indulgence for one other little matter to be discussed before getting on with this narrative. Boswell and Johnson began their Scottish journey in Edinburgh in the Scottish Lowlands. They proceeded up the east coast through Dundee, St. Andrews, and Aberdeen. They turned northwest toward the Highlands and Inverness before snaking southwest past Loch Ness into Fort Augustus and then by boat to the Isle of Skye, part of the Inner Hebrides chain. By land and boat they explored Skye and then the isles of Coll and Mull and Iona, getting back to the mainland near the end of their journey, passing through Glasgow to the south and Boswell's father's home at Auchinleck. Their trip finished where it began, back in Edinburgh. There was a logic behind what they did; it was all Boswell's, for the itinerary and everything else the travelers did was carried out under his guiding hand. Johnson acquiesced in everything that Boswell proposed. Boswell knew that he and Johnson would need to be away from the northernmost outposts before the worst of the fall weather hit in late October and November. I had similar concerns which altered my itinerary.

Like my earlier companions, I started and ended my trip at Edinburgh. But I had decided to retrace their journey backwards. My reasoning was calculated on the weather; I wanted to defer the most northerly portions of my journey to a time closer to spring in anticipation of less angry weather. No apologies for that, although I would find the weather I encountered to be nonetheless surprising almost every day. In addition my journey would carry me places Boswell and Johnson—indeed, hardly anyone in the eighteenth century and not many since—had no desire to go: to the Outer Hebrides and to the Orkney Islands, two of the most remote, isolated, and unimaginably different places to be found in all of Scotland. They were key parts of my belief that a greater familiarity with all of Scotland would give my accounts of Boswell and Johnson a sense of deeper knowledge and a wider perspective. Happily that plan proved providential, and I'm glad I did it; I believe it has broadened this book in many ways. What I found in visiting those extraordinary and out-of-the-way places gave me a greater sensitivity to what Boswell and Johnson experienced, the discovery of the new and the unexpected, as they shaped my awareness of Scotland's remarkable people, its history, and its culture.

So this will not be an exact re-creation of where and how Boswell and Johnson moved in 1773. Such a journey lies beyond my capacity, and I'm not convinced that an attempt at a geographic and geological re-creation of their experiences would hold readers' attention today. I like to think I have good company in not following the two men slavishly. Those books written since 1773 that have chronicled the journey have usually done so on their author's own terms and according to their personal inclinations, at least part of the way. Some authors have attempted a minute, precise re-creation of the journey; others have written more generally, and still others have been considerably more casual, hitting only a few high points here and there. A few authors seem to have used the trip as a backdrop for commentary only loosely connected to Boswell, Johnson, or even Scotland.

Whatever the merits of those authors, and whatever their motivations, I do believe that all of us came to Scotland, to this journey under the inspiration of Boswell and Johnson. All of us carried in our baggage a series of expectations, hopes, and our own gifts of observation and artistry. The earliest followers didn't have the benefit of Boswell's uncensored entries and so missed out on many of the pleasures to be found in the modern editions. Their advantage was that they were closer to the time of both men, and what they saw physically existed in much different form than what could be seen in the early twenty-first century. A house where the two men stayed overnight, perhaps, or a landing where they went ashore—those have disappeared through the wear of time or human carelessness. It's a trade-off, since the twenty-first century gives us an easier physical access that earlier writers would have envied. But all of us who have pursued the trail of Boswell and Johnson know we have been fortunate to been able to make the journey to whatever degree accomplished. We are the lucky ones.

I also believe that all of us have drawn solace and confidence and truth in one way or another from the words of Johnson, which serve both as a close to this chapter and a preface to the next: "I know not any thing more pleasant, or more instructive, than to compare experience with expectation, or to register from time to time the difference between idea and reality."

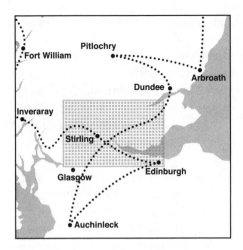

I

———⬥⬥⬥———

Stirling

After a brief exchange of pleasantries with the rental car agent and reminders of the differences between American English and Scottish English (the luggage goes into the boot, not the trunk, and the engine is housed under the bonnet, not the hood), and armed with directions to a nearby mobile phone store, I departed Edinburgh Airport to begin my journey. Thirty minutes later I was back at the airport after driving in a narrowing series of circles in hopeless search of the exit to the phone store, a trip made all the more exciting by the necessity of driving on the wrong side of the road.

The day was warm with temperatures near seventy, but I was sweating like a high schooler on exam day after attempting to negotiate one roundabout after another, keeping my car in the correct lane while searching for the proper exit. I didn't spot a person I could ask for help, although, as an overconfident male I'd never descend to actually asking anyone for directions. Besides, I couldn't find any place to slow the car, so help was out of the question. The thought did occur to me that in a bizarre way this experience was related to some unanticipated problems encountered by Boswell and Johnson, and that we were already becoming united by a similarity of travel stresses. Either that or I was getting tired really fast.

After nearly an hour of this foolishness, asking myself how important could a mobile phone be, I spotted a sign to Stirling, my planned first night's stop, and I abandoned plans for phoning in favor of a shower, some clean clothes, food, and a wee dram of Scotch. The M9 and M80 obliged, and with growing levels of confidence and weariness, I drove to my refuge near the base of the commanding presence that is Stirling Castle.

My home for the night would be an attractive, two-story bed and break-fast tucked into the side of the mountain of Stirling Castle Rock, several hundred feet below the castle walls. It certainly felt safe. It was operated by a pleasant couple; he offered to help me get my bags into the room, and she offered helpful advice about getting around the neighborhood. It would be the last time I would see him. He remained glued to the telly for football the entire period of my stay. Boswell and Johnson never got to Stirling, unfor-tunately, so I was on my own for a bit, shaking jet lag and getting to know this small piece of Scotland better.

This was not my first trip to Scotland—that occurred about thirty years ago when I spent ten days in Tayside, perambulating around some castles and historic scenery while demonstrating a keen knowledge of single malts. I was in the company of a small group of mean-spirited travel writers who seemed to regard me with nearly as much affection as Norwegians lav-ish on the Germans. In a bus in Oslo several years ago, a German couple boarded, speaking their native language. I'm not sure they heard the driver call them "fucking Nazi whores." I later asked the driver why he was so up-set. "Ever heard of the Second World War?" he snarled back to me. There are a lot of long memories out there, obviously. My travel writer compani-ons played a nasty trick, cashing in on my naiveté (witless even by ordinary standards of naiveté) when we visited gorgeous Blair Castle to meet its owner, the duke of Atholl. The duke was a delightful man, charming in a nonfussy sort of way, and rather laid back. Asking my "friends" how I should properly address the duke, I was told by several that I should be cer-tain to call him Duke. "Are you sure?" I asked. "Oh, yes," they reassured me, suppressing giggles I ignored.

And so, when my turn arrived I stepped forward and confidently, even loudly, blurted out, "Good morning, Duke." Not "Your Lordship." Not "Sir." Not nothing at all. Just "Good morning, Duke." It remains a low point in a life filled with them, and I still hear the raucous laughter from the writers as clearly as I see the duke's raised eyebrows and startled, then half-smiling response. He was a really nice duke, but can you say *cringe?*

Mercifully, let me change the subject. My first evening's dinner in Scot-land took place in a small stone pub located a few feet higher up on the rock. No bangers and mash here, just garlic chicken, perfectly roasted, with a side of fresh beans. It was not to be the last gustatory treat I'd find in Scottish restaurants. There was one slightly curious moment when I realized the music being piped in was not Scottish. In fact it was Glen Campbell, tune after tune after tune, followed by Ricky Nelson and the Byrds in an all-American 1960s pop fest, sounding ever more odd in a pub almost inside a centuries-old castle.

After dinner I drove to a grocery about a mile away to load up on water and snacks. The weather, curiously warm and sunny on my arrival, by now had collapsed into a very chilly rain followed by a drizzle and then by a hard rain. In the store I was paying for my stash when the cashier stopped and asked about my accent. "You from the States?" she inquired with her own Scottish accent. "I've got friends in Mount Pleasant near Charleston in South Carolina. You know them?" Well, no, but I lived for forty years in South Carolina and discovering a connection to the state through a cashier in the middle of Scotland was not what I had anticipated within my first hours in this country. And yes, I know, it's a very small world. And so, as Mr. Pepys put it, to bed. And to dream right through a lunar eclipse, a phenomenon that might have been construed as some sort of omen for my trip, had I been awake to know about it.

I awoke to a tasty Scottish breakfast of eggs, sausage, tomatoes, and tea. I would get used to that combination. Outside my window there was an interesting variety of wildlife: two owls on a tree, a fox lurking in the distance, and an unidentified rodent nearby. In the distance I could see a set of gorgeous snow-covered peaks. It was near freezing outside, but the rain had stopped. I decided first to resolve the issue with the phone, and my hostess directed me to a mall in downtown Stirling.

Because of the strategic importance of Stirling Castle through the centuries, the royal burgh of Stirling at its base has always been a thriving market. With the castle drawing half a million visitors each year, there's a splendid opportunity for merchants to make a little money. I located the mall with ease and negotiated a parking place with some unease given that the lines seemed drawn to fit bicycles more than automobiles. It took me a moment to realize with embarrassment that I had in fact tried to park in a slot reserved for bicycles.

Inside the mall I found the phone store and several young clerks who spoke an incomprehensible language which occasionally sounded Scottish. As we discussed various phone cards, the first one seemed to be saying something like, "Yuk nae come t' slip 'er here" while I repeatedly added, "What?" The first clerk then waved over a second clerk to better assist me. "Nae twim es 'er skurren?" he said pointing to the card. I figured they both must be immigrants from some bizarre planet until a just-arrived customer next to me explained, in a lovely, flowing brogue, "They're from Glasgow." With his assistance as translator, I got my phone card. I next acquired an umbrella and a toothbrush, decided I'd postpone the Glasgow portion of my trip until the very end, and headed for the castle as a cold rain began to fall.

Boswell certainly knew of the castle, and Johnson, too, given the pivotal role it has played in Scottish history and the seemingly endless conflicts between the Scots and the English. Over the years it has been both a fortress and a royal residence perched high on a rocky crag commanding the road linking the Highlands and Lowlands. For much of the last eight hundred years the surrounding lands have been swampy, and that, together with the rushing waters of the River Forth and the nearby mountain peaks, has made passage though this area pretty much at the pleasure of the occupants of the castle. The first known existence of a fortress on this site goes back to the twelfth century, though given its prominence—that's a pun, in case you failed to notice—it was likely occupied well before then.

The buildings that now comprise the castle date to the 1400s and 1500s and offer a memorable impression of the architecture of medieval and Renaissance Scotland. The castle is a test for the slothful; its up and downs can take the breath away from the out-of-shape, but the views from the perimeter are always bracing. It must have given the soldiers stationed here an occasional lift; and since they used to wash their clothes in urine, I would imagine almost anything would perk up their spirits. My stroll through the castle came as winds buffeted the walls and cold rain poured down. It certainly kept the crowds down; there was no one else in sight as I ducked in and out of the buildings. At the gift shop I bought a guidebook and three tiny, single-shot bottles of single malts; who knew gift shops could be so gifted?

Stirling Castle and Edinburgh Castle are the two most formidable castles in this nation, and one look tells you why: location, location, location. They are very high up, and to enemies they must have appeared mighty and impregnable. Trying to storm either one would have been folly. Stirling played a critical role in the Scottish resistance to invaders from England in the thirteenth and fourteenth centuries, and for the next couple of centuries it was a royal residence. King James V was crowned in the castle in 1513; he probably didn't remember much about it since he was seventeen months old at the time. Mary, queen of Scots, got her crown here in 1543. Once the kings departed—the English eventually won, you may know—the castle's upkeep diminished, and it wasn't until the twentieth century that efforts began to preserve and restore its undoubted grandeur.

Moving about between the showers, I walked through the courtyards, the royal apartments, the lovely Chapel Royal (which looks like but isn't the chapel where Mary was crowned), and finally the Great Hall, the largest ever built in Scotland. It is a huge rectangular space clearly designed for celebrations and great state occasions. Until 1964 it had been used as a military barracks for men of the Argyll and Sutherland Highlanders; now workers are returning it to its former glory, and already visitors can sense some of its earlier magnificence. Outside the rain stopped, and I walked over to the edge of a wall to get a better view of the countryside; there was a rainbow in front of me, and within minutes another developed to the north, and moments later one appeared to the south as well. The weather began clearing, and within fifteen minutes the rain had ceased, the sun was out, and the wind dropped. They weren't kidding when they said Scotland's weather was changeable. And quickly.

The castle's history and location have encompassed some of Scotland's greatest—and worst—historical moments and personalities. Robert the Bruce, a celebrated king of the Scots, enjoyed a resounding triumph over the English at the famous battle of Bannockburn in 1314; the battle site is located just a short distance south of the castle. It was also home to the Stewarts (that would be the Jameses, not the Jimmys) and, of course, to Mary, queen of Scots, whose colorfully tragic life has made her a central figure in the burgeoning Scottish tourist industry. She was at the heart of clashes between the Scots and the English, between Catholics and Protestants, between the nobility and everyone else, and her life was filled with exciting fireworks until she was imprisoned in the Tower of London and later beheaded by order of her cousin Queen Elizabeth I in 1587. Some of those fireworks—literally—occurred in Stirling Castle, which was the site of the first fireworks show in Scottish history when Mary celebrated the baptism of her son, Prince James, in 1566. While Mary's historic significance is unquestioned, I should note that tourist operators in Scotland are not shy about connecting her to just about any place they can since it encourages more visitors to stop by. Americans do the same with George Washington, Abraham Lincoln, and Elvis.

And speaking of icons, there is another Scottish figure impossible to overlook while you're in Stirling, or anywhere else in Scotland these days. I'm speaking, of course, of William Wallace, the consummate Scottish hero, better known these days as Mel Gibson's Braveheart. Of course there was a real Wallace, although actual information about him remains elusive, in part because he is a figure of the very distant past, and in part because almost everything we know about him contemporaneously derives from enemy sources. Their accounts, as you might imagine, are less than admiring. Bloody criminal, maybe, or thief and brigand. He was accused of everything but eating small English babies.

The real Wallace was born about 1270 and was a genuine hero who led an unexpectedly successful rebellion against the much larger occupying army of the nasty English King Edward I in 1297 in a battle at Stirling Bridge, just down the street from the Castle. He was a warrior, and he could be brutal, but by one account he was "a multilingual diplomat who was sent on embassies to France and Rome." Stories about Wallace began to appear in print just a few years after his death. One of the better known and most popular is Walter Bower's *Scotichronicon*, written in the 1440s, that gives us a portrait of Wallace: he had the body of a giant with a wild but pleasing look about him. He was "most liberal in his gifts, very fair in his judgments, most compassionate in comforting the sad, a most skillful counsellor, very patient when suffering, a distinguished speaker, who above all hunted down falsehood and deceit and detested treachery." Now we know why he didn't eat small English babies—clearly he was way too busy to have free time to munch on children.

Unfortunately his battlefield record was not unblemished. He had a re-match with King Edward's army in 1298 at Falkirk, just a few miles from Stirling, and was defeated. The story is that Robert the Bruce played a big role in the failure of the Scots on that battlefield; defenders of Robert deny this vigorously. Wallace was an outlaw to the English, a man with a price on his head. Though the Scots eventually submitted to King Edward, the English finally seized Wallace—or he was betrayed, take your choice. Betrayal is big in Scottish history. He was taken to England to be torn limb from limb in 1305 on the eve of St. Bartholomew's Fair at Smithfield, his remains said to be scattered around Scotland to discourage further disturbances. It was a terrible epiphany for Wallace, but he quickly became the greatest martyr in the cause of Scottish nationalism. He has been celebrated ever since. Robert Burns, Scotland's national poet, wrote in 1786, after a visit to one of Wallace's alleged safe havens in Ayrshire, "my heart glowed with a wish to be able to make a Song on him equal to his merits."

A few miles from Stirling Castle, near a bridge which is not the bridge where the battle was fought, is a five-story monument erected in the mid-nineteenth century commemorating Wallace. It's an impressive sight. Nearby is a smaller adornment that appears to celebrate Mel Gibson. Much less impressive.

So let's go ahead and confront the colossus that is Mel Gibson's Braveheart. That figure is an inescapable fact of life in Scotland these days, the eight-hundred-pound gorilla in contemporary Scottish history and the biggest thing since Bonnie Prince Charlie and the Jacobite Rising over two and a half centuries ago. The 1995 film *Braveheart* won five Oscars including

Best Picture and Best Director for Gibson. It made a mint worldwide and was a huge box-office smash in the United States and Scotland. It spawned a jump in the sales of kilts, brought hundreds of thousands of visitors to Scotland, and stoked the worst instincts of Scottish tourism entrepreneurs. (The Braveheart Museum at Loch Ness is in its own category as the most ghastly museum in the world, but please hold your eagerness to read about it until Boswell, Johnson, and I get to that vicinity in a few more chapters.)

The film was fun, I suppose, and informative in a way, but in the view of historians it emerges as a horrible concoction of half truths and total untruths, not entirely surprising given the paucity of genuine historical information. It was drawn in part from a poem about Wallace written in the late fifteenth century by a poet known colorfully as Blind Hary. The poem apparently had little truth to it, making it a fabulous source for the film. One historian recently observed that Blind Hary's creation "is the greatest single work of imagination in early Scots poetry." But before we all jump on the poor visually impaired scribe, I should note that other historians think there may be some factual elements in Hary's work, though they concede his first name probably wasn't Hary. (You can see some of the trouble with Scottish history here.)

No matter, and whatever the truth, lots of Scots and lots of others have praised Gibson and his film. It did neatly encapsulate one perspective on how the English have mistreated the Scots over the centuries, and it certainly gave new life to the Scottish Independent Party. The English may be forgiven for wondering why Gibson had it in for them since the film is unsparing in its treatment of English savagery, suggesting the Scots were bloody nasty only to pay back the English for their cruelty. History tells us that no one came away with clean hands. Nonetheless, Gibson, who has no family ties to Scotland, by the way, would seem to have assured Wallace—the man of the people—a preeminent position in the grail of Scottish mythology, a cup is already filled to overflowing.

And what of Robert the Bruce? For a long period, he was what Wallace has become today—the greatest national hero—having proclaimed himself king of Scotland in 1306 and having won the battle at Bannockburn over the King Edward II's English army in 1314. The battle was one of the most decisive in Scottish history, and certainly one of the most decisive battles that Scotland actually managed to win. It led to Scotland's independence, though before that conflict there had been questions about Robert's devotion to Scottish freedom. Bruce himself died in 1327, and the short-lived Bruce dynasty ended a few decades later. Historians commemorated Bruce's achievements with honor and praise, though declining support for the Scottish monarchy over the centuries continually eroded his reputation. The battlefield today boasts a visitor center and large equestrian statue of Robert that is viewed against the skyline of Stirling Castle. Incidentally there is still discussion about the precise location of the battlefield; things are seldom what they seem to be when it comes to getting a tight grip on history.

Back at my lodging, I was tired after a day of exploring. It was already evident that Scotland has a lot of history that I was going to need to digest to get the most out of my experience. But as long as there are gift shops selling single malts, I was confident that I was up to the task. As I fell asleep, I remember hearing the rain start up again. I pulled the blankets up a little closer and thought about the next morning's forecast of snow. I think I dreamed about already experiencing six different climates in my mere twenty-four hours in Scotland.

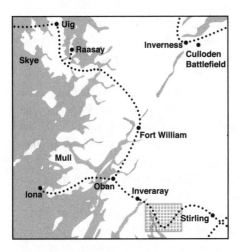

2

<del>——</del> ∞∞ <del>——</del>

Loch Lomond

At breakfast the next morning, the weather was overcast and quite cold, and the remnants of a light snow were on my car's roof (actually called "roof" in Scottish English). My host offered more eggs, sausage, tomatoes, and tea, and I learned that her mother had been a Druid. Well, after learning about Wallace and Bruce, I'm just relieved she wasn't English.

I was off to Inveraray, where I planned to pick up the trail of Boswell and Johnson for the first time. But there were a few sights to attend to before I got there, starting with Doune Castle, a mere fifteen minutes or so north of Stirling. Before arriving at Doune, however, I got another lesson in driving through Scotland. I was on a narrow road, sufficiently wide for one and a half cars, when, entering a curve, I spotted a sign that cautioned me about a bridge and oncoming traffic. As I rounded the curve, I realized that the road narrowed to one lane, and there were two cars on a bridge headed straight toward me, one after the other. On an instinct of survival I swerved onto a dirt road on the left just as the other cars whipped by me. I stopped, caught my breath, and wondered what the heck had just happened. That road sign apparently was telling me something I didn't quite get. I backed out to the road very carefully, saw nothing coming, and continued on my way across the bridge. I knew I had absorbed a very important driving lesson that would pay dividends throughout my trip; unfortunately, I had no clue what it might have been. I still don't. But I started paying a lot more attention to road signs.

Doune Castle sits on a high, easily defended promontory at the River Teith. The Roman governor Agricola's legionnaires put up a wooden fort near the current site in the first century A.D., on land now used by the local cricket club. The castle's construction began in the fourteenth century when it was envisioned as a dream home by a would-be king, Robert Stewart, duke of Albany, also known (I'm not kidding about this) as a "big spender." Alas, Albany died in 1420 before the castle was completed; his successors didn't keep their heads on—literally—long enough to enjoy it much either. Situated so close to Stirling Castle, it eventually lost its role as a fortress and became a really nice hunting lodge for royals and their families. It fell into disrepair centuries ago and lost its roof. The walls are imposing still, however, and inside there is some restoration in progress.

The castle has been the scene of some bloodshed over the centuries, nothing more outrageous than what occurred in 1974 when Sir Launcelot conducted a wholesale slaughter of men, women, babies, and nuns in the film *Monty Python and the Holy Grail* within these walls. That film is the reason Doune is popular today. Everyone wants to see the parapets over which cows, fowl, and a large wooden badger were hurled in French defiance of King Arthur and his invading Knights of the Round Table. In the film the castle was variously identified as Camelot and Castle Anthrax, but never simply as Doune.

It was well worth my stop in spite of very cold, blustery weather and occasional showers. Once again, given the off-season and the inclement weather, I found myself the only visitor, walking freely around the castle, up and down the chilly, medieval stone steps. The attendant preferred to stay intimate with a portable heater in her small office at the castle entrance-way. When I spoke to her I couldn't help but notice that in addition to the guidebooks for sale there were bottles of "Holy Grail Ale" and some single malts. I was disappointed that John Cleese and Eric Idle didn't step out and smile at me.

Loch Lomond, a relatively short distance to the west, blocked my path to Inveraray, and I couldn't resist a stop at the largest stretch of fresh water in all of Great Britain. So close as to be practically a suburb of Glasgow, the loch is famous for its "bonnie, bonnie banks." In the driving rain (I'm driving, it's raining), however, it was difficult to see any sort of banks or even the loch itself. I could tell it was off to one side as I crept through the blinding rain, and I was glad there was little or no traffic on the narrow road. It was definitely time for some hot tea or a little Scotch, and I wound up on another of those extremely compressed two-lane roads to a tiny village on the eastern shore named Balmaha. I was grateful that no one was coming toward me because it seemed certain one of us would have to pull into a field to allow the other to get by. I got soaked running from the car into the small inn, but I dried out quickly once I reached the cozy pub, warmed by a hot peat fire and some strong drink. While I calmed down, I looked for someone to join me, but only two men and their female companion at the other end of the pub were around, and no one gave any notice of me. I finished my tea, saw the rain had slackened, and decided to walk out to the loch for a view.

It was still cold, and I yanked my jacket closer around me and pulled on my gloves as I walked the hundred yards or so to water's edge. In the dank, gray afternoon light Loch Lomond did not sparkle. In fact it looked downright bleak. Only one person appeared on the water, a man in a wetsuit windsurfing in the distance. The rain began falling once again. I had a melancholic moment, and I thought of the famous ballad the chorus of which goes,

> *"Oh ye'll tak' the high road*
> *An' I'll tak' the low road*
> *And I'll be in Scotland afore ye,*
> *For me and my true love*
> *Will never meet again,*
> *On the bonnie, bonnie banks of Loch Lomond."*

It's a beautifully sad song that could wring tears from a stone, though it is sometimes treated rather offhandedly by singers, as if it were a little story of lovers by the banks of a pretty lake. Its origin and meaning, however disputed, give great emotional weight to the song for it connects to terrible times in Scottish history. No one seems exactly sure who wrote it; it appears in print for the first time in the mid-nineteenth century, and the lovely tune has been appropriated widely by many performers. I can remember one ghastly version by the 1950s rock 'n roll group Bill Haley and the Comets titled "Rock Lomond." In any event, in one version the ballad's story goes back to the first half of the eighteenth century and the Jacobite Rising when the Scots tried to put Bonnie Prince Charlie on the English throne (more about this later). The insurrection failed and some of the leaders were taken to London for trials (the English again). Their wives, sweethearts, and friends followed them the only way they could: on foot, trudging along poorly maintained roads. The trials were mostly for show; the men accused were convicted and put to death in vile ways. Their heads and other body parts were displayed on spikes along the "high road," the main road between London and Edinburgh. The families of the dead returned to Scotland the only way they could: on the "low road." Very grim stuff.

Or some maintain that the ballad is more centrally about a Scottish prisoner in 1746, about to lose his head to the English, who believes he will return to his homeland only in death (the low road). There are other versions, but whatever interpretation you prefer, it is evident the song is not a frolic, and singers who treat it as such are misunderstanding the background, whatever the details of that background might be.

Back in the pub, no one was talking to me yet, though the place was much more crowded for dinner. I couldn't even get the man behind the bar to chat with me in spite of using my most obvious Southern American accent (lots of *y'alls* and soft, slow slurring, and dropped *g*'s). I suppose I must have sounded too much like someone from the neighborhood, like maybe from south Balmaha? Dinner was pretty good, but I just couldn't seem to feel dry. I went to bed early, disappointed with Loch Lomond and a little discouraged. I'll bet Boswell would have been ashamed of me. If he'd been here he'd have been back in the bar, knocking back a few and talking boisterously and cleverly, maybe grabbing the wench at the other end of the bar for a little shagging. Thinking about it really left me depressed.

I woke up early. It was still dark outside, and the room was cold. I wanted to get on the road and get closer to Boswell and Johnson for the "real" portion of my journey. I read some in Johnson's *Journey* and then went to breakfast. The tea was hot and good, and the food was cold and inedible. It was hard to taste the difference between the eggs and the beans. The mushrooms seemed to have been freshly hauled in from the outdoors right after the inn owner's truck ran over them. Bad food and rain; ah, this was the Scotland I expected.

But in fact the morning turned absolutely gorgeous: sunny, eggshell blue skies and a brisk, uplifting wind. It was as if I had stepped onto another planet. As I drove around the southern tip of the loch and then began to ascend the A82 along the popular western shores, I begin to appreciate why the loch has such a storied name. The waters gleamed in the light, not a ripple in view, the snow-capped mountains reflected in mirrorlike images; it was a gorgeous view. I pulled the car over to get a better look and encountered an older, white-haired gentleman from Nottingham, who told me he'd been to South Carolina—Myrtle Beach, of all places, which he called "the hottest place on the face of the earth." He also had visited Chicago, which he found to be "the coldest place on the face of the earth." We separated before he had an opportunity to tell me about the rainiest place on the face of the earth, though I suspect we were already there.

My drive continued, slowly, as I enjoyed the views, the loch on my right and dozens of small but breathtakingly lovely waterfalls on the left. The road began climbing slightly, signifying the beginning of my arrival into the higher lands of Scotland. I wanted to stop for a late lunch in the picturesque little village of Cairndow at the northern tip of Loch Fyne. It was situated at the bottom of a very narrow one-lane road (I know this is getting repetitive, but it's true) angled down a steep hill, and I confidently headed in that direction.

Everything was fine for a hundred yards or so when I suddenly met an oncoming truck. Both of us were in the middle of the road because there was no where else to go. Even so, I immediately and instinctively tried to turn my car over to the right. Wrong thing to do. The truck also pulled to the right. We faced each other ever closer. I hit the brakes and stopped, bewildered and scared. The truck driver angrily swerved to my left and raced his engine as he whipped by me, passing within millimeters of my vehicle. I could feel his disgust. I resumed my trip down the hill, but my driving confidence plunged lower than Nessie's belly.

At the same time it seemed to me once more that I was having something of a twenty-first century adventure replete with surprises not unlike those Boswell and Johnson found on their eighteenth-century journey. That realization was a reminder that a trip isn't about the planning; it's about what happens while you're busy planning. Yes, I know that's a hoary cliché, but that's because it's true. This was, for me—even with experience traveling in the country previously—a largely new, unexplored land with new sights and challenges. The weight of Scottish history bears more strongly on me, and the joy of meeting up with Boswell and Johnson in Inveraray awaits. And if I can just remember to drive on the left I should be able to get there pretty soon.

3

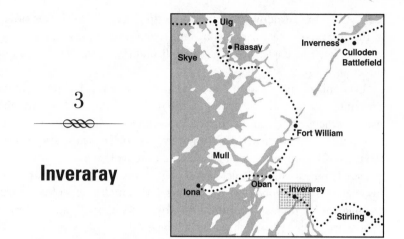

Inveraray

Boswell and Johnson arrived in Inveraray, one of the most important and entertaining stops on their journey, on the evening of October 23 following a rain-soaked trip from the west-coast village of Oban. The trip, the first leg of their eventual return to Edinburgh and the end of their journey, provoked some of Johnson's most majestic and vivid prose:

> The weather was tempestuous. . . . The night came on while we had yet a great part of the way to go, though not so dark, but that we could discern the cataracts which poured down the hills, on one side, and fell into one general channel that ran with great violence on the other. The wind was loud, the rain was heavy, and the whistling of the blast, the fall of the shower, the rush of the cataracts, and the roar of the torrent, made a nobler chorus of the rough music of nature than it had ever been my chance to hear before.

Think of it: the man who wrote this striking scene was an old man of sixty-four, who traveled mounted on a pony scarcely able to carry his weight and had ridden through a cold downpour, eaten in wet clothes, and yet could write at the end of the day of what an amazing experience he had had!

I arrived at Inveraray from the opposite direction under considerably nicer circumstances, including sunlight and a fully functioning automobile. Inveraray, perched at the edge of gorgeous Loch Fyne, was one of the first planned towns, although few living there at the time had any say about it. The duke of Argyll, whose castle—still in the family—sits only a few hundred yards from the town's perimeter, decided in 1744 that he had grown tired of the ruinous old castle he was living in and wished to construct a new and grander home. That naturally meant he would require sufficient space for proper landscaping of the grounds, a consideration I'm sure we all can recognize. In this instance it meant moving the town of Inveraray, which was encroaching on his project, to a new site farther away. The "New Town" took shape a decade later, and by 1776, just as the American colonists were breaking open their rebellion, the new Royal Burgh of Inveraray was opening for business. It apparently was just in time, based on what Thomas Pennant saw when he came here in 1772. "This place," he wrote, "will in time be magnificent; but at present the space between the front of the castle and the water is disgraced with the old town, composed of the most wretched hovels that can be imagined."

Inveraray today is considerably more pleasing, even a bit on the charming, genteel side, I have to confess. And it boasts the hotel, now known as the Argyll Hotel, built in 1755, where Boswell and Johnson settled in for their visit. Johnson described it as "not only commodious but magnificent." These things are a matter of some subjectivity, of course, and over a period of nearly two and a half centuries and a fire or two, one would expect standards of commodiousness and magnificence to change. They have. I arrived at 1 P.M. and was told by a rather pouty young female desk clerk that rooms would not be available until 3. When I returned at 3 she failed to recognize me—in spite of the absence of anyone else attempting to claim rooms—and bluntly advised me that rooms would not be offered until 3:30. I sat down on a sofa directly in front of her, and at 3:30 she managed to produce a slim smile of recognition. My room was close to the one where Johnson is alleged to have slept; it overlooked the loch, though getting to it up a creaky, steeply winding staircase surely would have taxed Dr. Johnson and perhaps even Boswell. I asked the clerk when I came back downstairs if she had heard of Boswell and Johnson. No, she replied, but she could get the manager for me. He might have seen them. This would be only the first of my discoveries that Scots, as a rule, don't have long memories or especially good thoughts for either Bozzy or Dr. J.

I departed for a haircut and a pint in that order. The haircutter turned out to be a woman in her thirties who trimmed men's and women's hair and said she had lived in Inveraray all her life. I asked if she had heard of Boswell and Johnson coming through the town, and she helpfully responded, "No, I haven't seen anyone like that lately." When I added that they passed through in 1773, she added, "Well, I wasn't here then." I didn't much care for the haircut.

The Royal Burgh is attractive, clean, and walkable. It has been affectionately described by the novelist Neil Munro, who was born here and poured out his love for Inveraray and for its closely knit Highland values in his 1907 novel *The Daft Days* (recommended reading before a visit here). Inveraray's neat, bright shops and pubs seem mostly to cater to the tourist trade. The tourists come here in summer, by the way, not for the pleasure of remembering Boswell and Johnson but to buy Scottish clothing at the many discount shops (all of which sell whisky in addition to the usual souvenirs, sweaters, and scarfs) and to see Inveraray Castle, the home of the latest duke of Argyll.

Boswell and Johnson had a remarkable time at Inveraray. Unfortunately for me, the castle was closed for visitors until April, though the grounds were open. That was especially disappointing because some of my predecessors on the Boswell/Johnson trail have made wonderful and occasionally bizarre entrances to the castle. In her quirky but readable 1956 book *A Hebridean Journey*, the English writer Elizabeth Stucley remembers how she, in the company of her eight-year-old adopted son David, knocked on the castle door, and when the duke opened it, "I explained I was Dr. Johnson and that David was Mr. Boswell." The duke graciously went on to give her a brief tour, and she and David slept that night in their van outside the castle. My teeth gnash at having missed such an opportunity. The Scottish writer Moray McLaren fared even better. In his engaging and insightful book *The Highland Jaunt* (1954), he recounts that when he got to Inveraray the duke-in-residence invited him to stay for a few days so that he could report that the castle "has not changed fundamentally" since 1773. I decided to venture back to the castle in the morning, partly because it had now turned cold and begun to rain steadily. But mostly because there was no one was there to invite me in.

Back at the hotel the clerk was smiling, though not at me. Her boyfriend had come in and was helping her pass the time. He looked surprisingly like her—solid, maybe even chunky, pouty, with at least as many facial rings as she claimed. His motorcycle was parked outside. I resisted any urge to ask him about Boswell and Johnson. I drifted into the empty hotel bar where Johnson and Boswell had lifted a glass. I ordered a pint and sat back to watch and wait. Twenty minutes later, I was still by myself with an empty glass. I decided to try another establishment.

Around the corner—the wind gusts blew me there quite easily—was the George Hotel, which had a lively, noisy bar and restaurant into which I happily slipped. The rain poured down in sheets outside, but a large, warming fire, hospitable neighbors, a delicious meal of Cullen Skink (smoked haddock, potatoes, and onions) and good drink kept me smiling until late in the evening when I returned to the Argyll. The bar was still empty. When Johnson arrived at the hotel on that rainy night 234 years ago, he did not change out of his wet clothes, noted Boswell. "We supped well; and after supper, Dr. Johnson, whom I had not seen taste any fermented liquor during all our travels [Boswell is wrong; see the section on Dunvegan Castle in a later chapter], called for a gill of whisky. 'Come,' said he, 'let me know what it is that makes a Scotchman happy.'" Boswell proposed a toast to their mutual friend Mrs. Thrale, but Johnson seemed offended and demurred.

Hester Thrale occupied an interesting place in the lives of the two men. Both were correspondents with her, and she and Boswell were something of rivals for Johnson's affection. Both had been given a blessing to write biographies of Johnson, and both pursued their relationships with some measure of self-interest. Boswell was far superior as a writer, but Mrs. Thrale held an important place in Johnson's heart—he was deeply saddened when she remarried and virtually abandoned him near the end of his life. She also was able to be with Johnson in more domestic situations, and hence gave a picture of the doctor in ways Boswell could not. I thought of all three—Boswell, Johnson and Mrs. Thrale—as I sat in the bar. But even with good whisky, it was way too depressing to be by myself.

Back in my room, which appeared to be a little larger than the one Johnson is alleged to have slept in, I prepared for the worst. The Scottish poet Robert Burns had stayed here, too, about fourteen years after Boswell and Johnson, and his stay wasn't so wonderful. He wrote in 1787

> *There's nothing here but Highland pride,*
> *And Highland scab and hunger;*
> *If Providence has sent me here,*
> *'Twas surely in an anger.*

The wooden floors were uneven and caused a near fall when I got up to go to the loo about 2 A.M. My bed, however, proved quite comfortable and, in spite of forebodings, I slept soundly. Morning brought clear skies and temperatures in the upper forties and a friendlier desk clerk who brought me a newspaper to go with my tea. Warmed and awake, I strolled briskly to the castle grounds, pastoral and quiet with elongated green patches and horse barns in the distance, lovely leafless woods, stone bridges, and sheep grazing peacefully. Do sheep ever graze aggressively? The castle exterior, at least seen from a distance, is a lot less imposing than, say, that of Stirling Castle or even Doune, having been much more scaled to domestic inhabitance. But it certainly played an imposing role in the visit by Boswell and Johnson.

The fifth duke of Argyll (sometimes spelled Argyle) was their host in 1773, and his castle was the seat of the powerful Clan Campbell, the most important family in the Highlands, if not in all of Scotland. The clan had been at the center of much controversial Scottish politics over the centuries. They were said to be allies of the popular Robert the Bruce in the fourteenth century, maintained loyalties to the royals, kept up remarkable cohesiveness among the individual members when other clans did not, and turned out to be rather aggressive and occasionally ruthless at the expense of their neighbors. Quite a few of them sided with the English at the Battle of Culloden in 1746, which resulted in a massacre of Highlanders and put a bloody end to the rebellion led by one of the most romantic figures in Scottish history, Charles Edward Stewart, better known as the aforementioned Bonnie Prince Charlie. More about him and the tangle of political history comes up later in this book.

Boswell naturally wrangled an invitation to the duke's home for himself and Johnson, though not without some soul-searching over a rather delicate matter. In his *Journal,* Boswell wrote: "The Duchess of Argyll, I knew, hated me, on account of my zeal in the Douglas Cause. But the duke of Argyll has always been very civil to me, and had paid me a visit in London. They were now at the castle. Should I go and pay my respects there?" Their disagreement came over a legal matter some years before when the wealthy and attractive duchess of Hamilton sought to have her son declared her rightful heir and Boswell supported a rival claimant, in the process treating the duchess with some legal and personal disrespect. The duchess of Hamilton was now none other than the wife of the fifth duke of Argyll. "I mentioned how disagreeable my company would be to the Duchess," Boswell wrote. "Mr. Johnson treated this objection with manly disdain. 'That sir,' said he, 'he must settle with his wife.'"

Boswell did go to pay his respects and at a time when he thought the duchess and her ladies might be gone from dinner. He found the duke most amiable, enjoyed a fine meal and good claret, and explained his most curious journey. At one point the duke introduced his wife to Boswell, who reported that she "took not the least notice of me." The two travelers returned the next day and Boswell introduced Johnson to the duke and recorded, with candor and clarity, his own feelings about a most un-dukely topic: "I shall never forget the enchanting impression made upon my fancy by some of the ladies' maids tripping about in neat morning dresses. After seeing nothing for a long time but rusticity, their elegance delighted me; and I could have been a knight-errant for them." How can you not love Boswell for his intimate frankness and openness? Who else would have the nerve to admit feeling horny around the little maids while one of the most powerful men in the country was showing his visitors around his estate?

If there was one person who could take Boswell's mind off those tasty maids, it was surely the duchess. And sure enough, at dinner later Boswell observed her "peevish resentment." Things got a little nastier after dinner when the duchess, who found herself enjoying Johnson's company, inquired as to why the travelers had gotten such a late-season start on their journey. Johnson replied that Boswell had been occupied in court. "'Why, madam,' said he, 'You know Mr. Boswell must attend the Court of Session, and it does no rise until the twelfth of August.'" Boswell quotes her reply: "She said, with spite, 'I know *nothing* of Mr. Boswell.'"

There were other delicious moments during the time Boswell and Johnson spent at Inveraray, including a testy exchange between Johnson and a dinner guest, more ruminations on the Douglas Cause, and Johnson's carefree "Meditation on a Pudding," a grand, quasi-scholarly and amusingly over-the-top ode to flour, salt, milk, eggs, and the natural and animal world that gives us—yes, pudding. The ode may have inspired Burns a few decades later when he wrote glowingly of the haggis. As for those who would find Johnson dour and unsmiling, this kind of evidence must be ignored, for it tells us clearly the good doctor was having a whee of a time for a good part of this strange yet refreshing journey. As for Boswell, simply being with Johnson over this extended period had given him not merely a devout intimacy but secured for him a literary mission as well.

But how about the Campbells? Did those dukes and duchesses at Inveraray carry any grudges over the years? At least one of them certainly did. In his excellent 1982 book *In the Footsteps of Johnson and Boswell,* the American-born journalist Israel Shenker recounts how he wrote a letter to Ian Campbell, the twelfth duke of Argyll, to ask permission to call on him at the castle. The duke didn't reply, but his secretary did, and I quote some of her reply as provided by Shenker: "For the Duke's part, he ventures to suggest that Johnson's and Boswell's visit to Inveraray was not perhaps their happiest one, certainly in Boswell's case, where he was received very coolly by the then-duchess, as you will know, and of the many distinguished visitors to Inveraray Castle over the centuries, these particular ones strike the least sympathetic note with the present duke; in fact, mention of them is inclined to make him wish 'to take to the hills.'"

She went on to suggest that the duke might prefer that Mr. Shenker take to the hills instead, and she ruled out any conversational possibilities. Shenker, being a good journalist, proceeded to take the pubic tour and get a look at the castle anyway. So much for peevishness unbounded, more than two hundred years after the Boswell and Johnson visit.

For those two men the journey was nearing its end. It was the end of October; the weather was worsening. They went to Boswell's home at Auchinleck, south of Glasgow, before returning to Edinburgh. For me, however, the journey was just beginning. On to Oban, following now the path that culminated in my literary companions' fascinating stop in Inveraray. Except, of course, that I was tracing the path in reverse.

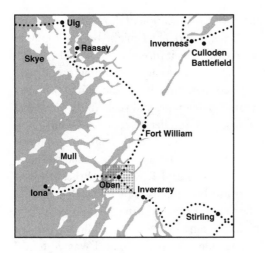

4

To Oban

Before departing Inveraray, I made a quick stop at the jail after the suddenly chipper desk clerk suggested it was worth a visit. She was right. An older gentleman of Inveraray, costumed as a nineteenth-century warder of the prison, escorted me around the damp, rather dismal place. I took a liking to him, though I once again discovered that the visit here by Boswell and Johnson excited no memory whatsoever. The old jail was built about 1820 for imprisonment. Men, women, and children were kept here, as many as twenty in eight small cells. The new jail, completed in 1848, was considerably more advanced in security, ventilation, and water closets. The warder took some pride in informing me that Argyll outlawed the death penalty well before the rest of Scotland got around to it. I stopped by the jail gift shop because I had never been to a jail that had a gift shop. In addition to a few books about the prison system and some woolies, glasses, and pencils, it featured a generous selection of Scotch whiskies for sale. Just the sort of thing every prison needs, I suppose.

Oban was about an hour away by car—you may recall that Boswell and Johnson needed a full day to slosh through the trip—so I took my time. The scenery was lovely, looping around the top edges of Loch Awe, which, at more than twenty-five miles in length, is the longest splash of fresh water in Scotland. Boswell and Johnson crossed this loch on a rain-swept ferry. According to travel guides, legend has it that the loch is inhabited by a monster "even more gruesome" than the one at Loch Ness. (That would make the monster "awesome," wouldn't it? Anyway, there are lots of legends to go around in Scotland, even more than to be found in Ireland.)

The ruins of Kilchurn Castle, once a fortification of those darned Camp-bells, were visible far in the distance. I thought I might be developing a potentially unhealthy addiction to castles; as it turned out it would only get worse. Much closer was a beautiful old stone church standing proudly on the banks of the loch. When I walked to it, though, I found that St. Conan's Kirk was barely one hundred years old—notable and venerable in America, perhaps, but historically speaking a mere toddler here, and, of course, no-where to be seen when Boswell and Johnson came through. The interior stones radiated a bone-chilling dampness, so I hurried along. And speaking of bones, the kirk is the repository of one of Robert the Bruce's bones, according to signage. I'm not sure just how that is known, but there is defi-nitely *somebody's* bone there. Back in the car the heater felt very good, and I drove past herds of shaggy highland cattle—the ones with horns—lots of sheep, and even some deer feeding calmly near the road. I was grateful I wasn't on horseback or foot.

I arrived in Oban in the early afternoon. Back when Boswell and John-son were here, it was but a hamlet, "a few families collected together with a view toward the fisheries," one traveler wrote in 1786. It had a post office and a customhouse, but since no one in the islands paid customs, there was no officer.

In the summer months this moderate-sized town becomes one of the busiest and most crowded in all of Scotland. It is the major jumping-off place for thousands of tourists headed via ferries to the Western Isles, and it bustles. In early March, however, it was largely deserted, and the tourist-shop owners were looking rather hungrily at me. Oban does have some things I badly needed: laundries, petrol stations, bookstores, and the like. The clerk at the bookstore said he had heard of Boswell and Johnson but couldn't tell me anything about them. Footballers, perhaps? At my urging he checked his computer and found one copy of an edition containing Bos-well's *Journal* and Johnson's *Journey* in stock. I bought it with the hope the store would have to reorder. It felt like a victory of sorts.

While I was so involved, the weather was rapidly deteriorating. By late afternoon it was raining heavily with gusty winds blowing in off the Firth of Lorn. By the time I walked four blocks to a seafood restaurant for dinner, the rain was horizontal and the winds felt gale force, keeping me unsteady on my feet. Cheered by a splendid dinner and ample drink, I very deliberately stepped through the puddles on my way back to the hotel, the wind howling in my ears and my clothes drenched through my supposedly waterproof jacket. With my first ferry ride coming up the next day, I was getting a little nervous about the weather, so I decided to reread the Oban entries from Boswell and Johnson.

The latter is terse about Oban. His only observation takes note of staying at a "tolerable inn." Boswell is, of course, a bit more voluble. The lodging the pair were pointed to was full, so they spent the night at another inn, "a slated house of two storeys, and we were well enough entertained; at least we were satisfied, though we had nothing like what is found in good inns upon a frequented road. . . . It was comfortable to Mr. Johnson and me after so many states of uncertain confinement in islands, to be now on the mainland." Another traveler who stayed at the same inn a few years after Boswell and Johnson found it clean and the food simple but good. He also reported on a bagpiper who "strutted up and down" in front of the inn. The piper was perceived as a rather accomplished musician and entertained the guests. When he was given—apparently unexpectedly—some shillings for his performance, his delight knew no bounds. In fact he refused to leave, playing far into the night until being forcibly escorted away.

I had a conversation with the desk clerk, who appeared relieved to have someone to talk with at such a barren time of the season. Most visitors, he told me, were stopping here on their way elsewhere; few made Oban their destination. He was a native of Thurso, which I only vaguely recognized at the time as a city on Scotland's northern coast, and had come south looking for work. "Don't like Glasgow and Edinburgh. Been there, too many people, too crowded," he said. He didn't have a driver's license and didn't expect to need or get one. "I've got friends. It's too expensive, you know?"

In my room later I picked up a postcard on the table opposite my bed and saw a cartoon panel depicting a heavily fleeced sheep standing in a downpour. The panel carried the description "British Winter." The next panel showed the very same sheep in the very same rain with the description "Scottish Summer." Outside, it was still, officially at least, Scottish Winter. I went to sleep with the sound of cold rain beating against my window.

5

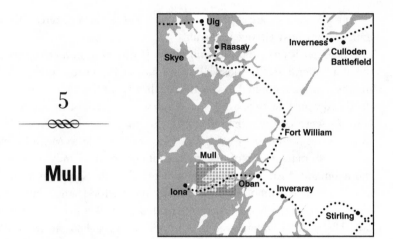

Mull

The appearance of the sun in the morning convinced me of one thing: it would be raining soon. And before I finished my first cup of tea, it was. Hard. Followed by blue skies less than a half hour later. I was headed to the Inner Hebrides, to the island of Mull, a trip Boswell and Johnson made in reverse on a small storm-tossed ferry, sitting on tree branches in the craft. I wasn't eager to see how closely I could duplicate their experience, and fortunately the weather seemed quite tolerable for a journey across the firth.

Thanks to *The Rough Guide to Scotland*, I knew Scotland has more than sixty inhabited islands, and nearly fifty of them have scheduled ferry service. The ferries are critical links between the islanders and the mainland, and in some cases, the only link. They bring not only passengers but also vital goods for residents and visitors. Small planes make trips to the islands, but it is the ferries that are the lifeblood of this sea-set nation. So naturally it is the ferries that are the subject of most of the whining. The reason why is that the ferry companies are virtual monopolies; they set the rates, they pick the destinations, they determine the service. They seem to annoy almost everyone. Either they charge too much or they don't go here or there often enough. Or their service stinks. Or they're slow. Or they just don't listen to what people want. For the trip from Oban to the islands of the Hebrides, the monopoly is Caledonian MacBrayne (known as CalMac to everyone).

I should report that in fairness I didn't have any serious problems with CalMac other than regretting the high cost of taking my car on board and struggling to understand the onboard announcements, given the combination of passenger din and a vaguely Glaswegian accent coming over the ship's PA. But I heard and read a bundle about the unhappiness of others, particularly on the Isle of Lewis where there were great public quarrels over Sunday ferry service. It's hard to keep everyone happy, I know, and I was grateful to CalMac for getting me where I needed to go and back without capsizing, even as I acknowledged that that seemed a rather minimal requirement for a ferry journey.

If the Scots are a reticent people, the ones on this ferry were atypical. They could hardly drink and chat fast enough, and most were eager to talk to an American, particularly an out-of-season visitor. Just about everyone who recognized my accent knew I was American and was eager to ask where I was from and what it was like there. They knew Atlanta from the Olympics, but no one had been there. They thought New York was "dirty" and San Francisco "gorgeous." They liked the South, and one elderly gentleman was so excited and admiring of Robert E. Lee that I thought it inappropriate to remind him that Lee had passed. One man told me he had an American car—a Jeep. "It's broken," he said. "Been broken. Terrible car. Bugger Chrysler." He must be smiling now.

It was a smooth forty-five-minute cruise to Mull, passing Duart Castle on a high promontory, a sight Boswell also noted, facing the Sound of Mull, I arrived at the very small ferry stop of Craignure on the southeast side of the island. Boswell and Johnson arrived and departed from a much higher point on the northeast, at the town of Tobermory, another thirty minutes away by ferry. They spent a rainy time here. Johnson called Mull "a most dolorous country." And indeed it can seem distressingly dark. Barren. Bleak. Unwelcoming. In rainy weather the treeless moorlands are aggressively dank and black. Getting around on the island can be difficult, for almost all of it is negotiated by single-track road. In the eighteenth century it was much worse. John Keats lived a short life perhaps because he chose to come to Mull. The twenty-three-year-old English poet visited the island in the summer of 1818, writing, "We have had a most wretched walk of 37 miles across the island of Mull. I have a slight sore throat." Arguably the sore throat would escalate into the consumption that would kill him in only three more years.

Boswell and Johnson were relieved to arrive on Mull; they had spent thirteen nights on the island of Coll to the west, trapped there by high winds and stormy fall weather that made their passage impossible. They were out of sorts, particularly Johnson, but grateful to be closer to the mainland, and their arrival at Tobermory was bracing. For Boswell, with his voluminous papers recording details of Johnson on the journey, it served to cement his determination to prepare a biography of Johnson. "I shall lay up materials for THE LIFE OF SAMUEL JOHNSON, LL.D.," he declared. "And if I survive him, I shall be the one who shall most faithfully do honour to his memory." Several years later, after Johnson read this observation and learned of Boswell's intent, Boswell reports that his friend "communicated to me at subsequent periods, many particulars of his life, which probably could not otherwise have been preserved." Allowing for some exaggeration on Bozzy's part, Johnson's cooperation and support seemed evident and the seeds sown for what would become the finest biography in the English language.

What remained immediately, however, was the negotiation of Mull, by horse and on foot, treacherous then, still almost unimaginable today. Johnson wrote in his *Journey*: "We travelled many hours through a tract, black and barren. . . . We found the country, for road there was none, very difficult to pass. We were always struggling with some obstruction or other, and our vexation was not balanced by any gratification of the eye or mind."

This portion of the trip produced some interesting entries. One recounts how the two had a moment of bad humor when they quarreled over whether Johnson's wish to put his thoughts on paper at too great a length might delay their passage across the island. In another Johnson describes the daughter of his hostess to be "the most accomplished lady that I have found in the Highlands. She knows French, music, drawing, sews neatly, makes shellwork, and can milk a cow."

At a home where they spent several evenings Johnson proclaimed that his was "the prettiest room we have seen since we came to the Highlands," while Boswell, who could be rather fastidious, found his bed sheets dirty and placed his overcoat between himself and the bedding. Earlier, during the long stay on Coll, he found himself forced to share a bed with a member of the same sex. He wrote, "I have a mortal aversion at sleeping in the same bed with a man; and a young Highlander was always somewhat suspicious as to scorbutic symptoms. I once thought of sleeping on chairs; but this would have been uncivil and unobliging to a young gentleman who was very civil and obliging to us. Upon inspection, as much as could be without his observing it, he seemed to be quite clean, and the bed was very broad. So I lay down peaceably, kept myself separated from him, and reposed tolerably."

When the trip resumed, Johnson was in low spirits because his small horse was unable to bear his weight and the good doctor was obliged to walk. And he had lost the favored oak walking stick that he had acquired in London in 1766 and used ever since. The travelers' goal was the island of Ulva, which lies only some one hundred yards off the west coast of Mull. Ulva was populated by perhaps four hundred people in the eighteenth century; when Elizabeth Stucley visited there in the early 1950s, she reported only twenty-five residents, all in one family. Today the residents are said to number about two dozen. The travelers spent just one night there; Johnson noted the practice of allowing the island's laird to share the bed of every bride on her wedding night. Their host, the laird, advised them that the custom was not practiced, but that upon every wedding the newly married were expected to provide a sheep in lieu of cash. One hopes that the laird wasn't supposed to sleep with the sheep.

Which brings up a pair of hoary Scottish jokes. To wit: Scotland is a place where men are men and sheep are scared. And, know why Scottish men don't marry sheep? Because sheep can't cook. I apologize to all immediately; Scottish men seem manly enough to beat me to a pulp, and that's not very funny. But you do hear these jokes around, probably circulated by the English.

Boswell and Johnson proceeded by boat to the tiny nearby island of Inch-Kenneth. There they encountered the only inhabitants: Sir Allan Maclean, chief of Clan Maclean, his two daughters, and their servants. Boswell enjoyed dancing a reel while one of the girls played a harpsichord. The visit provoked an outburst of piety when Boswell discovered that Sir Allan was not a big drinker ("riotous bottle companion," in Boswell's words). So he walked outside, knelt and prayed "that I may attain everlasting felicity." Such a moment recalls again the character of Boswell, so often slandered by his critics for his frequent failings. He was weak, as we all are, but he possessed a deep faith, an unquenchable hopefulness and a longing for goodness. The twentieth-century Scottish writer Moray McLaren, after tracing Boswell's path through the Highlands in the early 1950s, wrote: "It has been said of him that while other chroniclers, other writers of memoirs, have left portraits and sometimes even photographs of themselves to the world, James Boswell has given us an X-ray presentation of Boswell."

Before leaving InchKenneth Boswell expressed his delight at the island and indulged some serious if unlikely thoughts about buying it, as his brother David had always imagined purchasing an island. "Sir," said Mr. Johnson, "so does every man, till he knows what it is." Upon coming across a small barren black rock Johnson later mocked Boswell in this way: "This shall be your island, and it shall be called InchBoswell." Johnson's good humor could also be another man's undoing.

B & J and I took different paths across Mull. Theirs—beginning at Tobermory to the north of the island, proceeding via the west coast to the southwesterly tip and ultimately to the island of Iona—required the better part of two days. Mine, starting from Craignure, followed a gradual southwesterly road for about thirty-six miles to the small fishing port of Fionnphort.

I saw only six vehicles driving toward me on that entire thirty-six-mile trip, and I can remember each one with the kind of clarity and focus normally reserved for imminent tornadoes or ghostly visions. Single-track roads can do that to Americans.

About half a mile after leaving Craignure on the A849, the two-lane road shrank by half. Hills became steeper. Tree branches leaned closer to the road (where did trees come from on an island supposed to be devoid of them?). Vegetation appeared at road's edge as if spawned by Miracle-Gro. And here came a truck. Not a car, but a large lorry. A Mercedes, I remember. With an old man behind the wheel, grimacing. I'm going to be killed by a Mercedes. Is that better than being finished off by a Volvo? Or a Vauxhall? I began looking for a way out. And there, suddenly, a small twenty-foot strip of pavement appeared to my left, allowing me space to pull my vehicle mostly off the road. I did so, hurriedly, breathing fast, and the lorry dashed by at top speed. I know I should have been getting used to this. It took a few seconds to recover and realize that I had finally done what I was supposed to do—pull into the lay-by to my left and let the oncoming traffic go by. Whoever gets to the lay-by first is the one who stops. I finally got it. I was stronger now. The road, single-track or not, was no more threat, no more terror. I was exultant. I got past five more lorries and even managed to pull over to the left to allow another hard-charging lorry to overtake me. No more would single tracks cause me upset.

It was almost dinnertime when I pulled into the neat-looking B&B in the village of Fionnphort (pronounced finny-fort, by the way). My host John greeted me warmly, suggesting that he'd seen other Americans make it this far before. "Most of them get here pretty tense," he said with a big smile. "You look like you did pretty good." I was liking him already. The rain was beginning to fall and the winds were picking up. "It'll be a rough day tomorrow," John cautioned. His inn was made of granite, 120 years old, and it looked sturdy indeed. My room was quite comfortable. The B&B was a scant minute's walk to the ferry for Iona and half that distance to a pub that promised a snug fire, some Guinness, and maybe a little conversation with the locals.

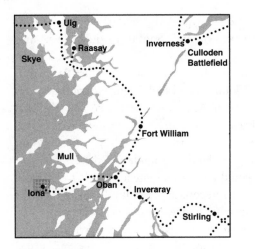

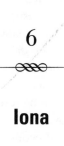

6

⎯⎯⎯⎯∞∞∞⎯⎯⎯⎯

Iona

Generally speaking, in Fionnphort the locals turned out to be as interested in Boswell and Johnson as just about everyone else I had encountered so far. The notable exception was the gentleman behind the counter at the local bookstore. He spoke brightly of the two, though he added a caution about some of the "not so nice" things Johnson had to say about the Scots.

It was more than amazing to find a bookstore in Fionnphort, a community which might number two hundred people but probably had fewer. I didn't notice it when I arrived the evening before, but there it was, about two houses away from my B&B, a can't-miss stop on the walk to the ferry. It carried a terrific selection of Scottish books as well as some groceries and, most significantly, whisky. When will bookstores in the States begin to offer the same level of amenities? I resolved to buy several books when I returned from Iona in the evening, but for the moment I had to rush to the ferry for the early morning's first trip, and the weather wasn't going to make it easy.

John, my host, a "recovering fisherman," warned me that the winds were nearing gale force 5, moving toward twenty-five miles an hour, and the one-mile crossing through the strong currents of the Sound of Iona was subject to cancellation when the wind-pushed waters made this brief trip too perilous. The wind was indeed very brisk and cold, waves were sloshing up, and the whitecaps were running hard as I looked out toward grayish, low-slung Iona in the distance. The ferry wasn't very big and was positioned next to a jetty. The bow ramp pressed into a concrete ramp at the toe-deep edge of the water, and I walked rather daintily up it, my shoes getting damp, and climbed up into the small passenger lounge, which was really just a bench seat on the port side. After a minute or two the ramp was pulled up and the ferry departed, already beginning to sway as the captain turned into the wind. I was terribly excited about Iona and, frankly, getting a little edgy about the trip across the Sound.

Boswell was especially excited by his arrival on Iona (then known as Icolmkill). For a change he and Johnson had had a rather smooth journey by boat, skirting the western coast of Mull (and missing completely what would be Fionnphort today). Their boat was unable to get close to the landing, so Johnson and Boswell were carried ashore, as Johnson wrote: "Our boat could not be forced very near the dry ground, and the Highlanders carried us over the water." It would have been quite a chuckle to have observed several people struggling to negotiate the bulky Johnson over the water—but that's apparently not what happened. Boswell later wrote that when the party landed, he and Sir Allan Maclean were carried on their crew's shoulders to dry land, but Johnson "sprang into the sea and waded out." Either story produces delightful images, but neither may give us the full account.

The editor of the latest (2007) edition of Boswell's and Johnson's writings on the trip, Ronald Black, has a bit more information about Johnson's actions, which were regarded as highly eccentric by everyone who heard about them. He includes remarks from a radio broadcast in 1936 or 1937 by the Rev. Dr. Coll MacDonald (it hardly gets more Scottish than that) which tell us that the incident was long remembered:

> Johnson was a massive, burly man, big-bellied and talkative. He was so short-sighted that he jumped out of Maclean of the Inch's galley before her stem had ploughed a furrow in the sands of Port Ronan. He was wet up to the thighs, and poor Boswell paid for the calamity. The huge old man exploded in rage and started berating and bullying him. "I have been tormented like the Apostle Paul by the tumult of waves and placed in danger of my life amidst the dark vales and horrid peaks of this uncouth land. Should this wetting bring upon me a fatal disease, pray take care that my corpse rot in London's soil, and by no means amongst the savage chiefs and plunderers of the Highland clans."

Yes sir, nothing like a little fear to get those real feelings out loud and clear. And yet, as we will see in a few pages, when Johnson was facing serious danger—not just thigh-deep wading, but the threat of his ship capsizing in a storm—he lay placidly below deck wondering what all the fuss was about.

The small island of Iona occupies a unique place in the history of Scotland. Boswell knew its significance well, and that heightened his anticipation of exploring the island with his companion. Iona is an enduring symbol of Christianity, and it has been a sacred destination for pilgrims over hundreds of centuries. It was here that Columba—later to become Saint Columba—is said to have arrived from Ireland in A.D. 563 to found a monastery that would become the heart of the Scottish church during the next several centuries. Columba spent thirty-four years on Iona, meditating, copying manuscripts, and leading monks in prayer, before his death in 597, as recorded by his seventh-century biographer Adomnan in *Life of Columba.* The magnificent gospel book, the *Book of Kells,* is thought to have been created on Iona before being removed to Ireland in the ninth century for safety.

There was a series of savage attacks on the island by Viking raiders in the eighth and ninth centuries, but the monastery persisted. Large-scale rebuilding operations on Iona took place in the thirteenth and fifteenth centuries, with Benedictine and Augustine structures replacing the old Columban monastery. Medieval pilgrims came regularly to the island. According to authors Anna Richie and Ian Fisher in their valuable and succinct guidebook *Iona Abbey and Nunnery* (2004), "the Scottish Reformation of 1560 put an end to monastic life in Iona and the abbey and nunnery gradually fell into the picturesque ruins so popular with the tourists of the eighteenth and nineteenth centuries." Restoration work beginning at the end of the nineteenth century and continuing intermittently afterwards has allowed modern travelers a better sense of the abbey's magnificence, and a community has been created on the island to assist modern-day pilgrims.

Boswell and Johnson were foremost among the eighteenth-century tourists. Johnson's first observations seem a bit supercilious in hindsight: "We were now treading that illustrious island, which once was the luminary of the *Caledonian* regions, whence savage clans and roving barbarians derived the benefits of knowledge, and the blessings of religion." But he warmed to the site quickly and added his oft-quoted comment, "The man is to be little envied . . . whose piety would not grow warmer among the ruins of Iona!" The two men arrived in the evening and spent the night in a well-provisioned barn (no longer in existence) with lots of hay, sheets for cover, and portmanteau for a pillow. Boswell's pleasure at having Johnson with him for this portion of the journey was palpable, and excitement courses through these pages in his *Journal.*

In the morning the travelers visited the religious sites, and Boswell gives us a memorable and quite Boswellian portrait of his experience in the abbey:

> I then went into the cathedral, which is really grand enough when one thinks of its antiquity and of the remoteness of the place; and at

the end, I offered up my adorations to GOD. I again addressed a few words to Saint Columbus; and I warmed my soul with religious resolutions. I felt a kind of exultation in thinking that the solemn scenes of piety ever remain the same, though the cares and follies of life may prevent us from visiting them, or may even make us fancy that their effects were only "as yesterday when it is past," and never again to be perceived. I should maintain an exemplary conduct. One has a strange propensity to fix upon some point from whence a better course of life may be said to begin. I read with an audible voice the fifth chapter of St. James and Dr. Ogden's tenth sermon. I suppose there has not been a sermon preached in this church since the Reformation. I had a serious joy in hearing my voice, while it was filled with Ogden's admirable eloquence, resounding in the ancient cathedral of Icolmkill.

I thought of that moment as I stood in the same place in the same abbey 234 years later. I did not possess a copy of St. James with me, nor did I claim knowledge of the works of Samuel Ogden, an eighteenth-century English-born churchman whose sermons were widely acclaimed. But I felt obliged to speak out loud when I found myself alone. "Bless all who have been here," I said. And then, merrily channeling Boswell, I added, "Hi Bozzy" without a trace of embarrassment. I turned around and saw a couple of other tourists behind me, looking quite puzzled. I excused myself and moved on, not wanting to go through more chatter about who has or hasn't heard of Boswell and Johnson.

The remains of the nunnery are the first things that greet visitors after passing through the houses and the shop or two that constitute the village of Iona at ferry's edge. I was dressed in a cotton turtleneck sweater, a wool outer sweater, and a heavy wind and rain parka with a drawstring hood. I was still getting soaked with the rain, and the cold, blustery wind whipped through all of my clothing as easily as a hurricane rolls through levees. I realized I had left my good gloves on the ferry. So much for doing anything with my hands except keeping them in my pockets. I walked much faster than I should have through those outdoor ruins.

A brisk five-minute walk away was the restored abbey cathedral, a welcome refuge from the wind and rain, though the stones made the damp cold feel oppressive. A soft-spoken woman gave a group of seven of us a tour of the sanctuary, her first of the season, she said. The other tourists were college kids from Aberdeen, red-cheeked and laughing self-consciously, snapping photos as quickly as they could turn around. Our guide mentioned Boswell and Johnson on the island, and I was shamelessly pleased. Later in the gift shop—no whisky here—the clerk found a copy of their books and told me that there had been a filmed reenactment of Boswell and Johnson's experiences on Iona some ten years ago, adding, "You know, Boswell and Johnson really discovered this part of Scotland for the rest of the world." I considered kissing her, but resisted. I've been unable to locate the video to which she referred.

The rest of the afternoon was spent wandering around various parts of the island. Iona is just over three miles long and a mile and a half at its widest point, but in the steady rain and wind it seemed larger. Iona is said to be the burial place for many of Scotland's kings, chieftains, and lairds, including Macbeth. There's a graveyard that is alleged to hold his remains, though the key words here seem to be *alleged to hold*. No one knows for sure, and most historians have lots of doubts. The story is one of those Scottish legends, perhaps, and another instance of the problem in separating historical reality from cherished myth.

It was hard to deny that the atmosphere of the island was special. Once a center for scholarship and spirituality, Iona still possesses an aura of peacefulness and solitude that was able to touch me in spite of the deteriorating weather all around. And while the ruins of castles and deserted buildings elsewhere in Scotland can evoke melancholy feelings, I experienced only gratitude that these structures on Iona have endured and are in use. I had a few minutes to talk with members of the ecumenical Iona Community who help ensure that the abbey and cloister are in daily use and who take responsibility for spiritual renewal programs on the island. One of them, a white-haired man named George, told me that the experiences there "speak to a grace within each of us, and allow us to renew our commitment to our God and our community." He spoke quietly, welcoming me and inviting me back when I had more time.

Boswell and Johnson made their way back across Mull, through country Johnson labeled "gloomy desolation." It was on this part of the journey that Johnson let Boswell know for the first time that he was contemplating writing about his experiences. "I rejoiced at the thought," Boswell wrote in his *Journal*. Once back on Mull, Boswell—in one of those moments his critics dwell on—once again slipped off the wagon, got drunk on punch, and found himself admonished by Johnson. "It humbled me to find that my holy resolutions at Icolmkill had been so ineffectual that the very day after having been there I had drank too much. I went to Mr. Johnson before he was up. He first said none of our (London) Club would get drunk, but then, taking himself, he said [Edmund] Burke would get drunk and be ashamed of it; [Oliver] Goldsmith would get drunk and boast of it, if it had been with a little whore or so, who had allowed him to go in a coach with her." I think we may conclude that with this refreshing conversation Johnson forgave his irrepressible younger companion. And hardly for the first time.

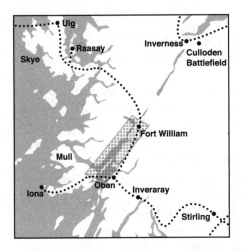

7

Mull to Fort William

Boswell and Johnson then returned to the mainland, to Oban, Inveraray, and southward as their journey came to a close. I wanted to go in the opposite direction, to Coll and to see the uninhabited island of Staffa, known as Fingal's Cave, with its giant rock face cut by the sea. My companions saw it during their trip toward Iona, and over a half century later it inspired composer Felix Mendelssohn's vivid, sea-washed work known as the "Hebrides Overture" or "Fingal's Cave," written during his visit there in 1829. That visit was part of a walking tour of Scotland which also gave the twenty-one-year-old composer the inspiration for his "Scotch Symphony." Both pieces are among my favorites. Even Queen Victoria was rowed by barge into the cave in 1847. I was eager, almost desperate, to get there for my own view.

But I first needed to get off Iona or face an extra twenty-four hours or more of delay. The wind was blowing hard, and the water between Iona and Mull seemed angry. I could see the small ferry struggling toward me through high seas. I was bone-cold waiting for it. The ferry finally made it as darkness neared, rocking and straining against the wind. Once I was on board a member of the crew walked up to my seat and asked if I had left a pair of gloves on the early morning ferry. I replied yes, and he handed them over. Scotland is amazing!

As we struggled through the sound, waves crashing over the side of the ferry, I wondered about my willingness to take a trip of an hour toward Staffa in this fierce weather. "Weather can be difficult here any time of year, but in the winter months, it's very hard," my Fionnphort host John said later that evening over a warming cup of tea. As a former fisherman, he not only counseled against going to Staffa but also said that I wouldn't be able to find anyone willing to take me there this time of year. He was right. My trip to Fingal's Cave would have to wait for another journey to Scotland. John also warned me about possible ferry cancellations to Coll. He would be proved right once again.

The next day I met a just-arrived couple of students from the University of Edinburgh taking a holiday. They knew of Boswell and Johnson and had planned a trip to Iona in part because they had read of the travelers. I shared a few impressions of Iona; their morning weather was much more forgiving than mine yesterday, though the forecast called for more storms on the way soon. After packing up I headed back to Craignure on the single-track road, pulling into the lay-bys with confidence, and even doing a little speeding in the sections where I had a long view ahead.

This part of Mull defied Johnson's desolate observations. The large tracts of moorlands nestled near the island's highest peak, Ben More (3,169 feet), appeared in a mix of gentle colors in the subdued sunlight, and the isolation of the island became a value not a threat. There were few farms visible, only a handful of vehicles in either direction and no one in sight. The feeling was one of suddenly finding yourself transplanted to another world where you are alone and the first to see the landscape surrounding you. It was dazzling, breathtaking, heart-stopping. A minute later the road ascended a plateau, offering an unobstructed view for miles. I pulled over and got out. A pure, clean smell, quiet hills. Nothing seemed to move, to speak. A gust of wind, then nothing. I held my breath for a moment. A quick movement to one side. A rabbit, perhaps? I felt myself teetering in place, almost dizzy, my senses overloaded by . . . well, by nothing, really. My mouth dropped open; I strained to hear something. Nothing. No stirrings as far as my eyes could reach, either. The moment stretched. I was afraid to move and force my canvas to change. And then . . . in the distance the faint noise of an engine, a car or truck, I suppose. The precious moment ended. I blinked for the first time in many seconds. I climbed reluctantly back into the car. I'm pretty sure I was smiling.

In Craignure the weather had turned nasty, and I discovered I had misread the ferry schedule. Going to Coll wouldn't be possible for at least another twenty-four hours, perhaps longer with the worsening weather. Boswell and Johnson would have appreciated my difficulty, I hoped. Their trip to Coll was nightmarish, or at least in Boswell's colorful description.

The travelers had set off in a small boat headed from Skye to Mull. The weather appeared favorable, the sort of omen that is invariably short-lived in Scottish waters. Boswell and Johnson would pass by islands engagingly named Rhum, Eigg, and Muck (which, when pronounced together, sound rather like the name of a hot toddy or perhaps someone's idea of a bad dinner). Boswell relates a bizarre, brutal tale of how some residents of Eigg murdered some members of the MacLeod clan who came hunting for them. When the people of Eigg refused to send out the accused killers, the MacLeods set a peat fire at the mouth of the cave and smoked everyone—men, women, and children—to death. For some reason Boswell regretted not getting to see the place. Once Boswell and Johnson were on board the ship, it didn't take long for the weather to change and make island stops impossible. Johnson wrote succinctly in his *Journey:* "We were doomed to experience, like others, the danger of trusting to the wind, which blew against us, in a short time, with such violence, that we, being no seasoned sailors, were willing to call it a tempest. I was seasick and lay down. Mr. Boswell kept the deck."

The prolix Boswell, however, gives us a much fiercer portrait of what they encountered, and, even allowing for some exaggerations, the trip indeed must have been frightening (more so for one on deck than for one lying below, I suspect): "As we advanced, the storm grew greater, and the sea very rough," he wrote. Darkness came, the winds howled, the sails were in danger of being ripped apart, and the crew was shouting in nervous tones. Boswell was understandably agitated.

> The boat lay so much on a side that I trembled lest she should be overset; and indeed they told me afterwards that they had run her sometimes to within an inch of the water, so anxious were they to make what haste they could before the night should be worse. . . . I saw tonight what I never saw before, a prodigious sea with immense billows coming upon a vessel, so as that it seemed hardly possible to escape. There was something grandly horrible in the sight.

Boswell feared his life would be lost. He thought of his wife. He prayed fervently.

> It was half an hour after eleven before we set ourselves on the course to Coll. As I saw them all busy doing something, I asked Coll with much earnestness what I could do. He with a lucky readiness put into my hand a rope which was fixed to the top of one of the masts, and bid me hold it fast till he bid me pull. This could not be of the least service; but by employing me, he kept me out of their way, who were busy working the ship; and at the same time diverted my fear to a certain degree, by making me think I was occupied. There did I stand firm to my post, while the wind and rain beat upon me, always expecting a call to pull my rope.

That, to me, captures much of the essence of Boswell. The scene is both funny and heroic. There can be little doubting Boswell's courage; he is on the deck of the bobbing ship, tossed by the mighty winds, soaked to the skin, but refusing to hide or turn away from whatever his fate will be. In such a moment many of us would have cowered or maybe even cried. A crew member gives Boswell a task—a totally meaningless one, probably, unless the mast collapses—which focuses the nervous passenger. Boswell knows it is an empty gesture, but he appreciates it. It gives him strength and prevents him from becoming a burden to the already overburdened crew trying to save the ship. How can you not like, even admire, Boswell at such a tempestuous moment? Boswell eventually went below, became ill, and struggled through the rest of the night before the ship landed safely at Coll. He found Johnson recovered, lying quiet and unconcerned about any danger, anticipating landfall.

I already knew what I would have to do; Coll would have to be dropped from my itinerary. I had a reservation coming up soon on the Isle of Lewis in the Outer Hebrides that couldn't be missed, and I needed some extra time to follow Boswell and Johnson on Skye. Rearranging plans in Scotland is hardly unheard of; nearly all of my predecessors in the pursuit of Johnson and Boswell have found themselves having to adjust their itineraries, and almost always because of the weather (although in several instances the pursuers decided they'd rather focus on one or two areas the men visited rather than the entire journey).

My alternative was to head back to the mainland and drive up the coast to Skye, my jumping-off point for Lewis. I had some time before the ferry back to Oban arrived, so I read again what Boswell and Johnson had written about their much longer-than-intended stay on Coll. The island doesn't seem to offer much now nor did it then. The *Rough Guide to Scotland* tells of the possibilities for bird-watching and the sandy beaches, but it seems to me a long way to come just for a stretch of sand blown by the untrammeled breezes off the Atlantic.

Coll is about twelve miles by three, fish-shaped, and a two-and-a-half-hour ferry ride from Oban. It has a resident population of about one hundred, roughly one-ninth of what it was in 1773. Johnson said of it, "there is not much to amuse curiosity, or to attract avarice." What struck me most compellingly was never what the travelers thought of the island as much as the incredible, dangerous journey they endured getting there. Once he was forcibly marooned on Coll by the weather, Johnson wrote a bit dryly about the history, work habits, and religion of the islanders. Boswell, typically, was much more personal, endorsing the "primitive heartiness" of some lodgings and the odd custom of some islanders donning cow skins for special celebrations; observing Johnson's insatiable curiosity and confessed disgust with the coarse manners he found ("I cannot bear low life"); and, of course, reporting on the regular bouts of stormy weather, which is unusual, and even surprising, for a native Scotsman.

It was time for me to depart from my two literary companions for a while until we reunited on Skye. The ferry crossing back to the mainland went smoothly, and once on shore I zipped up the A828 and the A82, with an overnight stop planned at Fort William. The route had beautiful strips of water off to my left—Loch Linhe, Loch Creran, and pretty little Cuil Bay—and under temporarily sunny skies my spirits soared.

Near the village of Portnacroish, which I reached an hour or so later, there was a restaurant beside the road with a spectacular view of a castle surrounded by water a few hundred yards away. It was Castle Stalker, which, like Doune Castle, played a role in *Monty Python and the Holy Grail*. Near the end of the film the castle stood in for a French-occupied fortress which once again rejects King Arthur and his knights. Arthur is seen knee-deep in water, dejectedly walking away from Stalker at the end of the movie. Stalker (which means hunter or falconer) is quite unbelievably picturesque even at a distance. The present structure got its start under the Stewarts in the fourteenth century, and by 1620 it had fallen into the hands of the powerful and ubiquitous Clan Campbell. They occupied the castle when they repulsed a Jacobite invasion in 1745. There were other bloody clashes before the castle was abandoned and began falling into ruin by the end of the nineteenth century. Restoration began in the mid-twentieth century, and Stalker now has been made habitable and is once again occupied. From any angle, it is a spectacular sight. I was told that it's been the castle most often used in movies, though I later heard the same about three or four other castles. I couldn't take my eyes off it, even as I ate a sandwich in the restaurant. The skies had darkened and rain began falling hard, but I still couldn't resist walking outside to make some photographs before I got back in the car.

Fort William was rather gray and gloomy on this rainy afternoon. I didn't realize that such is pretty much its regular demeanor. The central business district had lots of closed shops, and only a couple of bars and tourist stores seemed to be open. The town is a lure for visitors in the summer, though mostly for its location: it's only a couple of hours drive to Skye toward the northwest and much less to Loch Ness and Inverness to the northeast.

That puts Fort William within easy reach of Glencoe, perhaps the most renowned of all Scotland's magnificent glens and one whose name still leaves an unpleasant anti-English taste in the mouths of many Scots. It was the scene of one of the great acts of treachery in a history that reverberates with scheming and plotting. The betrayal occurred in 1692 after King William of Orange, whose policies alternated between coercion and consent, attempted to enforce loyalty from rebellious Highland clans. Most of the clan chiefs agreed, however reluctantly, to pledge their support to the crown. One of them, Alasdair MacIain Macdonald of Glencoe, missed the deadline for doing so by a few days, though he eventually pledged himself. That gave William an opening to make a point about his power. He had his army—mostly the Campbells—ingratiate themselves with the Macdonalds. The two sides enjoyed meals and company together for a couple of weeks until the king gave the order to exterminate the Glencoe Macdonalds.

The king's soldiers moved first to block off the northern and southern entrances to the glen. Then they began the extermination. Old man Macdonald was shot to death in his bed. The clan members began running, half-naked, toward the icy hills. Both of Macdonald's sons and his grandson escaped. Thirty-eight other clan members—men, women, and children—were systematically slaughtered, and uncounted others died in the raging snowstorm that soon hit the area. It could have been worse—hundreds of women and children could have been murdered—if some of the plans hadn't proved too complicated to pull off.

News of the massacre hardly produced the subservience King William had wanted and expected. The sympathies of the Highland clans would never be with the king in any numbers, and their enmity would be important in the coming wars between Scotland and England in the first half of the eighteenth century. Because of the distastefulness and public revulsion over the Glen Coe massacre, the English government did what governments usually do in a time of crisis: it appointed a commission to look into the matter. To its credit the royal panel found the massacre was an act of murder, and the government was condemned for having "barbarously killed men under trust." The king's secretary of state in Scotland became the scapegoat, but of course no one officially blamed the King. As bad as it was, Glencoe was only one of several atrocities committed by the government in the Highlands in the seventeenth century, setting the stage for more bloodshed to come on an even grander scale.

My accommodation for the night in Fort William was a former distillery upgraded into a comfortable, modern hostelry. With a fine dinner of fresh Scottish salmon and some single malts—how could anyone resist when you're spending the night in a building that smells like good drink?—I was in a most agreeable mood. At the hotel's quiet bar I found myself in an easy conversation with a couple of local men close to my age, from whom I kept my own counsel about the ragged condition of Fort William. We talked about the weather (too cold), the tourists (I seemed to be accorded a different status for being here in the winter), the cost of whisky and petrol (too high), and the attractive if slightly slutty-looking young woman (too cheap) who passed through the bar with her boyfriend. Having just read about the Glen Coe massacre, I managed to work it into the conversation, wondering if my companions might have any thoughts about that event that occurred so long, long ago—315 years ago, to be exact.

You would have thought that I had just insulted William Wallace.

"You know what those English bastards did, do you?" one of them asked, his tone growing fierce. "Took 'em in for dinner, drank with them, just like us, and then turned around and cut them up, cut the little children and the women, raped them, beat them, the bastards!" he said even more loudly.

The other man was nodding faster and faster, and both had put their drinks down on the bar so they could gesture with their hands. "Cut them like that," the first one said, swooping his hand down to the bar top with a thud. And then he stopped. "You know," he said a little more quietly, "they did it before, and they did it again. We were always their favorite chopping ground."

I raised my glass to them, and we all drank without a sound for a moment. I wasn't sure what I should say. It seemed another bold reminder that history lays close to the heart in Scotland. As it does in Ireland, Poland, the American South, and many other lands. William Faulkner was, of course, right when he observed that "The past is never dead. It's not even past." We all sat quietly and nursed our drinks for a bit. Then I excused myself and went to bed. Quite sober.

8

—⚉⚉⚉—

Skye, Part I

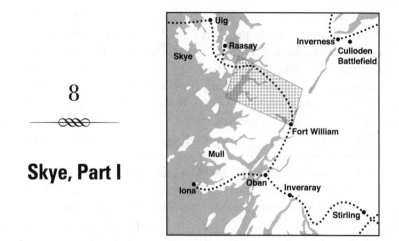

There were nothing but blue skies above when I climbed behind the wheel the next morning, pointing northward on the A82 and then west on the A87. I was eager to get to Skye; every time I strayed from Boswell and Johnson I quickly began missing them. The journey on this lovely morning proved spectacular: gorgeous mountains topped by fresh snows and framed by those deep blue skies and a few puffy high whites. Scotland's highest peak, Ben Nevis (4,406 feet), was off to the right, and later the Five Sisters, peaks that range up to 3,000 feet, were glowingly displayed in the sunlight. The glen was breathtaking, the waters of Loch Duich, cold and clean, running along the roadside and offering polished mirror images of the distant peaks. I must have stopped the car a half dozen times. In summer, I was told later, buses with thousands of visitors headed for Skye barrel through here with little opportunity for reflection. None could have a finer weather moment than I was enjoying now; I snapped photo after photo. I've never spent two hours in the presence of any more stunning scenery than that before me this morning.

I made the tough decision to pass by another terrific-looking castle as a step in my faltering struggle to overcome castle addiction. It was Eilean Donan Castle, one of Scotland's most photographed edifices and the one featured in such films as *Highlander, The World Is Not Enough,* and *Rob Roy.* The last appeared in 1995, the year of *Braveheart,* though it drew considerably less attention. Liam Neeson starred as the title character, which the moviemakers pitched in their usual modest way: "Honor made him a man. Courage made him a hero. History made him a legend." It wasn't the first film about the man; that would have been the 1911 *Rob Roy,* the first "major" motion picture produced in Scotland. No prints of it survive, but like the most recent version—the fourth to hit the screen—it was probably all about a kilted Highland hero in a romantic landscape.

There was a real Rob Roy, a MacGregor born in 1671. He became a romanticized figure over the years, thanks largely to Sir Walter Scott's somewhat fanciful and very popular 1818 novel, *Rob Roy*. The 1995 film didn't hurt that romantic portrayal, either. Like *Braveheart*, it looks great on the screen with numerous lovely shots of the Scottish countryside. The actual story of Rob Roy has a stirring reality about it that connects with some of the deepest strains in Scottish history.

As a teenager Rob Roy joined his father in the uprising against King William of Orange. He was wounded in one battle, and his father was jailed by the English for treason. When the father was released, his wife was dead, their lands taken, his spirit crushed. Having survived that, the son eventually settled into life as a respected cattleman. He wound up defaulting on a loan to increase his herd, and his chief creditor—the powerful duke of Montrose—branded him an outlaw and evicted him from his land. That led to a blood feud between the two men that lasted for five years until he surrendered to the duke and was imprisoned. Rob Roy was eventually pardoned. He died quietly in 1734 and remains a figure celebrated by most Scots.

The original fortified structure on the island of Donan went up in the thirteenth century to protect against Viking incursions. The castle expanded over succeeding centuries and witnessed many periods of bloodshed. Eilean Donan played a role in the Jacobite uprisings in the seventeenth and eighteenth centuries, which resulted in its near destruction at the hands of the English. Abandoned and neglected for most of the next two hundred years, it was rebuilt between 1912 and 1932 and has been open to the public since. On the day that I was there, there were only a few cars in the visitor lot, but I had decided to push on to meet up with Boswell and Johnson. Within minutes I was driving over the Skye Bridge, which opened in 1995, replacing the old ferry, and which now links the island to the mainland. Mine was a much easier trip than Boswell and Johnson had when they took a slow boat to Skye to launch the Western Isles portion of their journey that would include, as we now know, the islands Skye, Coll, Ulva, InchKenneth, Mull, and Iona.

Skye is the largest of the Hebridean Islands in both land mass and population. In the eighteenth century very little was known about it. The first printed history of the west coast of Scotland had appeared just one year before Boswell and Johnson's journey when Thomas Pennant published his still readable book *A Tour in Scotland and Voyage to the Hebrides.* Pennant was a fellow of the Royal Society, a zoologist and, in Johnson's words, "the best travel writer" of the time. He spent eight weeks sailing around the region and produced a surprisingly thorough survey. He didn't get to the Outer Hebrides, but his writing on the Inner Islands, including Skye, "goes a long way to explaining why the Hebrides are so different from the rest of Britain in culture, language, and tradition," according to historian Elizabeth Bray. "He shows the Hebrides have been heirs to a different legacy; separated from the rest of Britain not only by their geographical remoteness but by accidents of history and climate and language that make the Highland line—the division between Gaelic-speaking Highlands and Islands, and the Sassenachs (the 'Saxon' or English-speaking Lowlands) and south Britain—a border of as great significance as the border between Scotland and England."

Boswell and Johnson spent more time on Skye than anywhere else on their trip. It was, most observers feel, the true goal of their immense journey, carrying the romantic thrill of Bonnie Prince Charlie and the Jacobite Rising of 1745. It was and is a magnificently beautiful island, though neither Boswell nor Johnson devoted themselves much to describing its glories. (By contrast, Sir Walter Scott in 1814 found his imagination elevated by the beauty and grandeur of what he observed.) That said, the trip to Skye prompted some marvelous writing by the two men along with a series of memorable encounters, some historically significant, and at least one divertingly ridiculous. There would be few dull moments on this journey.

There should be no doubting the challenges before Boswell and Johnson at Skye. The island was large and largely mysterious in 1773, exceedingly difficult to traverse in the best of weather (and we know how often that occurs here, don't we?). Isolated, even potentially dangerous, the scene of warring less than thirty years in the past, it may as well have been the jungles of Borneo in the minds of educated Londoners. But unfamiliarity did not deter either man, for this was the place they had long aimed for, and Skye would prove well worth the excitement they felt on landing at Armadale on the southeast coast of the Sleat peninsula.

It did not take long for matters to get out of hand, however, and as usual Boswell was at the heart of the distress The two men spent their first night on Skye at the home of Sir Alexander Macdonald, ninth chieftain of the Macdonalds and lord of the Isles. He was not a man, as described by Johnson, who had been "tamed into insignificance by an English education." He was a proud Highlander, and by accounts very much the pedantic, priggish figure Boswell—the exact opposite—found him to be. Worse, Boswell didn't think much of the accommodations. Dinner was "ill-dressed," and there was no claret. He and Johnson almost had to share a bed until Boswell complained enough to have them separated. "I was quite hurt with the meanness and unsuitable appearance of everything." He pumped other guests for stories that reflected unfavorably on his host, finally confronting and belittling Sir Alexander to his face. "Had he been a man of more mind, he and I must have had a quarrel for life." The next morning, it seemed all had been forgiven, but Boswell this time got Johnson involved: "Sir, we shall make nothing of him," Johnson said. "He has no more ideas of a chief than an attorney who has twenty houses in a street and considers how much he can make of them. All is wrong." Johnson went on to insult Lady Macdonald with his celebrated observation recorded by Boswell: "This woman would sink a ninety-gun ship She is so dull—so heavy." Then Boswell got drunk, and, as hard as it might seem to believe, things slipped even farther downhill. Even after their departure, and throughout the rest of his writings, Boswell never stopped referring to the unpleasantness at Armadale.

Matters did not end there. Boswell and Sir Alexander would get into it a few years later over what Boswell had to say in his *Journal*. Their relationship apparently had continued—somehow—on a relatively even keel until 1785 when Boswell's book was published and Sir Alexander read a watered-down version of the stay at Armadale (he didn't have to read between the lines with too much effort). He sent Boswell a long and insulting letter, and things almost degenerated to a duel before Boswell recanted and took out a few lines. (Modern versions of the *Journal* include what Boswell originally wrote and the version to which I refer.)

Boswell was genuinely upset by the reaction he stirred, though most of us would have to say that what he wrote was on the rude side and could indeed have made the Lord Macdonald angry. (And what he quoted Johnson as saying would only have added fuel to that fire.) Still, Boswell wasn't one to pull his punches, and he always felt that if he told the truth, people would understand. When they didn't, he was surprised, disappointed. That was part of Boswell's ingenuous character. But enough of this; back to Skye.

I was driving on to Sconser on the northwest coast for the night. I passed Coriechatachan, now a very small community beside the A87, where there is virtually nothing left to suggest the good times the travelers enjoyed here at a farmhouse with their tenant hosts, Mr. and Mrs. Mackinnon. They were well fed, hospitably entertained, and after dinner Bozzy joined with them in singing and drinking (he would suffer an epic bout of drinking when he made a return visit there a few weeks later) before retiring (in a bed by himself) in what was a dormitory sleeping situation. The next night

Boswell watched another guest, a minister, come into the dormitory room to prepare for bed; the maid helped him undress, and he turned his naked back away from her to use the chamber pot. "A remarkable instance of the simplicity of manners or want of delicacy among the people in Skye," Boswell observed.

I spent my night in a private room Boswell would surely have preferred in a picturesque Victorian-era hunting lodge on the wind-lapped waters of the Sound of Raasay. My host Philip and his wife Debra came here three years ago from England to run the inn and have been pleased with their success so far, in spite of quickly rising costs for everything on Skye. Philip maintained a fine library for the use of guests, and we chatted a bit about Johnson and Boswell—he proved well acquainted with their journey—before the subject got around to the weather. "It's windy here even when it's not windy," Philip said, and indeed it was, though rain held off the entire day. I was going to sit up and read, but it was too chilly in the house, so I went up to the bedroom. It was even colder there, and I turned off the light and snuggled under the blankets, feeling a wee bit of communion with B & J.

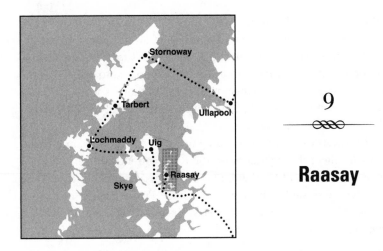

9

Raasay

The wind was still blowing briskly and a light rain was falling when I boarded a small ferry to Raasay the next morning. My car and one other were aboard, and the number of passengers was only six, including a small child. I was weary; my back was hurting from too-soft beds, a common problem on this trip. The pillows everywhere were worse. The matter of heating was interesting, to put it mildly. It had been cool or cold every night, and my rooms had gotten progressively chillier. Most innkeepers turn off the heat from 10 P.M. to 6 A.M. or so, though I can scarcely tell the difference between the heat being on and being off. Climbing into bed at night means pulling up as many covers as can be located. As a champion of fresh air I've gone so far as to open windows some evenings, only to turn my lodgings into a meat locker by the time I was up for the bathroom at 3 A.M. By the way, there's a reason no one puts toilets in meat lockers; the seats are cold enough to inhibit even the most urgent needs. But I digress.

It was only a fifteen-minute ride to Raasay, a place where Boswell especially had a deliciously good time. The four days he and Johnson spent on the island were among the happiest of their journey, maybe as some have suggested, the happiest of Boswell's entire life. And Boswell's writing has an undoubted lightness for this part of the trip, suffused with the great pleasure he felt sweeping up his imagination when he arrived on the lovely island. Readers should savor it for themselves in full, but I'll try to offer enough samples to give a sense of Boswell's palpable energy and exuberance.

Boswell and Johnson, the latter seated high on the stern "like a magnificent Triton," were rowed across the sound in a boat sent by John Mac-Leod, the laird of Raasay. The crew sang as they rowed, and the words echoed those of reapers laboring on the shore. The crossing turned rough, as usually happens. Johnson likened it to being in an open boat on the Atlantic, as the wind roared and water splashed into his face, but he held his good humor, imagining the day's short journey compared to one across the Atlantic in an open boat and laughing at how Londoners would shudder with fear at his recklessness. Johnson at this moment hardly seemed an ailing, melancholic man of sixty-four.

He and Boswell were accompanied by two marvelous companions who would be with them throughout Skye: the Reverend Donald Macqueen, a minister in the Church of Scotland, and Malcolm MacLeod of the House of Raasay, who was said to have helped Bonnie Prince Charlie escape his pursuers on this island in 1746. Boswell's oft-quoted description of Malcolm's person gives us a much admired prose portrait of a keen Highlander:

> He was now sixty-two years of age, quite the Highland gentleman; of a stout, well-made person, well-proportioned; a manly countenance browned with the weather, but a ruddiness in his cheeks, a good way up which his rough beard extended; a quick lively eye, not fierce in his look, but firm and good-humoured. He had a pair of brogues, tartan hose which came up only near to his knees and left them bare, a purple camblet kilt, a black waistcoat, a short cloth green coat bound with gold cord, a yellowish bushy wig, a large blue bonnet with a gold-thread button. I never saw a figure that was more perfectly a representative of a Highland gentleman. I wished to have a picture of him just as he was. I found him frank and *polite,* in the true sense of the word.

Boswell could have done no better had he snapped a camera's shutter.

Boswell liked the view of the rocky coast with fine houses in the near ground, trees, and beyond them hills ascending into mountains. The island prompted from him rare comments on the beauty of the physical and natural world he observed. Johnson's doubts about the expedition were quickly laid to rest, too: "We found nothing but civility, elegance, and plenty. The general air of festivity . . . struck the imagination with a delightful surprise."

On the first night the travelers enjoyed a feast with plenty of drink. There was dancing ("nor did ever fairies trip with greater alacrity," wrote the bemused Johnson) and singing, and Boswell and Johnson relished good conversations, warm hospitality, and a people "polished" and "pleasing" in all manners.

Johnson wrote about the island's topography, admired its wooded areas, and drifted off to a discussion of national culinary preferences when he noted the presence of eels in Raasay waters and the population's disinclination to eat them. (They were believed to cause madness.) "It is not easy to fix the principles upon which mankind have agreed to eat some animals, and reject others; as the principle is not evident, it is not uniform," he wrote. "That which is selected as delicate in one country, is by its neighbors abhorred as loathsome."

Johnson then turned philosophical, examining the prevalence or absence of certain wildlife and the suitability of land for harvests before offering a concise portrait of a small eighteenth-century community. He guessed the population numbered between six hundred and nine hundred, down from the previous centuries, and while there may have been little about the place to stimulate his intellectual curiosity, he concluded his observations with an affectionate note, hailing the hospitality of his hosts and the vividness of the setting: "Such a seat of hospitality, amidst the wind and waters, fills the imagination with a delightful contrariety of images. Without is the rough ocean and the rocky land, the beating billows and the howling storm: within is plenty and elegance, beauty and gaiety, the song and the dance."

Boswell, meanwhile, so full of energy, could not restrain himself. With several hardy companions he took a long walk around the island—apparently close to twenty-four miles in all, a task that hard-bodies still find formidable today—exploring the coast and the island's highest peak, Dun Caan. There occurred a most unforgettable moment: "We mounted up to the top of Dun Caan, where we sat down, eat cold mutton and bread and cheese and drank brandy and punch. Then we had a Highland song from Malcolm; then we danced a reel to which he and Donald and Macqueen sang." My goodness! Think of it: Old Bozzy, half a day on foot, climbing to the top of a 1,400-foot peak to dance a Highland reel and sing boisterously! The description conjures up a very special scene, and in fact many artists have offered their views of that moment, both seriously and comically, over the centuries since.

There was more fun, more dancing—every night, in fact—and more talk, but Johnson was eager to get away, and Boswell reluctantly concurred. They had stayed at the Raasay House, still intact but now an outdoor center (and closed when I visited; it was damaged in a 2009 fire). I stayed at the nearby Isle of Raasay Hotel, a short, curving drive uphill from the ferry pier, passing small houses and their neatly tended gardens. It was a charming hotel, usually full, but I was the only guest this evening. David, who has owned the hotel since 2006, was conversant with Boswell and Johnson. He had carefully explored the Raasay House and other places where the two men spent time, but he admitted "There's not a lot left that really connects directly to them. You can go to the top of the mountain where Boswell danced. That's fun, and you can get a nice view on some days, but it doesn't look like it did back then."

I walked back to a small chapel behind Raasay House, but it was impossible to tell if it was the one referred to by Johnson, and nearby was a graveyard, again similar to one he briefly described. With rain beginning to come down heavily, I took a short drive to a thickly wooded area toward the middle of the island; the sight of so many trees in this one spot, Raasay Forest—when there have been so few on the island—was arresting, even as the rain poured in my half-open window. The forecast called for storms and discouraged me from further exploration, though I confess I had imagined myself doing a few twirls on the mountaintop.

I savored a terrific dinner of tuna steak prepared for me exclusively by Giovanni, the Italian chef recently hired for the hotel. It felt quite luxurious to have the chef checking in with me to discern my levels of satisfaction every few minutes, though I appeared to be the only diner. After dinner David talked with me more about the island and its fewer than two hundred residents. He says he gets on with them well, but that most are strict fundamentalists in their religious practices. He told about a friend who died recently and was buried on the island. The friend's name could not be spoken aloud in the church during the service "because he wasn't a religious person," David said. That seemed harsh, but times have been harsh on Raasay and its most immediate neighbors, an archipelago of three islets, Rona, Fladda, and Eilean Tighe. Raasay is far and away the largest at fourteen miles in length and two and one-half miles across; Eilean Tighe at half a square mile is the smallest. Roger Hutchinson calls this group "the Hebrides in tiniest microcosm," and I'll use his splendid book *Calum's Road* to excerpt a bit of the islands' tortured history. Rona is mostly rock and today uninhabited; it has been little fit for humans throughout its past. Nevertheless in 1841—half a century after Boswell and Johnson—987 people lived on Raasay, a productive land, and 110 on Rona. Fifty years later, in 1891, Raasay's population had fallen to 430 and Rona was home to 181 people, jammed together and trying to eke out a living. Why?

What happened was the mass eviction of the crofters of the land on southern Raasay by their nineteenth-century landlords, who wanted to improve their bottom lines by converting the land to raising sheep and breeding deer. The tenants, who had held to their land for centuries, were resettled to the less desirable parts of northern Raasay and to Rona. One owner of Raasay constructed a stone fence across the island, a precursor to the hated Berlin Wall, if you will. To the south sheep, deer, and rabbits grazed; to the north, men and women attempted to use their miserable slices of land for their animals and crops and to remit an annual rental, which, if defaulted on, would ensure another eviction.

The owners of Raasay after World War I were absentee landlords, and servicemen returning from their military duty were angry at the existing state of affairs. Five men sailed from Rona in 1921 to claim squatter's rights on land they had been denied in southern Raasay. The brave, decisive action by the "Raasay Raiders" led to arrests, court decisions, anger and ultimately lots of bad publicity for the island's owner, but it finally worked. The population began to decline; people living in northern Raasay and Rona moved back south. But not everyone.

As the population dwindled Calum MacLeod and his wife became the only two people left in the north of the island of Raasay. And MacLeod— a crofter, postman, and tender of the Rona lighthouse—wanted a road to his isolated house. A group of crofters who had lived in the area had sought repeatedly road-building assistance from the government, but it was never forthcoming, and they had slowly drifted away to the south. Only Calum was left, and he decided to undertake the creation of the road by himself. He began in the mid-1960s, and worked, six days a week, through gale-force winds and rain, until the road was done, in 1982. His story is a chronicle of great personal achievement and persistence, and Hutchinson's book tells it memorably.

What happened on Raasay happened all over the Highlands and Islands. Mass evictions, the banishing of crofters from good lands in favor of mostly sheep. The tragic process is known as the Highland Clearances and it requires some explanation. Maybe it's best to begin with the Rising of 1745, to which I've referred several times in connection with its most famous participant, Bonnie Prince Charlie. The Jacobite Rising possesses a powerful resonance, as it certainly must have for Boswell and Johnson, traveling through the heart of a proud, independent nation torn and bloodied by the rebellion a mere twenty-seven years earlier.

In early-eighteenth-century Scotland warring with England had become a fact of life. The relationship between the English crown and Scotland was unsettled, to put it charitably. The Stuarts had been on the throne, except during the nasty, forgettable period when Oliver Cromwell seized power. When Charles II died in 1685, he was replaced by James, the seventh Stuart king of the Scots and the last. James was Catholic and willfully and pointlessly alienated non-Catholics in Scotland and England. It wasn't exactly a surprise when he was overthrown in the largely bloodless Glorious Revolution of 1688 and succeeded by his daughter Anne and her husband, the

Dutchman William of Orange. James fled to France, where he proceeded to nurture grudges and plot his return. Meanwhile many of the Highland clans found encouragement from James's political policies, even as he sat in exile, and their backing of the banished ruler gave rise to the Jacobite (derived from the Latin *Jacobus,* or James) faction. There were clashes beginning in 1689 at Killiecrankie; clan members were killed—Glen Coe became a rallying cry in 1692—and resentment and antagonism against the English hardened. James VII died in 1701 and passed the torch of Jacobitism to his son James, who became known as the Old Pretender and who would press his case—his pretensions, if you will—as the rightful heir to the throne. Disputes between the Scots and the English abounded. Many were unresolved bloodbaths. There was some hope that approval of the Treaty of Union between the two countries in 1707 would settle issues, but it resolved little. England assumed responsibility for external affairs for the two nations, and the Scots were supposedly allowed to run their own internal affairs as they had been. The treaty quickly provoked more anger than hope; the Scottish parliament that affirmed it was branded as "bought and sold with English gold." Historians have some disagreements over its impact, but hardly any Scots liked the fact that promised economic benefits from the treaty weren't forthcoming.

The treaty, however, did reliably set the stage for escalating political and battlefield clashes. The Catholic Old Pretender continued to agitate from France, hungry to regain the crown for the Stuarts the way a dog is hungry for a bone. Protestant English remained deeply suspicious of him. There was a short-lived war in 1715 between the Jacobite supporters and the English that brought James back to Scotland in hoped-for triumph, but he hot-footed it back to France when his men were defeated. Another such venture in 1719 also failed.

And so we come to James's son, Charles Edward Louis John Casimir Silvester Severino Maria Stewart, our Bonnie Prince Charlie, also known as the Young Pretender because he was, of course, younger and was beset with the same pretensions. Born in 1720, he arrived in Scotland from France in 1745 at the inexperienced age of twenty-four to proclaim his father king and himself as regent. Many of the Highland clans, nursing their grievances against the English, lined up in support of the prince, though many Lowland Scots had little use for the pretenders and were loyal to the King. Nonetheless, Prince Charles and his army advanced deep into England, threatening the crown and forcing Londoners into a panic. The government put evacuation plans into effect. But the army stalled and was forced to begin a ragged retreat back to Scotland, pursued by the vengeful English. In the early spring of 1746 the two armies clashed for the final time at Culloden near Inverness in the Highlands, and the men of William, duke of Cumberland—soon to be known as "the butcher"—triumphed in a massacre that forever smashed the authority of the Highland chiefs. The victorious English banned the playing of bagpipes and the wearing of tartans, took land away from the chiefs, and forbade them to raise an army. The clan system was effectively destroyed.

As for Bonnie Prince Charlie, he scrambled to escape from the duke's armies, hiding successfully all over the Highlands and Islands over the next year with the help of a small but dedicated group of loyalists, until he was able to slip back to France. The episode was extremely bloody and vicious, but over time it became quite a romantic yarn spun by the Highlanders and eventually picked up by others.

The clearances didn't quite follow the same easy-to-see timeline, but in general they began in the wake of the Jacobite downfall when the clan chiefs no longer needed armies or could afford tenants. The *Oxford Companion to Scottish History* calls the clearances "one of the most evocative and symbolic but least understood episodes of Scottish history." It is, however, hard not to sympathize completely with the men, women, and children who were evicted from their land and separated from their families. The clearances occurred primarily between 1770 and 1860; landowners used their unrestricted authority in the absence of legal obstacles to evict and relocate people who had been occupying their lands for generations. They acted in their own economic self-interest, in many cases by introducing sheep to lands previously tilled by their tenants, and the consequences were devastating for the poor victims. Imagine you and your family have lived on a parcel of land for as long as you remember, and one morning someone shows up and announces that you have to leave immediately. There is no option, no choice; your livelihood is over. You may either be sent to another place you have never heard of, or you may simply be told to go. Period. No more land. No more earning a living as you have become accustomed to doing.

Some men thus evicted joined the English army and fought and died in America. Many of the tenants tried to immigrate to America; some made it. For others, their fate was like that of the Scots who perished in a terrible accident at sea off the coast of Skye in 1853 when 333 of 385 immigrants on board drowned. Landowners recognized the need for redistributed labor, and successfully lobbied the government to tighten the restrictions on anyone trying to depart Scotland. Tenants in Sutherland in the northeast Highlands, for instance, were resettled into coastal crofting communities where tiny pieces of land could not support the people living on them, thus forcing them into laboring in the landlords' kelp and fish exploitation. The Sutherland clearances were particularly cruel—the homes of tenants who refused to leave were burned in front of them—and there were tens of thousands of Highlanders and Islanders whose lives were forever altered. Once-populated areas became pastures for sheep or simply stood empty; between 1745 and 1811 the population of the Outer Hebrides fell from nearly twenty-five thousand to just over thirteen thousand. Famine resulted, and in spite of the difficulties leaving the country posed, many did so.

There is a vivid firsthand account of an eviction on Skye in 1854. A witness observed this tragic scene recorded in Eric Richards's book *The Highland Clearances:*

> There were old men and women, too feeble to walk, who were placed in carts; the younger members of the community on foot were carrying their bundles of clothes and household effects, while the children, with looks of alarm, walked alongside. . . . Everyone was in tears; each wished to clasp the hands that had so often befriended them, and it seemed as if they could not tear themselves away. When they set forth once more, a cry of grief went up to heaven, the long, plaintive wail, like a funeral coronach [Highland dirge]. . . . Not a soul is to be seen there now, but the greener patches of field and the crumbing walls mark where an active and happy community once lived.

The tragic results of the clearances remain into the twenty-first century, witnessed in still-declining populations and the lack of employment opportunities for those who remain in certain places throughout Scotland. There is nothing amusing about this process, and I can only hope that government and private efforts to reverse these problems will ultimately succeed.

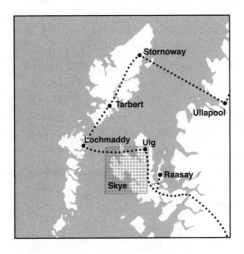

Skye, Part II

Boswell and Johnson departed Raasay in good spirits with the aim of traveling across Skye to the northwest coast and Dunvegan Castle, home of the MacLeods. They found no roads, no paths. "A guide," wrote Boswell, "explored the way, much in the same manner as, I suppose, is pursued in the wilds of America, by observing certain marks known only to the inhabitants." The weather was miserable; stretches were so boggy they had to dismount from their horses and walk. Part of their journey was taken by boat, or else they would have spent days winding through the island. On the way they stopped at a farmhouse in tiny Kingsburgh on Loch Snizort (Scotland's funniest-named loch; say it out loud several times and you'll hear why. It sounds like someone sneezed in German).

Here they met the remarkable Flora Macdonald, whose history was so amazingly intertwined with Bonnie Prince Charlie, and, curiously, America. As a young woman she had taken the prince, fleeing for his life after the disaster at Culloden, from Lewis in the Outer Hebrides, disguised him as her maid, a certain "Betty Burk," and escorted him away from pursuing soldiers across the treacherous waters of the Minch to Skye. Once back on land she saw him to safety and turned him over to other Jacobite sympathizers (Malcolm, Boswell's companion, was foremost among them) who conveyed him across the island to Raasay in search of a safe haven. For her courageous actions she was seized by government troops and imprisoned in the Tower of London, eventually winning a pardon.

On the way to the tower she left a vivid and amusing portrait of the prince donning his disguise:

When the Prince put on women's cloathes, he proposed carrying a pistol under one of his petticoats for making a small defence in case of attack. But [Miss Flora] declared against it, alleging that if any person should happen to search them, the pistol would only serve to make a discovery. To which the Prince merrily replied, "Indeed, Miss, if we shall happen to meet with any that will go so narrowly to work in searching as what you mean will certainly discover me at any rate." But Miss would not hear of any arms at all, and therefore the Prince was obliged to content himself with only a short heavy cudgel, with which he design'd to do his best to knock down any single person that should attack him.

Flora's story hardly ended there, however. She returned to Skye in 1747, married Allan Macdonald, and remained there until 1774, a year after Boswell and Johnson visited her. She and her family then joined so many other Scots in the immigration to America and settled in North Carolina, where they became entangled in the revolution. Now supporters of the English crown she once disdained, they joined the loyalists, and her husband and son were captured and imprisoned. Flora returned to Skye by herself. Her son died in America, but she was later reunited with her husband, and she died on the island in 1790. An astonishing personal story, to be sure; she is unquestionably among Scotland's most famous and bravest women.

Many readers have wished that Boswell had provided a fuller description of her; even so, he devoted page after page to Flora ("A little woman . . . of mild and genteel appearance" is pretty much all we get), detailing the colorful stories of the prince on Skye. They are entertaining and show how absorbed he was with the prince (these pages are the longest devoted to any one person to be found in the entire *Journal*), but they are a bit out of place in this narrative. Suffice to say the Young Pretender made it off Skye on his retreat to France, barely keeping ahead of his would-be captors. When Boswell prepared to publish this section of his book he requested permission from King George III to use the name Prince Charles, fearing some hard feelings about the Jacobites might persist in the current English monarch. The king couldn't seem to care less, but Boswell pestered him by mail and in person until he got approval.

Neither Johnson nor Boswell was an overt Jacobite sympathizer; their feelings were much more complex. Johnson had a curiosity about the uprising, and Boswell—more of an admirer certainly—admitted to a "liking" of the Jacobites. Boswell was excited, he wrote, at the sight of Johnson lying in the very bed where the prince had lain twenty-eight years before. And

Johnson seemed genuinely pleased to hear Flora Macdonald tell of her exploits. He left a note in Latin which read, "With virtue weigh'd, what worthless trash is gold?" Boswell later took that to be an appreciative reference to the loyalty of Highlanders who shunned government gold—up to thirty thousand pounds—as reward for the capture of the prince. Ironically Johnson referred to Flora Macdonald in only two sentences, ending with the note that hers is "a name that will be mentioned in history, and if courage and fidelity be virtues, mentioned with honor."

They arrived at Dunvegan, a dark, imposing castle on a rocky promontory, in the late afternoon and immediately found welcoming hospitality. After their arduous journey, to find warmth, large rooms, family portraits, and a graceful welcoming must have been bracing. The MacLeods were most agreeable, and the two men settled in for a delightful visit. The conversational topics, so splendid to Johnson's mind, were an embracing blend of history, politics, and . . . well, everything else, including the fidelity of women, prompting this outburst from Johnson: "Where single women are licentious, you rarely find faithful married women." Consideration of a book about gout with conclusions Johnson disputed led him to observe that "No man practices so well as he writes." The good doctor was even persuaded to take a little brandy before bedtime to help a cold, something he almost always refused. The castle may have been remote and the weather dreary, but sitting by the fire reading and talking provided long moments of happiness and inspiration for Boswell and Johnson, who observed his sixty-fourth birthday on the morning of September 18 there.

Part of the conversation led to the unlikely subject of cloth with some unexpected conclusions. "We talked of the highlanders' not having sheets; and so on we went to the advantage of wearing linen," Boswell wrote in his *Journal*. Johnson got into the topic, explaining, "All animal substances are less cleanly than vegetable. Wool, of which flannel is made, is an animal substance; flannel therefore is not so cleanly as linen. I remember I used to think tar dirty. But when I knew it to be only a preparation of the juice of the pine, I thought so no longer. It is not disagreeable to have the gum that oozes from a plum-tree upon your fingers, because it is vegetable; but if you have any candle-grease, any tallow upon your fingers, you are uneasy till you rub it off."

After this edifying commentary Johnson launched a thought that almost blew Boswell away. He said, "I have often thought that if I kept a seraglio, the ladies should all wear linen gowns, or cotton; I mean stuffs made of vegetable substances. I would have no silk; you cannot tell when it is clean. It will be very nasty before it is perceived to be so. Linen detects its own dirtiness."

At this point Boswell couldn't believe his ears: the noble, elevated Johnson talking about owning a seraglio? "To hear the grave Dr. Samuel Johnson, 'that majestic teacher of moral and religious wisdom,' while sitting solemn in an arm-chair in the Isle of Skye, talk *ex cathedra* of his keeping a seraglio and acknowledge that the supposition had *often* been in his thoughts, struck me so forcibly with ludicrous contrast that I could not but laugh immoderately." Johnson was upset by Boswell's reaction and apparently responded with some sharp words, which caused Boswell pain.

The pain was such that Boswell agonized over how to tell the story in his published *Journal*. There are several versions. To give one example: Johnson retaliated "with such keen sarcastic wit and such a variety of degrading images, of which I was the object, that though I can bear such attacks as well as most men, I yet found myself so much the sport of all the company that I would gladly expunge from my mind every trace of this severe retort." Boswell neither wanted himself reflected in that way nor Johnson made an object of ridicule for his comments.

For all the raillery, and the serious talk, their nine-day stay at Dunvegan was a thoroughly enjoyable one. Their host seemed equally pleased, writing of his "good fortune" in welcoming Boswell and Johnson. Less than three years after the visit he raised an army of Highlanders to fight against the colonists in America, was captured and imprisoned, and came to know well General George Washington before his release.

Historian G. B. Hill visited Dunvegan and wrote in his 1890 book *In the Footsteps of Johnson* that the doctor slept in the Fairy Bedroom in the castle's Fairy Tower. "The legend runs that this part of the castle was built 450 years ago by that very uncommon being, a fairy grandmother. . . . Had Puck peeped in and seen Johnson wearing his wig turned inside out and the wrong end in front as a substitute for a night-cap, he might well have exclaimed that his mistress kept a monster, not only near but in 'her close and consecrated bower.'"

My own trip to Dunvegan stopped first in the small port of Portree, where I dodged on-and-off showers while getting my laundry done. The city was attractively laid out on a hill overlooking a bay filled with small boats. The picturesque scene, with brightly colored sails on bobbing boats, glistened brightly when the sun made a brief appearance in the late afternoon and required my dark glasses. My Raasay host had warned me that Portree merchants enjoyed separating tourists from their money, and sure enough, the Royal Bank of Scotland wanted to charge me a hefty fee to cash some pound sterling travelers checks, the first bank to insist on imposing additional charges. I asked for the manager and complained that other branches of the same bank did not ask for extra money. "Sorry, that's our policy," was the best I could get. I went next door to another bank and got my checks exchanged, without fee, from a very attractive young teller who smiled warmly, almost as if I were a lot younger and handsomer.

I dined at McNabs Inn, where Boswell and Johnson were said to have supped. I don't think any of us would have remembered the mediocre meal. Next door was the Royal Hotel, where Flora Macdonald is said to have bade Prince Charlie goodbye. It had nothing of the look of an eighteenth-century establishment; it looked whitewashed and tired, and I stared at it for a moment and wondered if there could possibly be *two* Royal Hotels.

I spent the night at the classiest (and most expensive) hotel so far on my journey and savored some fine Finnan Haddie (smoked haddock) at dinner. It felt wonderful to have a really comfy bed, room-controlled temperature (warm at least!), and a delicious breakfast. In chats with others at the hotel I learned that I'm a rare American visitor for spending much time on Skye. "Most Americans come in here and ask for a three-hour tour of Skye," said one hotel employee. "And that's pretty much what they get." I inquired about Boswell and Johnson; he pointed me to McNabs and suggested I be sure to go to Raasay and Dunvegan. "You'll get a really good picture of what they did on Skye. It's pretty amazing when you think of it. There was nothing but a few farmhouses and villages on Skye back then, and no roads. It was very isolated. They were brave and took a lot of risks to come here and then spend so much time." Turns out he used to be a schoolteacher, and he knew whereof he spoke.

Off to Dunvegan, twenty-five miles away, and into a dark, low cloud mass that let go of high winds and a horizontal rain. The road was two lanes but quite narrow, and not knowing the way, I drove with extra caution. There was, however, only one way to go, so little chance of getting lost. When I got to the car park for Dunvegan, the rain was still coming down in torrents, and I feared the castle would not be open. When I completed my rain-soaked five-minute walk to the entrance, I was greeted with warmth that seemed to echo the reception given B & J and also belied my appearance and my pedigree. Back when Johnson and Boswell visited the castle was entered upward through a series of stone steps and could be accessed only when the tide was low; now the entrance is level with the footpath from the car park.

I discovered that I was by myself in a sumptuously furnished castle, open to the public since 1933 and overrun by visitors in the summer. Dunvegan, I learned, is the oldest ancient house in Scotland to have retained its family and its roof and has been the seat of the chiefs of MacLeod for more than eight hundred years (with one short exception during the mid-nineteenth-century potato famine). These chiefs, while good lairds in the main, have warred with other clans and had some rather unsavory moments in their past, including reports that at least one of them sold his tenants into slavery in America in the early eighteenth century before Britain halted the slave trade.

The castle boasts a fascinating and lengthy history with occasional interruptions of bloodshed, and the tour of its interior proved highly entertaining. I headed, of course, to the Business Room where Lady MacLeod entertained Boswell and Johnson (above it is the Fairy Room where Johnson slept, and Sir Walter Scott, too, when he came here in 1814). It still exuded conviviality, and it was easy to imagine my Bozzy and Dr. J seated in the room enjoying good drink and lively conversation. Johnson's portrait hangs over the fireplace flanked by the charming, gracious letter he wrote to his hostess thanking her for her hospitality: "I hope you believe me thankful, and willing, at whatever distance we may be placed, to show my sense of your kindness by any offices of friendship that may fall within my power," Johnson wrote a week after his departure. "Lady Macleod and the young Ladies have by their hospitality and politeness made an impression on my mind which will not easily be effaced. Be pleased to tell them that I remember them with great tenderness and great respect." Boswell also noted that "I cannot enough praise the genteel hospitality with which we were treated."

The earliest parts of the castle date from the 1300s; regrettably some of the oldest areas were shut down because of the bad weather, and some others because they were the living quarters of the twenty-ninth Clan MacLeod chieftain. But there was plenty to see including a gorgeous dining room surrounded by ancestral portraits on the walls, a pit dungeon in which enemies were hopelessly encased and placed adjacent to the food preparation, presumably so they could smell the food and be assured of not getting any. Another room held some Jacobite relics including a lock of Bonnie Prince Charlie's hair. I spent more time here than I had anticipated, but it was well worth it. Even so, it was getting late and I had to walk back through the heavy rain, strong winds, and bone-chilling cold for my return to Portree. Any hope of following Boswell and Johnson on the rest of their visit to Skye had disappeared in the storm forecast and my too-extended visit to Dunvegan, It was getting too close to my scheduled departure to the Outer Hebrides.

From Dunvegan Boswell and Johnson set out on a somewhat convoluted path to the south to Ullinish and Talisker before returning through Sconser and Coriechatachan and back to Armadale for their sailing to Coll and ultimately Mull. Along the way the subject of Ossian arose, as it had earlier and would again before the journey ended. Because Ossian and James Macpherson appear several times in the texts of Boswell and Johnson, and because their mention connects to an important issue of the day, I think readers today will benefit from a little background.

After the Treaty of 1707, and certainly after the Jacobite defeat in 1746, the Scots went looking for a way of expressing their national identity. They possessed a long, rich history apart from England, now their political master; what could they mine from that past to give their culture meaning and substance? (The American South went through this same reexamination following its defeat in the Civil War.) James Macpherson rode to the rescue. A would-be Highland clergyman, Macpherson showed up one day with the exciting news that he had stumbled across a manuscript bearing examples of ancient Gaelic poetry. Those who saw it in Edinburgh couldn't read Gaelic and asked for a translation; Macpherson obliged with an excerpt of a poem by the legendary Scottish bard Ossian that was epic in scope, a romance, a drama, breathtaking in its story-telling artistry—in other words, nothing like what was known of Gaelic poetry at the time.

Macpherson had clearly discovered not just another Scottish poet but the nation's equal of Homer. With the help of impressed scholars Macpherson published a collection of translations of Ossian's work in 1760. Voilà, Scotland had the greatness of its cultural identity confirmed and the glories of the Gaelic people assured. Macpherson probably should have stopped there, but he opted to discover, translate, and publish more volumes of Ossian. People began getting suspicious. Undeterred, Macpherson and his supporters hailed the books as the equal of *The Iliad* and *The Odyssey*. Others, including Dr. Johnson, doubted their authenticity. Johnson wanted to know where the originals were and why Macpherson kept promising to show them but never did. "Why is not the original deposited in some public library, instead of exhibiting attestations of its existence? Suppose there were a question in a court of justice whether a man be dead or alive. You aver he is alive, and you bring fifty witnesses to swear it; I answer, 'Why do you not produce the man?'"

Johnson also thought the works themselves to be worthless. Asked if any man of a modern age could have written such poems, Johnson replied, "Yes, sir, many men, many women and many children." He added later that he could write that sort of stuff if he could "abandon himself to it." Comically, Macpherson is said to have threatened to beat up Dr. Johnson, though he never did that either. Johnson's letter to Macpherson (not a part of his *Journey*) is fun reading: "I hope I shall never be deterred from detecting what

I think a cheat by the menaces of a ruffian." The argument raged on as Johnson and Boswell made their Highlands journey.

The coda to this story is interesting. In 1805, after Macpherson's death, the Highland Society of Edinburgh investigated his papers. It found that Macpherson *was* in fact Ossian; the clergyman had borrowed and stolen some lines of Gaelic poetry along with language and concepts from the Bible, Milton, and so on, to create his books. The critics were right. And yet many people—and writers such as Sir Walter Scott, who seriously doubted Ossian's truth—had embraced him because he supplied, if fraudulently, their need for a national literature at the midpoint of the eighteenth century. The late Sir Hugh Trevor-Roper finished the story: "If the Scottish belief in the authenticity of Ossian weakened in the course of the nineteenth century, that was not because the Scots, however belatedly, yielded to reason. . . . Ossian's poems lost their authenticity, not when they were disproved, but when changing circumstances made them no longer necessary. . . . With the rediscovery of genuine traditional Scottish poetry and the creation of genuine modern Scottish poetry, Scott had filled the void, and Ossian was no longer necessary."

Boswell's lengthy account of this mostly agreeable period makes for good reading. On his second stop at Coirechatachan Boswell indulged far too many bowls of punch and got quite drunk, not getting to bed until 5 A.M. "I awaked at noon, with a severe headache. I was much vexed that I should have been guilty of such a riot, and afraid of a reproof from Dr Johnson," he wrote. When he got to Boswell's room, however, Johnson offered no upbraid, instead answering Boswell's plaint that "they kept me up" by observing with good humor, "No, you kept them up, you drunken dog." His hosts offered him some "hair of the dog," a little brandy, which Johnson approved: "Fill him drunk again. Do it in the morning, that we may laugh at him all day. It is a poor thing for a fellow to get drunk at night, and skulk to bed, and let his friends have no sport."

In later years there would be some criticism of Boswell for showing Johnson endorsing, in effect, the drunkenness. Boswell's response eloquently points to the biographer's responsibility: "In justice to him I would not omit an anecdote, which, though in some degree to my own disadvantage, exhibits in so strong a light the indulgence and good humor with which he could treat those excesses in his friends, of which he highly disapproved." Johnson, in spite of his professed aversion for the lower classes, got into a lengthy and apparently enjoyable conversation with Mrs. Mackinnon, a kinswoman of Flora Macdonald, about her stories of Prince Charles and his escape. Boswell savored the two of them together, and she told everyone,

"I'm in love with him. What is it to live and not love?" Johnson's response, if any, is unknown.

In addition to the exchanges with Mrs. Mackinnon, while he and Boswell were trapped by the inclement weather there Johnson indulged in some remarkable, if innocent, flirty play with a neighbor's sixteen-year-old wife. "She was a neat, pretty girl," Boswell recounts with relish. "She sat down upon Mr. Johnson's knee, and upon being bid by some of the company, put her hands round his neck and kissed him. 'Do it again,' said he, 'and let us see who will tire first.' He kept her on his knee for some time (I'll *bet* they could scarcely have pried her off) while he and she drank tea. He was now like a *buck* indeed. All the company laughed in great glee, and they were all pleased to see him have so much good humour. To me it was a very high scene. To see the grave philosopher—the Rambler—toying with a Highland wench!" My guess is that Boswell was a tad bit jealous of his companion at that point. Nonetheless, the picture is a funny one; for a man whose appearance could literally frighten small children to be so catered to must have been a delightful moment for him. Some critics have suggested that Johnson was probably very uncomfortable, but given his appreciation of sexuality, I doubt it. Besides, Johnson later read portions of Boswell's notes and pronounced himself pleased.

"The more I read of this, I think the more highly of you," Johnson said.

"Are you in earnest?" Boswell asked.

"It is true, whether I am in earnest or no."

Boswell added a poignant note about the islanders' increasing immigrations to America: "Mrs. Mackinnon told me that last year that when the ships sailed from Portree to America, the people on shore were almost distracted when they saw their relations go off; they lay down on the ground and tumbled, and tore the grass with their teeth. This year there was not a tear shed. The people on shore seemed to think that they would soon follow. This is a mortal sign." As I said, there was nothing amusing about the clearances and what they did to the soul of Scotland. Still, Skye had been a wonderful experience for Boswell and Johnson, and so it had for me.

II

—∞∞∞—

The Outer
Hebrides

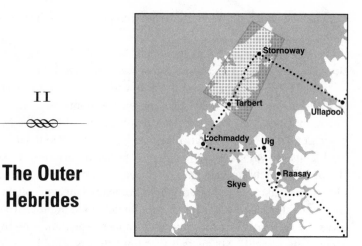

I was now separating myself from Boswell and Johnson for several weeks. I was going where they and hardly anyone else in the eighteenth-century could have imagined going: to the Outer Hebrides, known as the Western Isles, the farthest western reaches of Scotland. Actually not that many people in the twenty-first century go there, either. It's remote even from the places I've been that are remote.

It was there Bonnie Prince Charlie first thought himself safe, and with good reason, although the English were so passionate about revenge that they followed him even there. Skye native Martin Martin (his father so loved his name that he named him twice) traveled to the Hebrides, and his 1703 book—*A Description of the Western Islands of Scotland,* which so impressed the young Johnson, you may recall—is one of the first published accounts of what was there. (A Scottish clergyman named Donald Munro had visited some of the islands in 1549, but his published account lacks the clarity, thoroughness, and fame of Martin's.) Martin noted how little others knew about the islands: "Foreigners, sailing thro the Western Isles, have been tempted . . . to imagine the Inhabitants, as well as the Places of their residences, are barbarous." London's Royal Society in 1690 knew virtually nothing of life in the Hebrides. In fact, as related by Martin, the people were civilized—with some quirks—and lived relatively harmoniously, at least once the Vikings finally stopped invading and left them alone.

It's difficult for anyone to know much about a place that doesn't exist on maps. And the Outer Hebrides didn't appear on maps—at least on any kind of map that got them in approximately the right order and the right place—until John Elder's, which was published about 1543. One of the reasons it was so hard to map these islands was the necessity of mapmakers having to do their task in two ways, not just by land but also by sea. It was almost impossible to get a sense of the Hebrides, and except for the Vikings, there were few geographers with enough maritime experience and willingness to accomplish that formidable task.

These "outer isles" form a 130-mile-long archipelago stretching from Lewis and Harris (they share one island but seem as if they are separate) in the far north to the Uists and Barra in the south. There are some two hundred islands and islets that comprise this area, though most of them consist of only a few rocks and remain uninhabited, reachable only by boat, and lacking much reason to visit them under any circumstances. The population of these islands now is about twenty-seven thousand; the capital, Stornoway, has about eight thousand people. There is a lot of empty space here. To get to the Outer Isles requires a boat in most cases; there is limited air service from the mainland, because it is always subject to the weather (as is everything in Scotland). There are surprisingly good roads for travelers, a few single tracks, and markings are good if you can read Gaelic. There are bilingual maps available since few visitors have a clue what the Gaelic words mean (Steornabhagh is Stornoway, for example).

The Outer Hebrides remains the heart of Gaelic culture, not just because of the road signs, but also on account of the way of life. A majority of the islanders can speak Gaelic, though its usage is threatened by the dominance of English and incursions of everyone from travelers like me to business-men from the mainland. The government here is determined to preserve the language, and it survives in the schools (where it is taught as part of nurs-ery school, play school, and primary education) and in the church, where it is the means of communication in the services. Gaelic is lovely to the ear, less so to the eye, I'm sorry to say. Here's why: This sentence in English— "In Scotland, there are some 66,000 Gaelic speakers and at least as many again in other parts of the world"—in Gaelic becomes, "A' Ghaidhlig an SgoileAnn an Alba, tha mu 66,000 a' bruidhinn na Ghaidhlig agus uimhir eile co-dhiu air feadh ant-saoghail." The survival of language seems clearly worth much more than anyone's inconvenience, however.

Tourism isn't nearly as important on the Outer Hebrides as the Inner Hebrides; clearly the distance and difficulty in getting here makes most travelers opt out. Boswell and Johnson would have struggled to find a boat to get them over the Minch, the name for the treacherous, wind-blown waters that separate the Outers from the Inners. When they were on their mid-fall journey, few boatmen would have had the courage to make that crossing; indeed, such a proposal would have been deemed foolhardy, and not many knew the waters. Boswell knew no one on the islands, so he could be assured of no warm welcome or even acceptable accommodation. No, a journey here would have been outrageous, and neither man would have considered it seriously.

My CalMac ferry departed from Uig (pronounced Weeeg) near the northern tip of Skye in the morning. The weather was stormy, the rain stronger than the wind. I got my car in line for the ferry about an hour before departure, then stepped into the ticket office for a cup of tea. I would be on the ferry for three hours, crossing first to Lochmoddy on North Uist and then, after a short pause to offload a handful of passengers, northward to the coastal town of Tarbert on the island of Harris. From there I would drive to Lewis and the house I had rented for a week's stay.

The crossing weather began on the stormy side, and when I stepped outside the passenger lounge, the wind slapped my face with rain. The large ferry offered a surprisingly smooth and comfortable ride (thank you, CalMac; once again I was grateful not to have to contemplate capsizing), but the skies grew portentously dark, the water increasingly churning, and when I tried to step outside a second time, the door was blown shut by the wind. High waves crashed against the bow, and the ship's side-to-side motion became more noticeable. Back inside over some hot soup, I heard radio announcements of a major storm with gale-force winds bearing down. One of the crew members told me that the wind already was up to gale force 8, more than forty miles an hour, and strengthening. He assured me we would make it to Tarbert, but there were no guarantees for the return trip today.

I drove off the ferry at Tarbert on Harris after a three-and-a half-hour journey, convinced that the Outer Hebrides were indeed way outer. The temperature was cold and falling. The wind was howling; I could hear it through the closed windows, and I began to worry about keeping the car on the narrow two-lane pavement. There was little choice; to my left were black peaks rising up to a blacker sky, and to the right was a drop-off to rocky waters. That's where the wind was coming from, and I had a white-knuckle grip on the steering wheel. The rain was pelting down, and the landscape looked like an uninhabited planet in a sci-fi movie. My pace was slow, deliberate, and I made cautious headway against the wind. Within twenty minutes or so, however, I entered more hospitable surroundings: buildings, cars, and signs of Stornoway. The rain eased up, and so did the wind.

I located a grocery in town, bundled myself against the elements, and raced inside to load up on supplies for the week. The store was packed with shoppers on a Saturday afternoon. Everyone was talking about the approaching storm and filling up carts in preparation. Not a good sign, I figured; these people are used to whatever is going to happen, and I'm not. Nonetheless, several customers paused and commented on my American accent. They couldn't have been more friendly and curious, especially wanting to know why I had come here in such an off-season. This time I had no Boswell and Johnson story; I've come, I said, because I've always been intrigued by the remoteness of this place. Because I expected it would not be like anywhere else I've ever known (which was certainly the case this far). And because I liked an adventure, though a very cynical friend back home suggested I could have an adventure just by driving Interstate-285 around Atlanta on a rainy-afternoon commute and save all the expense of going to Scotland. Cynics always miss the point.

The grocery—one of two in Stornoway—wasn't like an American grocery. It was considerably smaller with fewer choices than the average American supermarket. The produce and the meats and eggs and dairy products all had listed a point of origin, a specific county or shire, indicated on their packaging if they came from Scotland. Sometimes even an individual farm would be noted. I liked that accountability and the likelihood that something from nearby would be fresh. The portions of meat and produce were smaller than in the U.S.; typical portion sizes of meat were three to four ounces; the roasts appeared to be about half the size of roasts back home. One big difference: when I had to ask for directions to a specific product—and I had to do that a lot—no one seemed to know anything about Saltine crackers—a clerk would not point the way but personally guide me. I was impressed with this invariably courteous service. The bread and vegetables were pretty much picked over, most likely because of the stormy forecast. But the store still had a splendid supply of liquors, lawn furniture, and washing machines. I opted out of the latter two and focused on the liquor. The storm could last a while, I figured.

My sturdy stone rental cottage was about twelve miles from Stornoway across the peat bogs, near the west coast village of Barvas, less than a mile from the North Atlantic. I knew a little about Barvas, just a fascinating tidbit of history. It's only a small community now with a convenience store selling supplies and petrol and an assortment of housing around the road. The early explorer Martin Martin, however, wrote about a curious custom in this area:

> The natives in the village of Barvas retain an ancient custom of sending a man very early to cross the Barvas River, every first day of May, to prevent any female crossing it first; for that they say would hinder the salmon from coming into the river all the year round; they pretend

to have learned this from a foreign sailor, who was shipwrecked upon that coast a long time ago. This observation they maintain to be true from experience." In my short experience here, it seemed reasonable to expect the salmon might be blown across the river quite easily, sparing everyone the necessity of crossing the water.

My host, bundled up in what appeared to be three sweaters, met me at the cottage to provide instructions about the heating system, the oven, the television, and so on. She said the house was a "good, renovated crofter's home" and said to call about any problems—if the phone lines didn't go down in the storm. She also warned that the storm was supposed to be a serious one overnight, and snow was likely tomorrow. Given that the wind blew me off my feet as I tried to walk from my car to the house with a bag of groceries, I took her words seriously. That night the storm hit in a fury. I found out later wind gusts reached one hundred miles an hour, and sustained winds were more than seventy. The rain seemed as if it would blast the house sideways. But nothing happened.

The house was a rock. With walls three-feet thick, it neither budged nor made a sound even as the wind screamed outside. What I remember most, though, was the cold. It was so cold. It was colder than a demon spawn's diaper rash. The electrical system put out only a miniscule bit of heat, and the house stayed frigid. I made a light dinner and climbed into a bed with sheets that must have been stored in an igloo. I've had frozen carp warmer than those linens. It was colder than the Bonnie Prince's corpse. It was so cold . . . well, you get the idea.

In the morning it was still cold, it was still raining and the wind was still blowing, though gusts were now only fifty miles an hour or so. The phone worked. Wearing my own three sweaters, I made breakfast and looked out toward the ocean. I couldn't believe my eyes—next door, about fifty yards away, there was an elderly white-haired man walking through the wind, carrying a feed bag and heading toward a flock of sheep hunkered down on the ground. He calmly fed his flock, then gracefully walked back to his house, barely bent by the maelstrom around him. How did he do that? I fell over on a paved path just crossing the twenty feet from my car to the front door. I felt very much a visitor in this unusual place.

And then it snowed, not a lot, but it snowed. In the cutting wind I stayed inside all day. It was "Silent Sunday," and on this Calvinist Presbyterian island, nothing was open: petrol stations, groceries, shops. It was a good day to make a hot peat fire—there's lots of peat on this island; it's been the preferred fuel for centuries—and my host left me fifty pounds for starters.

It was hard to get the flame going, but once lighted the fire remained hot and easy to maintain. I read, and I could scarcely do better than my two choices: Adam Nicolson's *Sea Room,* an eloquent account of a man taking ownership of the Shaint Islands off the southeast coast of the Western Isles, and David Yeadon's *Seasons on Harris,* a lovely and perceptive true story by an American who spent a year in the Outer Hebrides. Both are packed with valuable insights on the people and the land and should be required reading for anyone who even imagines a trip here. The house was surprisingly roomy; it even had a glass-protected sun porch attached to the back, though I never used it—no sun, naturally—and wondered how much use it could possibly get even in the middle of summer.

Imagining trips here has been a cottage industry for generations. The islands have inspired some passionate and beautiful words from writers who never got farther physically than the Scottish west coast. Few have produced more moving words than the English poet William Wordsworth in "The Solitary Reaper." Here is his poem:

Behold her, single in the field,
Yon solitary Highland Lass!
Reaping and singing by herself;
Stop here, or gently pass!
Alone she cuts, and binds the grain,
And sings a melancholy strain;
O listen! for the Vale profound
is overflowing with the sound.

No nightingale did ever chant
More welcome notes to weary bands
Of travellers in some shady haunt,
Among Arabian sands:
A voice so thrilling ne'er was heard
In spring-time from the Cuckoo-bird,
Breaking the silence of the seas
Among the farthest Hebrides.

Will no one tells me what she sings?—
Perhaps the plaintive numbers flow
For old, unhappy, far-off things,
And battles long ago:
Or is it some more humble lay,
Familiar matter of to-day?

Some natural sorrow, loss or pain,
that has been, and may be again.

Whate'er the theme, the Maiden sang
As if her song could have no ending;
I saw her singing at her work,
And o'er the sickle bending;—
I listened, motionless and still,
And, as I mounted up the hill,
The music in my heart I bore,
Long after it was heard no more.

We don't know what specific girl might have inspired those lines, but it is not unlikely that the solitary reaper was an island girl. Lowland Scottish women often went to the islands for the harvest after their own had been completed. And her song suggests as much; music has always been an accompaniment to work in the islands, and a voice in Gaelic would have been unfamiliar to Wordsworth when he visited the west coast in 1803. Gaelic songs and hymns were published in the mid-nineteenth century; might they not have been the words that the poet heard and responded to earlier?

Historian Elizabeth Bray, whose commentary on Wordsworth informs my own, tells the story of one of the great Hebridean laments drawn from an almost unbelievably tragic story, that of Annie Campbell of Scalpay (a tiny island off the southeast coast of Harris), who was engaged to marry a sea captain, Allan Morrison of Stornoway. On his way to Scalpay for the ceremony, the captain's ship foundered on the rocks, and all aboard were drowned. Brokenhearted, Annie died of grief a few months later. Her body was taken for burial, but on the voyage to the church a storm came up, and her coffin had to be tossed overboard to lighten the load and save the ship. Not long after that Captain Morrison's body was found washed up on one of Shiant Islands in the Minch. A few days later Annie's body washed up on the very same beach. You can understand easily why this lament achieved a certain stature among Gaelic laments.

Human habitation on these islands is said to go back 6,500 years; prehistoric evidence abounds. At the famous Callanish Standing Stones a few miles south from my cottage, nearly fifty giant stone monoliths—some as high as fifteen feet, dating back to maybe 3000 B.C.—are stark and imposing. Not only are they easily accessed, but on the day I visited, I was alone. The small visitor center was closed, and in the light snowfall—with intermittent sunshine—I walked to and through the monoliths. I confess to touching them and walking close by—and I doubt I'm the first to do so—even though it is officially prohibited. Callanish is quite a contrast to the slightly larger, better-known site at Stonehenge in England, where the stones are fenced off to keep visitors back. I stood quietly for a few minutes to allow the magic of the site to sink in. It is certain that these stones did not arrive here by accident, though what the plan in their arrangement may have been—a predictor of seasonal cycles for the farming community? forming the shape of a Celtic cross for religious purposes?—is lost to the ages. My guess is that they served a religious need for people in a remote area who needed strength and certitude in their beliefs. This is a boldly constructed site, not a casual one. Its symbol is enduring strength.

The Vikings made their mark on the Western Isles, largely because they were such good sailors and no one else could get there. For several centuries, until the 1200s, they ruled, and the Norse influence is still prevalent throughout all of northern Scotland and the Orkney and Shetland Islands. After the Vikings the MacLeods ran things for a few more centuries until their archrivals, the Mackenzies, took over for several hundred more years. Eventually the potato famine in the 1840s forced people out, and many who remained were later thrown out in the clearances. The evictions were as harsh here as elsewhere, but there are reminders that all over the Highlands and Islands there were people who resisted. In 1849 on the island of North Uist in the outer Hebrides, police enforced eviction orders, and when several houses were demolished, crowds gathered. There was violence between authorities and the evictees, according to historian Eric Richards. Similar scenes were enacted in other locations, but sadly, the results were the same.

Survival has been a struggle ever since that period. Employment opportunities have been limited, and until the last century so was education. The immigration of younger people to the job-rich cities of Edinburgh, Glasgow, Manchester, and London continues as a major problem into the twenty-first century.

The next day brought some broken clouds, dabs of blue sky, and only brisk winds, so I headed off for a day of exploring. Temperatures hovered in the thirties, and during the day I encountered sun, rain, sleet, and snow, and not necessarily in that order. At one point on the road south of Barvas I had sun on the right and sleet on the left, a description that probably translates into a single word in Gaelic. Literally I was in the middle of that meteorological muddle and marveled at the most peculiar weather I have ever experienced. To deal with the cold in my house I purchased a small electric space heater in Stornoway. It immediately became the best thing I bought on the trip. Well . . . maybe I wrote that in haste . . . there are those bottles of Scotch, after all. Nonetheless, when I got home I could move the heater from room to room: I could go to bed in a warm room, I could make dinner in a warm room, and I could step out of my shower into a warm bathroom (luxury!). After that purchase I think my affection for Lewis grew a bit warmer, too.

The interior of Lewis is mostly a peat moor, barren and marshy. It's the plentiful fuel source, but it's bleak-looking. And yet—off in the distance are the beautiful snow-topped peaks of Harris, as pretty as anything I've seen. These islands are contradictions; parts of north Harris are as bleak and alien-appearing as can be imagined; they were used to depict the planet Jupiter in Stanley Kubrick's film *2001: A Space Odyssey*. The south has a coastal beauty that can steal your heart (at least when it's not storming). The Atlantic coast of Lewis, where I was staying, is battered by the strong ocean winds and tides; there are many small bays and high cliffs, all showing the roughness of repeated exposure to the elements. At the peak of the Butt of Lewis—no jokes, now, for this is actually the northern tip of Lewis and not the bottom—I looked off to the west, a sea span unbroken by land until you get to North America, and to the north, where there is no land until the Arctic. The feeling of isolation, of being at the end of the world, is inescapable. It isn't a bad feeling, or a scary one, just a very unusual sense of being at the edge. The wind blew fiercely at the Butt of Lewis—mind those jokes—and with temperatures near freezing, the feeling of wanting to get back in a warm car proved just as inescapable.

Back in Stornoway I shopped for more groceries, but the pickings were on the slim side, particularly when it came to fresh vegetables. The storm had shut down ferry service for forty-eight hours, and stores over the island ran short on a lot of supplies. The rain finally slackened, but the wind remained high, and there was no certainty the ferries would return right away. I wandered over to the Lewis Loom Centre, a storehouse of Harris Tweed coats, sweaters, scarves, hats, and gloves. It was a well-worn establishment just off one of Stornoway's main roads, and the fellow in it looked a mite well-worn, too.

He was tall with unkempt white hair falling over and around his face, and he was wearing a rumpled blue sweatshirt. He was a Mackenzie, quite a character, and he had been working there for many years. Since I was the only person in the store, he spent a long time chatting and helping me pick out a Harris Tweed sport coat with heather blue/green shadings. Quite handsome, we agreed, and at 245 U.S. dollars it seemed a bargain. Our conversation continued about Stornoway and the Western Isles, about which

Mr. Mackenzie had no lack of opinions to share. He had been saddened by the exodus of people but understood the few jobs and fewer alternatives. He needed more customers to keep business up, of course, and he worried about the future for Harris Tweed, a hand-woven cottage industry unique to these islands for centuries.

The clatter of the loom and the warm, moist aroma of pure wool have been an integral part of the Outer Hebrides for generations. Finlay Macdonald, who grew up on Harris in the 1920s and 1930s and whose mother spun wool, remembered that everyone on the island was very poor, and the only means for removing the extreme oiliness of the fabric was with the use of community urine pools. Everyone would contribute, and after the urine had stood for a time in a rain-safe location, becoming "mature," it could be incorporated into the process.

That particular practice has long since gone, but the rich tradition of Harris Tweed itself has been threatened as orders worldwide have declined, the number of skilled weavers has diminished and fabric imitators have been on the rise. David Yeadon in *Seasons on Harris,* published in 2006, wrote with knowledge and compassion about what has happened, and his words gracefully speak to the concern of a handful of weavers who carry on the traditions on the island. But Mr. Mackenzie was not optimistic: "It's dying now. A few more years maybe you won't find this Harris Tweed any more. A pity, a great pity."

But there are some good signs. The Harris Tweed Act, passed by Parliament in 1993, acknowledged that the industry "is vital to the economy of those islands" and "should be maintained." There's now a statutory body charged with safeguarding the industry and, by implication, a critical slice of the economy of the islands. Terry Williams, writing in a 2008 issue of *Scottish Life* magazine, noted that in 2006 production of Harris Tweed almost closed down for good. Since then a coalition of private and government officials have been working together to physically and financially connect the remaining weavers and the tweed mills; the industry cannot survive without both. The most recent evidence seems to point to modest success.

Lewis has lots of sites that I wanted to see before my time ran out. With slightly improving weather I paid a visit to the small village at Arnol where a marvelously preserved blackhouse was open for exploration. Once inhabited by crofters on the island, the blackhouses were built low to the ground to withstand the strong winds off the Atlantic. They were dark, of course, their interior lit mostly by a peat fire never allowed to go out. There was no chimney as such, only tiny openings in the thatch roof, so much of the smoke stayed inside. It sounds pretty grim, but in fact the smoke served several important purposes: most important, it kept out the midges. Midges are a subject that must be addressed here, because they are a part of the Scottish experience no less than tartans, pipes, shortbread, and the Loch Ness Monster.

In most guidebooks midges rate their own entry. And how fitting, given the general tenor of Scottish history, that they involve bloodshed: *yours*. The midge is a very tiny fly which gets its joy from taking your blood, and it does it efficiently and very, very annoyingly. The females have twenty teeth and do the biting; the males are rather gentle, which brings up a thought about how you tell the difference between a male and a female midge. The answer, I think, is somewhere close to the same way you tell the difference between a male and female crocodile. The only people who know for sure are in no condition to respond. Midges are found all over the Highlands and the Islands, and here's the really bad news: their swarming coincides almost perfectly with the tourist season. (That is only tangentially connected to the fact that my visit ended just about the time the midges began organizing for their attack season.).

Midges love the twilight hours and overcast days, and they are like angry bees, only a lot smaller and more persistent. Someone in the middle of a midge attack may be forgiven for feeling like King Edward's soldiers must have felt while getting clobbered by William Wallace's men. And while midges are not the only troublesome insect of the Highlands and Islands— there are stealth clegs (horseflies), ticks, fleas, lice, and more—they have earned a special place in the country's hall of obnoxiousness fame and have been recognized by travelers over the centuries.

In the 1720s one account included this note about the midges: "The violent heat of the sun among the rocks, make my new companions . . . such voracious cannibals that I was obliged to lag behind, and set my servant to take vengeance on them for the plentiful repast they were making at my expense, and without my consent, and by which I was told they were become as red as blood."

And this, from 1737: "They are so very small that, separately, they are but just perceptible and that is all; and being of a blackish color, when a number of them settle upon the skin, they make it look as if it was dirty; there they soon bore with their little augers into the pores, and change the face from black to red." So enough of blood; you undoubtedly get the point here. Boswell and Johnson were smart travelers; they arrived after midge season.

For people who live in the area, however, midges are a matter of real concern every year. And that's why—to get back to the subject of blackhouses again—the smoke is important for keeping the nasty little insects away and enabling everyone to sleep at night. The smoke also served another purpose: it turned the sod and thatch roof into next year's fertilizer. Crofters, their families, and their animals—cows, sheep, chickens—all stayed inside together in winter. Some crofters permitted the dung to accumulate inside throughout the winter; the smell must have been intense. Others swept it out regularly. The last person who actually lived in the blackhouse I visited occupied it for eighty years and moved out in 1966. What is left attests mutely to a way of life that has completely disappeared.

I returned to my cottage for more reading, some dinner, and heard a strange sound: the sound of nothing, an absence of wind. It was the first time since I arrived here that there was no wind blowing. I slept poorly overnight; I think that was because it was too quiet outside. In the morning I drove back to Stornoway for some cash, and my friends at the Royal Bank of Scotland—recall the shady moneylenders at Portree?—were asking ten dollars to cash travelers checks written in pound sterling. I reminded the teller that I paid nothing at their banks in Inveraray and Stirling; I was bluntly reminded that their policy is to charge a fee. It's only ten dollars, but I vowed I'd sooner beg on the streets of Stornoway than pay them their miserable little fee. I walked several blocks to find another bank willing to cash my checks for nothing. And I resolved to be absolutely certain I mentioned the Royal Bank of Scotland unpleasantly throughout my book.

Over a cup of tea I imagined what Boswell and Johnson might have written in their respective books over such an incident. Johnson would put it this way: "Sir, disagreeableness need not deter you. It is the pebble in the shoe that may be removed with but a gentle shake." And Bozzy, surely, would have opined something like, "I could not conceive of a more onerous action to confront; you did well to move on to that place where you will be well received." I'd like to think they would have been so moved. The truth is I was missing both of them here on Lewis.

At home that evening I watched a show on the telly called "Britain's Worst Weather." The announcer didn't waste any time; he walked to a map, pointed to the west coast of Lewis—just about exactly where I was sitting—and said, "Here's where you don't want to be." That was followed with a litany of ghastly storms, shipwrecks, drownings, houses washed out to sea, and people being blown about. Outside, it started to rain. And then I heard the wind starting up. I knew I'd be sleeping well.

Morning brought sunny skies and relatively light breezes off the ocean and time to check out a weird bit of history in these islands. It involves a nineteenth-century soap baron with a lot of money, a lot of ambition, and a lot of unworkable plans, who almost wrecked these beautiful places. The soap baron was William Lever, the heir to a large wholesale grocery business in England. He was successful, and ultimately, as Lord Leverhulme, he turned the business into the giant Lever Brothers group, a commercial empire extending from Wales to Africa. In 1884 he visited Stornoway and fell in love with the Hebrides. In 1918 he bought the Isle of Lewis, and the following year he acquired its neighbor to the south, Harris. He thus became the landlord for some thirty-four thousand people and more than half a million acres. A colleague said of him, "The ruling passion of his life was not money or even power, but the desire to increase human well-being by substituting the profitable for the valueless." In other words, he would be judge and jury for everyone. You can see the problems starting.

Specifically he wanted to leave his mark as planner and philanthropist. He thought the land was useless and saw no purpose to crofting, which was how most everyone on the islands made a living, so he set about raising the standard of living by moving everyone off their land and into fishing and tweed factories. Residents of Lewis liked his lordship personally but couldn't abide his notions, which were especially unpopular with servicemen returning from World War I—and the islands had more than their share of volunteers for the army—who wanted their land and felt they deserved it after giving up years for their country. And they had been promised land in return for service, so there was a clash between what the law said and what the landlord wanted. The government finally refused to evict men from their land, and Leverhulme abandoned his plans—at least for Lewis. Instead he "transferred his benevolence," as Ian Mitchell put it, to Harris, where he encountered a more receptive population. He built a port which he modestly called Leverburgh as the base for a mammoth fishing fleet to serve MacFisheries, a chain of fishmongers he had earlier created in Great Britain. His project included docks to accommodate up to fifty ships, huge fish-curing sheds, a refrigeration plant, accommodations for hundreds of workers, and—most peculiarly—parking lots for twenty cars on an island where cars and roads were a rarity. It was, again quoting Ian Mitchell, "the largest scheme of social engineering ever undertaken in the Highlands of Scotland, possibly anywhere in the British Isles." And, duh, it also failed.

Why? Well, for one, the waters in which he expected his fishing crews to sail were too dangerous for navigation in all but perfect weather, and as we know, there is no such thing for an entire day anywhere around here. The outcome? He landed one summer's catch in 1924, and only because he used an English fishing fleet he summoned up to Harris, as well as importing women to work in the fishing factories. His accountant called it a disaster;

Lord Leverhulme abandoned his scheme and died the next year. The accountant, meanwhile, offered his epitaph for Harris and Lewis: "The best thing you can do with your islands is to sink them in the Atlantic for four hours, and then pull them up again." The corporation sold the islands. Leverburgh today is a small, somewhat rundown village that serves as a CalMac ferry stop on the treacherous run through the Sound of Harris to the extreme south of the Outer Hebrides.

The accountant wasn't the only one to hold a low opinion of the people of these remote islands, however. The late Scotsman Alasdair Alpin Mac-Gregor relentlessly chronicled a series of offenses committed by the residents in a 1949 book entitled *The Western Isles*. MacGregor wrote knowledgeably about the islands' geography, archaeology, and history, but when it came to the drunken, lazy, whoring, useless people who inhabited the islands—his ideas, not mine—he was extremely negative, and his attitudes expressed in the book grow from barely tolerant to almost abusive. Let me count the ways. "Two characteristics of the people, which the stranger to the Western Isles is swift to observe, certainly so far as the male population is concerned, are laziness and drunkenness." Women, on the other hand, are never idle. "Indeed, they are not allowed to be," he writes. And a darned good thing, too, because the women are "on the whole, plain, and many of them exceedingly so." The women of the Outer Hebrides "bloom early, and fade early . . . and are spent within a few years after marrying."

The problem, you'd have to think from reading his book, is that everyone in the Outer Hebrides has been having too much fun drinking, dancing, and screwing around. "Morals, in the sexual sense, are extremely lax in the Western Isles," he writes, proceeding to conjure up enough feverish couplings and dance-inspired fornication to make modern-day readers imagine he's describing Las Vegas or maybe Amsterdam.

Not to belabor his points, but he finds parts of the Hebrides—actually most of the Catholic parts to the south—to be rife with promiscuity, resulting either from people dancing with one another or from hanging out too closely together when it rains and there's nothing else to do (which pretty much covers every day in the year). There was way too much drinking going on, especially among Catholics, and especially at Catholic weddings and funerals, the latter nothing like his Presbyterian-preferred funerals where the deceased were allowed to slip quietly into their graves without everyone hoisting a few. The people of the Western Isles tended to be unclean in other ways as well; that apparently was not a Catholic thing, but rather came about because no one bothered to take baths. And did I mention that they are vindictive? Poor MacGregor gets so riled up in the middle of one chapter that he begins foaming at the prospect of government agencies spending money on the degenerate islanders and insists there can be no rebuttals for his book's "facts."

Far be it from me to cast aspersions on old man MacGregor. I went searching for the pockets of promiscuity he promised, but after an investigation it appeared that I'd have to be a whole lot closer to Glasgow to succeed. There definitely was some drinking going on, but I observed that mostly by checking out the contents of my cottage's liquor cabinet. And, regrettably, it rained too much for me to get a really accurate sense of how many people might have been dancing or hanging out too closely together, but it was cold, and we all know what happens when it's cold and rainy outside, don't we?

One of the sources for MacGregor's fury at excessive drinking resulted from an incident that occurred in the Sound of Eriskay in the southern sections of the Hebrides. Back in 1941, a time of rationing everything in the United Kingdom including whisky, a merchant ship, the SS *Politician*, wrecked in a storm. Its cargo included 264,000 bottles of tax-unpaid whisky destined for sale in the United States to raise money for Britain's war needs. Word got around the islands quickly, and men from all over descended for nocturnal, quasi-secret sojourns out to the stranded vessel to off-load the precious cargo illegally. What they couldn't drink right away, they hid for later imbibing.

Compton Mackenzie, the prolific English-born author, intelligence officer, broadcaster, champion of the gramophone, and president of the Siamese Cat Cub, wrote an enchanting novel about the incident, *Whisky Galore*, in 1947; it was made into a charming movie two years later. Mackenzie, who died in 1972, lived for many years on Barra in the Outer Hebrides and owned the Shiant Islands in the Minch. He set his story in 1943 on the fictional but recognizable Hebridean islands of Great Todday and Little Todday. His is a very funny book, with a respectful, light-hearted treatment of the islanders, and it serves as a graceful introduction to Gaelic culture as well.

But it doesn't tell the truth about this near-mythical incident, which is fascinating and merits a lengthier retelling. The islanders did off-load the whisky illegally, and they drank and hid the bottles all over their landscape. It was, in the words of one author, "the largest happy hour in the history of the Hebrides." But there were villains in this story: two men who represented His Majesty's Government as the local and regional customs officers. Their maniacally dedicated efforts to find the stolen whisky and persecute those who took it left a bad taste in the mouths of many islanders. They sought jail sentences for men, women, children, pensioners, and even soldiers recently returned from war. They tragically lacked any sense of perspective or justice, and they remain in sharp contrast to what most of us now perceive as the high jinks of a poor, deserving group of islanders. Read Roger Hutchinson's splendid *Polly: The True Story behind Whisky Galore* (1998) for this full and factual fairy tale.

But to return to Lord Leverhulme. His legacy has been limited. He left Harris with serious employment issues, and those mostly remain intact. There is a small fishing industry and the tweed industry, but apart from those, subsistence is largely scrubbed out on occasional public projects and the small tourism industry. I suppose you could say that the road network on Harris is at least partly attributable to Leverhulme since he started construction on several roads before his death, apparently eager to have people get their nonexistent cars into those twenty empty parking places. In Stornoway there is Lews Castle, built by Sir James Matheson in 1863 after he evicted the crofters who lived on his land. Matheson, who made his mint pushing opium to the Chinese, had purchased the island in 1844 and wanted a monument for himself. When Leverhulme acquired the island, he got the castle, too, but at his death he returned it to the people. It is now in a state of disrepair, and given its history, no one seems terribly enthusiastic about coming up with the money to restore it. The castle grounds, however, have a lovely bunch of trees, a most unlikely sight in the Outer Hebrides, thanks to thousands of tons of soil imported from the mainland decades ago by Matheson, who longed to see greenery every time he looked out his castle window. Money apparently will get you almost everything but someone to mourn for you; Matheson's name is less remembered now than Leverhulme's.

It was soon time to pack the car for my trip to the Stornoway ferry. I was headed back to the mainland and a road trip around the northern edges of the Highlands, more places that Johnson and Boswell never imagined visiting. My goal ultimately would be the Orkney Islands—is the word *remote* getting to be a little overused?—before resuming the trail of Bozzy and Dr. J in the Highlands near Inverness and Loch Ness.

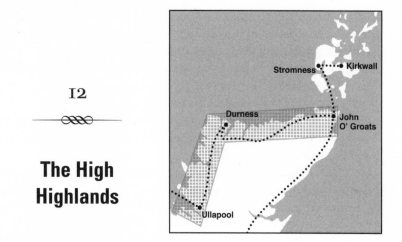

12

The High Highlands

After the experience on the ferry getting to the Outer Hebrides, I was prepared to rock and roll back across the Minch. But the crossing was uneventful under sunny skies and mild breezes coming up from starboard. It was a lovely scene when I arrived back on the northwest Scottish mainland at the town of Ullapool. Several candy-colored homes on a small peninsula jutting into the water with snow-capped mountains in the backdrop made an eye-catching scene as the ferry pulled in.

Ullapool has about four thousand residents; it has been a fishing village since its founding in 1788. It's got some tidy, attractive residential streets, a community center where the Ullapool Junior Pipe and Drum Corps was rehearsing, some delicious fish-and-chips restaurants, not just one but *two* well-stocked bookstores, and a very comfortable bed and breakfast with a third-floor view of the picture-book-pretty harbor. There was also a handy little book available, *A Guide to Ullapool*, put together by a group of towns-folk; it was a very smart little publication and showcased community pride. Before drifting off to sleep, I read in a local newspaper about a man in Fort William arrested for "interfering with himself" in front of a neighbor woman. Odd expression. I got the drift, though.

The sun was out again the next morning, and it was a cold, clear, crisp day, just made for a little walking. A word about the sun in Scotland. (Yes, Virginia, there is a sun in Scotland.) The light in the Highlands is very bright and almost piercing, rather like the light that skiers find at high elevations. It can hurt the eyes without dark glasses to tame it. That day, the skies were as blue as anywhere I had seen, and the few clouds stood out in sharp, puffy relief. In the afternoon the sun's angle gave the landscape a dramatic look; the loch's reflections intense, the colors richly defined. The harbor waters here changed colors, too, from deep blue to light greenish to dark green depending on the play of the sun across the surface.

Today marked the beginning of "British Summer Time"—the equivalent of Daylight Saving Time in the States—so I had an extra hour of daylight, much appreciated as I entered these northerly climes. And now that I thought about it, this was the fourth day with little or no rain; spring in Scotland had gotten off to a wonderful start, and Ullapool had been a delightful place to celebrate it.

Before heading north I made a forty-five-mile detour south to one of Scotland's unusual and unlikely attractions: Inverewe Gardens. Along the way I passed Loch Ewe with its drop-dead gorgeous harbor, so well protected that it was used as a staging point for Russian-bound shipping convoys in World War II. There were gun emplacements still dotting the shore. The harbor currently serves as a refueling port for NATO ships, and there were two warships at anchor when I was there. A few miles farther south were the gardens, a tribute to one man's remarkable vision, now operated by the National Trust for Scotland. I'm not really a garden person, but my host in Ullapool urged me not to miss these since I was so close, and of course he was right.

This twelve-thousand-acre nondescript plot of land was inherited in 1862 by a fellow named Osgood Mackenzie who decided to create a garden because of the area's surprisingly temperate climate (the result, so the guidebook says, of the Gulf Stream drawing a warm sea current from Mexico to these shores). Mackenzie collected plants from all over the world—China, Tasmania, California, Italy—and planted and nurtured them. By the time he died in 1922 his garden sprawled in most unlikely beauty all over the rocky peninsula. Even in March, when I arrived, dozens of flowers were blooming, and hundreds of visitors were walking about (it's more like thousands in the summer). The visitor center, alas, was closed, meaning that there was no place for anyone to go to the bathroom. That circumstance no doubt accounted for why people kept suddenly disappearing off the paths into the woods, where perhaps they were providing fertilizer for another generation of blossoms. On television back home in the evening, the BBC offered a sterling production of Jane Austen's *Northhanger Abbey* followed by a put-me-sound-asleep show on the care of hedges. I did say I wasn't a garden person, didn't I?

At breakfast I chatted with the new arrivals, a talkative couple from Glasgow on their way to visit friends on Lewis. They made a short visit to the States several years ago and found Bostonians "rude." Their daughters made a Greyhound bus tour of the eastern United States which they found fun and their parents thought to be "a crazy idea." We fell into a discussion of politics, and they wanted to know how Americans could elect a "lunatic" like George Bush. I dodged the talk about politics. The man has worked on a North Sea oil rig for twenty-five years; he flies to the Shetland Islands and is helicoptered to the rig for two weeks work at a time. Then he's off for about ten days. The pay is good, and he likes the schedule. We parted, and I was briefly struck that I'd been in Scotland for close to a month and this was the first conversation about politics—unless, of course, you count the chat about the Jacobites.

A jacket felt good as I drove out of Ullapool, but the skies were sunny once again. A succession of motorways beginning with the A835 guided me to the northwesterly tip of Scotland and the town of Durness. Along the way the roads, the A894 and A838, changed from dual carriage to single track, and the landscape became ever more barren. There were no trees; small farmhouses became more infrequent; towns were farther and farther apart and became smaller in size. There were few cars or lorries; I seemed to have wandered into a very different place from the comparative bustle of Ullapool and its neighbors.

The bare mountains and dark glens were not so much forbidding as tranquil or tranquilizing. I stopped beside the rushing waters of a small creek tumbling down a mountain, got out of the car, and walked up the top of the hill. The steepness was surprising, the absence of any sound once I passed the creek was stunning, as it had been on Mull. Once again I could detect no sign of human presence. In the cloudless sky I could see off in the distance to the coast, blue-green Atlantic waters splashing against the shore. A timeless landscape. I walked on further, stepping across a tiny creek bed, weaving my way through medium-sized boulders. I must have walked for forty-five minutes before I realized I wasn't certain how to get back; the landscape looked the same no matter where I turned. And it seemed endless. I took note of the sun and began walking back in the direction of the car. In the high, dry altitude I got very thirsty and finished off the bottle of water I had brought with me. It took almost an hour to get back, and I was exhausted. And in all that time I never saw another vehicle or another person or an animal of any sort.

I drove on to Durness, arriving in the late afternoon. This is a part of Scotland not many visit; there is occasional bus service from the lower lands, but those who come here mostly come by car, and few do, given its isolation at the top of the country. It would never have been a consideration for Boswell and Johnson; no roads existed in the eighteenth century, a trip by boat would have been too dangerous, and there would have been virtually no likelihood of locating a knowledgeable guide. There was no place to stay and there were no welcoming faces, no services needed to sustain travelers. The landscape was all but deserted.

Oddly Durness had a small tourist information office. Not so oddly, it was closed at this time of year. There was only one place for dinner—a small pub—and I wasn't optimistic. The crowd inside looked mostly young and faintly hostile to strangers; I couldn't find a table and so stood around uncomfortably hoping someone would offer me a place. Finally someone did. The menu looked so ancient that I feared Bonnie Prince Charlie might have used it to place his order. But to my wonder the beer was warm and delicious and so was the fresh cheese and curried chicken dish I ordered. I even ate dessert, though I've now forgotten what it was. I remembered the many warnings of lousy food and low expectations for culinary experiences in Scotland; there's some real history behind that.

Cookery books from eighteenth-century Scotland contain some pretty bizarre tales, including suggestions, for whatever bizarre reason, on how to fool diners. For instance, "To make a tame duck pass for a wild one," one author suggests, "knock it on its head with a stick." Yum. One traveler in Scotland in 1679 wrote that he was most often served carrion, but only after it had been kept for a fortnight and "perfumed with the aromatick air, pass thro' the clammy trunks of flesh flies" and then heated and served with butter. Well, you certainly wouldn't want to eat your fly-strained carrion without butter, would you?

Boiled sheep's head was considered something of a delicacy. Most important in the preparation was holding the head over the fire to singe off all the wool; some chefs sent the head to the local smithy to be certain it was fully singed. Makes you hungry, doesn't it? And, of course, there's the national dish, the celebrated haggis, the soul and glory of Scotland, a compilation of oats and offal usually boiled in a sheep's stomach. It prompted Robert Burns's admiring description ("Great Chieftain o' the puddin' race," an ode that is quoted when Scottish societies gather to celebrate Burns's birthday) and the disparagement of others, to quote here one example citing haggis as "a dish not more remarkable or more disgusting to the palate, than in appearance." I had sampled haggis for myself in a visit to Scotland years before, and didn't find a need to repeat the experience now. I found it edible then, but it took more than a few drams of whisky to get me to that point.

Fresh vegetables—or even any vegetables—were seldom found on Scottish menus. The only vegetable mentioned in most cookery book recipes, according to historian Marjorie Plant, is pickles. Martha Bradley, writing in *The British Housewife,* does mention the various vegetables in season, but appends a warning that "in all these articles the Housekeeper is to remember, no Stress is to be laid upon them in the Entertainment, but coming as slight inconsiderable Dishes, they give Variety and always please."

My experiences, however, proved quite different. I encountered an abundance of fresh, well-prepared vegetables even in the late winter / early spring months. Fruits were imported and easily available. Meats were cooked with imagination, and servings were completed with style, even in the most ordinary of dining establishments. Pub grub, much maligned, was of a high order on my trip, often outstanding. Even simple soups tasted delicious, made fresh with local ingredients. Nothing tasted canned. Overall I found better, more consistent food in Scotland than back home. In early 2008 the food critic for the *New York Times* reported himself pleasantly surprised by what he found when he visited several Highland restaurants, and he visited more acclaimed establishments than I.

Drinking was another matter. The pubs where I drank seldom ventured beyond the expected, and that included modest varieties of Scotch blends and single malts along with a few bottles of other whiskies, and a slim selection of beer, usually just one or two brands. The barkeeps weren't going to be eager to whip up a Mimosa for you, or a Cuba Libre. It appeared to me that you might not get your Scotch if you asked for some ginger ale dumped in it. The pubs were almost always full, and the drinkers were usually drinking beer. I didn't see many people getting drunk, which is another case where history didn't seem to match up to the present.

The Scots enjoy—literally—a reputation for heavy drinking; Boswell was hardly alone. Breakfast in the seventeenth and eighteenth centuries was often served quite late in the morning, so everyone, men and women, hoisted a drink of ale or spirits after they arose to keep them going until time to eat. "The Scots as a whole were noted for being immoderate drinkers," Plant writes, "although not so intemperate as the Germans." Then again, the Scots never had the idea of invading Poland.

The Scots used their drink for medicinal purposes as well. A glass of whisky laced with linseed oil was supposed to cure a variety of ills (but probably not the taste of linseed oil). And brandy was recommended as the favored treatment for scarlet fever. And here's the good part: if the patient was an infant, it was urged that "the nurse should drink it for the child." Good news for nanny dear.

Highlanders could put away three or four quarts of whisky at a sitting (they must have sat for a long time afterwards), but drunkenness, in fact, was not common. Plant records one gentleman whose bottle was so large that it had to be brought into his room in a wheelbarrow. Now that's drinking. Reports of such excesses did begin to decline a bit after tea became the preferred drink around the middle of the eighteenth century. Still, it was reported that when Flora MacDonald, the heroine of Skye and savior of Bonnie Prince Charlie, was buried in 1790, the funeral procession, on its sixteen-mile journey to the graveyard, put away three hundred gallons of whisky.

My host at the small B&B at Durness, Martin, was a sheep farmer on a working croft. He had a large flock of cheviots and a fleet of Border Collies who were skillful and well trained when they brought in the sheep as darkness fell. Martin clearly was a hard worker, up well before dawn to begin preparing breakfast and with little spare time for conversation. He said the grass that grows around Durness is not rich enough to raise his sheep up to market size. So he gets them only to a certain size, then sells them to another farmer further south who rears them on richer lands until they can be sold for the highest price.

It was another sunny morning, and a chilly one, and my room, which didn't have any heat overnight, didn't seem to have any when the sun came up either. But Martin's breakfast was delicious: choices of smoked fish, sausage, eggs, bacon, and fresh fruits. Wonderful hospitality from a taciturn host whose wife appeared only occasionally in the background. She seldom spoke and seemed to have no obvious role in the care and feeding of visitors.

On my way out of town a few minutes after breakfast, I saw a sign pointing to a bookstore. In this remote, tiny corner of extreme northwest Scotland, could there really be an operating, profit-making bookstore? Yes there might be, but unfortunately it was on the verge of opening and wasn't yet ready for business. I have no idea how anyone could make a go of it in this economic climate (not to mention geographic climate), but I silently wished the owners well. I read a year later that the Loch Croispol Bookshop and Restaurant is now open, advertising itself as "the most north-westerly bookshop/restaurant on the mainland" (can't be much competition for that, I'm guessing). It has a lot of books on Scottish history and literature, apparently, and an "extensive wine list." Clearly Durness is now an uptown place. I hope the booksellers are succeeding. I had another surprise departing Durness when I stopped for a moment at a small roadside memorial; it was a stone tribute to the late Beatle John Lennon. Lennon and his family used to vacation in the Durness area when he was a youngster, and the community wished to recognize his presence. I took a photo for my son and son-in-law, both big Beatles' fans.

Forty or so miles away was the crofting township of Tongue where I had decided to spend the next night. There was a small Royal Bank of Scotland branch there, and I couldn't resist walking in to inquire about cashing a travelers check, even though I didn't need the cash at the moment. Certainly, sir, the teller told me. Fee? No sir, none at all. Couldn't have been nicer and quicker. Now I wondered if I should have said those ugly things earlier. In the spirit of impartiality, I decided to wait and see what the rest of the trip brought.

So close to the sea, Tongue enjoyed a surprisingly temperate climate and boasted Scotland's most northerly palm tree, the sort of claim that should warm the heart of any chamber of commerce representative. I find myself at a loss for anything to say about a palm tree, however.

From Tongue to Thurso the next morning—sunny again?—I passed a nuclear technology plant quite out of place with sheep grazing in the near pasturelands. In the distance a herd of wind turbines whirred strongly in the breeze off the North Atlantic. The nuclear plant has meant jobs for hundreds of people in a relatively jobless area of Scotland, and many think that the wind turbines are the future here. Getting close to Thurso, my sense of isolation faded as I pulled into what seemed a real city near the tip of northeastern Scotland. I had driven across the least- traveled section of the country. Inland just a few miles from me was empty land, no homes, no people. Well, hardly any. The area surrounding Thurso is an extremely remote piece of land within a landscape that is itself extremely remote. Things seemed a little more expensive in Thurso: food, lodging, petrol. Everything had to be trucked in, and it's a long trip. I realized I was closer to the Arctic Circle than to London. I ate dinner at an Indian restaurant and noticed that outside people parked their bicycles loaded with packages without using locks. I checked the local paper later for news of thefts; there weren't any, but there were two separate columns about bird-watching activities.

After a ragged night's sleep on a bed that sagged practically to the floor—yes, I know the only person who cares about my whining one whit is me, but it's what travelers do—I took a short jaunt over to the extreme northeastern edge of the county at John O'Groats, a curiously named collection of buildings that constitutes a tourist slag heap of cheap souvenirs, expensive food, and pay toilets. It's a port for travelers headed to and from the Orkney Islands, and that is the only reason anyone comes here. The weather was beautiful, albeit cold and windy, and I drove a couple of miles further to what is actually the most northeasterly point in the United Kingdom, Duncansby Head. It has an odd square lighthouse designed by Robert Lewis

Stevenson's father and is situated on a two-hundred-foot high cliff over-looking the dangerous intersection where the North Atlantic crashes into the North Sea. The wind blew fiercely, but the view out toward the Orkneys was gorgeous. No one was around, and I suddenly had the urge to dance, to make up for what I missed on Dun Caan's peak on Raasay. I wanted to shake my booty for Bozzy. And so I did, twirling, bebopping, ending in a modified twist, arms and legs in quick motion. I had finally made my trib-ute to Boswell, and I was really happy—especially since neither he nor Dr. Johnson nor anyone else was around to see me. On the way back I passed through East Merkle, then Merkle, and finally West Merkle in the space of maybe half a mile. Was this geographical division really necessary? There can't be more than sixty residents in all three communities together. Couldn't we all just get along, people?

I was going to the Orkneys, but I had decided to leave from the much closer ferry port of Scrabster near Thurso. It was a longer ferry ride, but it was another pretty, bright day, and I didn't want to ruin it by heading back to John O'Groats.

13

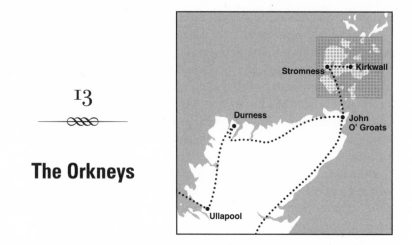

The Orkneys

I had left behind my friends at CalMac because Northlink provided ferry service between Scrabster and the Orkneys and Shetland Islands. Northlink's ship was large and very comfortable, and I crossed in a quick ninety minutes. I had now traveled from one vast, sparsely populated area to the sparsely populated archipelago of seventy or so islands that comprise the Orkneys. It was time to reorient myself.

The Orkneys are as close as ten miles from the Scottish mainland and are a part of Scotland, at least to most people living on the Scottish mainland. There are dissenters: "The place is no more Scottish than Wimbledon," wrote the Englishman Charles Jennings. Gordon Donaldson, the late "historiographer royal" (an absolutely impeccable-sounding title), pointed out a few years ago that while the Northern Isles were clearly de facto parts of Scotland, "*de jure* there is less certainty." Jennings, somewhat the cynic, added: "Orkney passed into Scottish hands at the end of the fifteenth century in compensation for the non-payment of the dowry of Margaret of Denmark. And before that it was all Norsemen and Danes. . . . The place is just too far north."

If you live in the Orkneys, however, you are an Orcadian, and a reference to the mainland is a reference to the largest island in this group and *not* to the Scottish mainland. It's not a secessionist sort of thing, though, but as much as a fact of geography and history. The Orkneys are a long way from Edinburgh and Glasgow, although the islands are just over the horizon when you're standing at John O'Groats (and wishing you weren't).

Those populous centers of Scottish influence really don't exert a lot of influence here because they are so far away, and because the history and geography have long pointed to other places, notably Scandinavia. There were Stone Age people here at 4000 B.C. and later some Christian settlements. It was a Pictish kingdom for a while, and then came the Vikings, warriors who arrived about the ninth century and created a formidable outpost that lasted for more than three hundred years. Norway then took over until 1468, when Christian I, the king of Norway and Denmark, mortgaged the islands to Scotland on the occasion of his daughter's marriage to King James III of Scotland. One of history's earliest recorded cheapskates, Christian never paid off his debt, so there's always been a little legal argument about who owns what, although it's been generally quickly and fairly resolved over a beverage of some sort. No matter, the Orkneys have been mostly a Scottish preserve since, but the Norse and Danish influence remains much in evidence and helps impart a unique flavor to these islands.

So much for history. The reality is that when you look at a map the Orkneys—and the Shetlands even farther to the north—are a long way away from most everywhere else. The explorer Martin Martin described them in 1695, but his words didn't exactly prompt a tourist stampede to the islands. Boswell and Johnson never mentioned them, understandably. The construction of oil rigs in the North Sea brought important new commercial interests (albeit more to the Shetlands than to the Orkneys), but the rise of tourism as a major industry in these beautiful, sneakily seductive, fertile islands has been a relatively recent phenomenon, only a few decades old. "It's a place you have to want to come to, not somewhere you come by accident," an Orcadian native told me one sunny afternoon as we sat outside St. Magnus Cathedral in the city of Kirkwall.

I had really wanted to come here. That old quest for the unusual was certainly part of the reason, but mostly it was the music that got me to these islands. Specifically it was Sir Peter Maxwell Davies, one of the current generation's finest classical composers, who was born in England but has lived in the Orkneys since 1971. Much of his music has been written here and written about places here. I had listened to his operas, symphonic and chamber scores for nearly thirty years, finding in them a deep satisfaction and refreshment that evoked an intense curiosity about the land that so inspired him. I know it sounds a tad daft to insist that music got me all the way here, but it's the truth. Alas, I was not here at the right time of year for the St. Magnus Festival, a musical event that draws thousands, and for which he is responsible. For anyone needing an introduction to Maxwell Davies, I'd suggest his gently evocative piano piece "Farewell to Stromness" and his witty, rambunctious orchestral work with bagpipes, "An Orkney Wedding with Sunrise." Be careful, though; these could provoke a sudden desire to go to the Orkneys.

Of course the music I heard on the islands mostly was either some vague European rock or American pop music from the 1960s, as if Glenn Campbell and the Byrds had never gone away. I wondered if the Wichita Lineman was hanging over my shoulder as I drove off the ferry at the lovely little Victorian-era port of Stromness. The port has one-and-a-half lane streets and two-way traffic, posing some interesting challenges if you don't know your way around. Finding a parking place—a task roughly on par with locating a one-dollar gallon of petrol—consumed about forty-five minutes. I parked on a hill and hoped the brakes would hold. I walked the steep, tiny alleys connecting the upper and lower city, finding bookstores, neat little restaurants, almost everything charming, except for the poorly stocked grocery. But I made a great discovery there: the ice cream. Who knew Orcadian ice cream is the stuff of gods? So rich, so pure tasting, so chocolately. Was I in Italy? It was the single best treat I ate on the entire trip, and I ate it every day, sometimes more than once.

Back in the car, I headed out of town and across the mainland into Kirkwall. With picturesquely narrow streets and medieval-looking architecture in its central market area, Kirkwall is the largest city in the Orkneys, home to about nine thousand people. Fewer than sixteen thousand live elsewhere on the islands, so here was the metropolis, complete with a good grocery, bookstores, clothing shops, and teens on bicycles. I bought my groceries without comment—no one remarked on my "Americanness," and I didn't need help locating the pickles—and headed into the country, past attractively kept green, small farms, toward my rental cottage.

No stone walls here; the modern-style, single-story rental house—the walls were nonetheless pretty thick—doesn't get hit with the same kind of wind blasts I encountered on Lewis, I was told. And yes, that was true, as it turned out, but not by much. The wind never stopped on the Orkneys. It blew lightly some times and hard at other times, but it was always an accompaniment to whatever else the weather was doing. Cold, fine. Rain, okay. Warm, maybe. Wind, oh my yes, how did you want it served today? There is some good news, however; the wind kept the midges at bay most of the time.

The weather on the Orkneys proved much milder than on Lewis. Thanks to the Gulf Stream, I was told, there's little snow here, mostly rain when precipitation falls. I confess I can't figure out how the Gulf Stream gets up here, but more than one person insisted that that was the case. In spring and summer days are long this far north, and the weather can be very pleasant (and windy). From late fall to early spring it can be pretty cold (with extra windy winds). It was partly mild, partly cold, and always windy during my week's stay.

That's probably a lot more than anyone who isn't a meteorologist wants to know, but it's not fair to avoid the topic since it affects everything else, including how much time you spend outdoors, whether you're walking, shopping, or sightseeing. The weather never compromised my experiences, except that on several occasions I got so cold standing in the wind at an outdoor monument that I ducked inside early.

The interior of the mainland offered surprising scenery: gently rolling hills, rich, efficiently cultivated, green pasturelands, a calming, sculpted beauty, and few trees. Blame the lack of trees on the incessant winds. One cloudless night I looked out from my house over the Wide Firth, reflecting the moon's light and in the background the lights of Kirkwall. The scene appeared like a brightly colored circus illumination. The next night, the clouds were full of dramatic contrasts in the partial moonlight, and the wind-driven sea water was a foamy wash of whitecaps. Both nights the sun set after 10 P.M.

Historic and prehistoric sites abound on the Orkneys, so it was hard to be there more than a few days without discovering my inner archaeologist. At Maeshowe, a five-thousand-year-old site on the mainland, a breathtaking neolithic (Stone Age) village bumps up against spectacular ritual and burial monuments, and visitors easily slip back in time. Maeshowe is a large grassy mound with a chambered tomb inside. I entered it by squatting and duck-walking through a narrow, tight stone tunnel for about twenty-five feet. I was sweating from acute claustrophobia the whole time. I could then stand up in a small, high-ceilinged and watertight stone chamber with side cells. This was for hundreds of years a burial site, apparently, and the effort to create it without machinery thousands of years ago was extraordinary to imagine. The passageway to the tomb was aligned by its builders so that at three weeks before and after the shortest day of the year (December 21), the light of the setting sun perfectly illuminated the back of the chamber.

But that's not the best part of the site. The Vikings came through here in the mid–twelfth century and stopped at Maeshowe for a time. They left something–of a calling card—a series of runic inscriptions carved by knife on the inner chamber walls that are visible and easily interpreted today. These were not the mighty, sacred words of kings and lords and leaders;

these were the words of the grunts who did the fighting, the rowing, and most of the complaining. What they said—hilarious, bawdy, light-hearted, precursors to "Kilroy was here,"—tells us a lot about how people really haven't changed over the centuries.

"Otarr carved these runes," reads one. Another bears these words: "Ingigero is the sweetest woman there is." Yet another appears to say that "Thorni bedded Helgi." Someone else carved his name and apparently mentioned Helgi, too, suggesting she might have been something of a twelfth-century Viking tart, but I admit that's just conjecture. Maeshowe is absolutely fascinating, a burial place the Vikings made their own. I have to admit, though, that I couldn't get back out of the claustrophobic tomb fast enough.

Not many miles away was the village of Skara Brae, like Maeshowe a site inhabited some five thousand years ago, well before the Egyptian pyramids were built and centuries before Stonehenge was constructed. And what is most remarkable about Skara Brae is not its age but the degree of its preservation. A number of structures of the semisubterranean village have survived, but how? I found out that the answer is midden, right after I found out what midden is. It's a durable material formed from the decomposition of organic matter, sort of like a gardener's compost heap. And that, with the sand that filled up and buried the village after its abandonment in approximately 2500 B.C., accounts for the splendid state of preservation. Skara Brae was uncovered accidentally because of a storm in 1850 that revealed the midden heap; archaeologists now call it one of the most important Stone Age sites in Europe. Another amazing site to explore.

I made a detour a few miles from Skara Brae to get over to Skaill House, the finest surviving mansion on the Orkneys and a home with a long history, mostly an unhappy one for the owners. Bishop George Graham is recorded as having lived here with his wife and nine children in 1615. Alas the Bishop was deemed too lenient with the local witches (I'm sure the English could have helped him with a few nasty executions) and way too lax in enforcing the incest laws (he may have loved his family a little too much, if you get my drift). He was forced to resign his position in 1638. The mansion apparently sat on fertile land; the next occupying laird also had nine children. One of the next owners, an eleven-year-old, was accused of stealing gold ducats from a shipwreck. Another child was also accused of theft. More modern generations turned out a little better, and the mansion got improved in the process, too.

I was so excited by everything Orcadian at this point that I bought a bottle of the soft drink that everyone around here seemed to love: Irn-Bru.

It was some sort of concoction of citrus flavor, carbonated water, orange color, and some minerals. It's been around since 1901 and has assumed something of a cult status, outselling even mighty Coca-Cola here. But, my Lord, the minerals tasted old enough to have come from Skara Brae, and the liquid was so sickly sweet I felt a diabetic alert going off. One swig induced a nauseating, carbon aftertaste. How could the people who created God-approved single malts also manufacture this . . . well, I'll be charitable and call it stuff? Throwing out the rest of the bottle was among the best decisions I made in the Orkneys.

I later asked my landlord to please explain the popularity of the drink. "Can't tell ya," said Greg. "Terrible stuff, isn't it?" Why didn't I ask him earlier? Greg and his wife Lesley and I talked a bit of politics after we polished off some tea. He spoke quickly with a heavy brogue that made understanding him difficult, and he apologized for that: "Most Americans can't figure me out at all." The conversation eventually got around to Boswell and Johnson when he asked about the book I was researching. I related a little of the background to Boswell and Johnson's journey, and he remembered reading about them in school. "They didn't get up this way now, did they?" We chatted some more and I told him a few stories about the travelers' journey, and his face brightened with genuine interest. He rather liked Boswell—"He seems a bit of a real person, ya' know? A lot of things going on inside him"—and a bit cooler to Dr. Johnson, although he suspected that the doctor "enjoyed flirting with the girls on their trip, didn't he?" It was fun to talk about B & J here in the Orkneys; I wondered what they would have thought about these islands had they been fortunate enough to get here.

We talked some about the character of Orcadians—what struck me as their quiet certitude—and in what ways they differ from the mainland Scots. "I think we're very easy-going, ya' know," Greg said. "There's not a lot of us, and we've got a fair lot of room here, and we try to get along. There aren't many who are trying to push themselves in others' way." I described the attentive responses of the Hebrideans on Lewis to my needs, and their surprising (to me) warmth toward a visitor. "I've not been there; that's a way off for us, you know. I've heard they were friendly people, too."

His words echoed what I had read in Hebridean native Ian Mitchell's *Isles of the North* about his sailing trip to the Hebrides and the Orkneys a few years back. He was told that the Orcadians are independent-minded and laid back and that they seem to want to get along: "There's very little exertion of rules and regulations. It's very much live and let live. I guess there's room for everybody."

Edwin Muir, who was born in the Orkneys in 1887 and grew up there, wrote with affection of his friends in his classic account *Scottish Journey*. A visitor, he said, "will find a population of small farmers and crofters, naturally gentle and courteous in manners, but independent too, and almost all of them moderately prosperous. . . . But he will not come to know much about the place unless he lives here for quite a long time, habituating himself to the rhythm of the life, and training himself to be pleased with bareness and simplicity in all things."

Seventy years ago when he wrote, Muir found few extremes in class and poverty. Agriculture dominated; unemployment was uncommon, "and the result is an alive and contented community." By and large, that still seems true, but now tourism must be added to the mix of a flourishing community.

The calendar now had turned into April, and I needed to pick up my pace in order to get back to the Scottish mainland to link up again with Boswell and Johnson. I made a special point of visiting the lovely eight-hundred-year-old St. Magnus Cathedral in the heart of Kirkwall. Magnus, "an innocent sufferer and a man of piety" of Orkney, was killed in 1117 and soon proclaimed a martyr. The cathedral holds relics of Magnus, including a skull which shows a head wound that conforms to the story told of the death of Magnus. Curiously, for a church, there is a small area behind the chapel that was used as a dungeon; there are records showing men and women imprisoned there as late as the eighteenth century. (For lack of piety? Failure to attend Sunday school? Failure to deposit into the collection box?) And, curiously, the cathedral is owned not by a church but by the Orkney Islands Council, a secular body that permits its use as a parish church in connection with the Church of England. No matter, the sandstone cathedral is quite a spectacular sight inside and out, and during my visit the organist was producing magnificent music for the choir. The sound reverberating off those stone walls was indeed inspiring; how could anyone hearing this glorious sound have failed to support the collection box?

On my way out of town I stopped by the 210-year-old Highland Park Distillery for a quick tour and a free wee dram. The twelve-year-old single malt was very good, the twenty-five-year-old sensational, dark, woodsy with an edge of peatiness, and about six times as expensive. It's a bit amazing that the whisky here is so good when you consider the fact that when the distillery was closed during World War II, soldiers stationed here used the huge vats for communal baths. They must have enjoyed it immensely, but I'm supposing the distillery got some new vats after the war. Regardless, I bought a bottle of the twelve-year-old to remind me of the Orkneys for the next few weeks.

I'm not a diver, but if I had been, I probably would have made a stop at the great harbor at Scapa Flow my first order of business on arriving in the Orkneys. For the first half of the twentieth century this natural harbor served as the main base for Britain's Royal Navy, and although it sees little war-like activity these days, it is a fascinating reminder of the prominent role the Orkneys played in the two World Wars. There are many ships sunk in these waters, German and British, and the harbor is a mecca for undersea divers from all over the world.

Of two British wrecks there the best known is the *Royal Oak*, which was sunk on October 14, 1939, by a German submarine. The attack was audacious attack, the German skipper bringing his sub into the harbor on the surface, successfully dodging ships sunk by the Brits to block the harbor. The sub was picked up by a car's headlights and the driver reported the sighting to the authorities. As happened at another harbor—Pearl—two years later, the authorities ignored the report, believing that such a sneak attack would be impossible. Their behavior cost the lives of 833 sailors from the ship's complement of 1,400. The sub slipped out through the narrow channel to safety.

The other British ship in the harbor is the HMS *Vanguard*, which went down on the evening of July 9, 1917, after an internal explosion that killed all but two of the nearly one thousand men on board. The force of the explosion was so powerful that the battleship's gun-turrets, each weighing several hundred tons, were hurled more than a mile through the air. Even so, the sunken ships are not what brings divers here. They come because of a footnote in history. In Scapa Flow's most celebrated moment, the entire German High Seas Fleet—seventy-four ships—was interned here awaiting the outcome of the Versailles Peace Conference. Fearing that the treaty would require handing over all of the ships to the Brits, the German commanding officer ordered the entire fleet scuttled. Within minutes every single one of the ships was beached or sunk. Some of the wrecks were raised between World Wars I and II, but plenty remain, and squadrons of divers go down after them year after year.

One other thing about Scapa Flow is too amusing to ignore, and it doesn't involve the folly of German fleet commanders. Because of the presence of the Royal Navy during the two World Wars and the men and matériel necessary to ensure the fleet's safety, the population of the Orkneys soared. In World War II while the island's resident population was estimated at about twenty-five thousand, there were close to one hundred thousand servicemen and women stationed here. The islands were unsuited for such an invasion force—even a friendly one—and the soldiers and sailors found themselves in the middle of one huge, colossally boring experience on these remote landscapes. One of those men composed a song, doggerel really, which expressed some pretty universal soldierly feelings:

> *This bloody town's a bloody cuss—*
> *No bloody trains, no bloody bus,*
> *And no one cares for bloody us—*
> *In bloody Orkney.*
>
> *Everything's so bloody dear,*
> *A bloody bob for bloody beer,*
> *And is it good?—no bloody fear,*
> *In bloody Orkney.*
>
> *The bloody flicks are bloody old,*
> *The bloody seats are bloody cold;*
> *You can't get in for bloody gold*
> *In bloody Orkney*
>
> *No bloody sport, no bloody games,*
> *No bloody fun, the bloody dames*
> *Won't even give their bloody names*
> *In bloody Orkney.*
>
> *Best bloody place is bloody bed,*
> *With bloody ice on bloody head;*
> *You might as well be bloody dead,*
> *In bloody Orkney.*

There are many more verses, but you get the idea. And more than a few singers were happy to insert the "F"-word in place of *bloody* just to give the ditty a creative twist.

The wind was blowing strongly when I arrived at the ferry for my trip back to the Scottish mainland. The sky had grown dark, and a cold rain was falling nearly sideways while I waited to board. I was taking a different ferry line to a different port, Gill's Bay, which is slightly to the west of John O'Groats. The trip was scheduled to take only some forty minutes, but the ferry was considerably smaller than the Northlink vessel I came over on, and the worsening weather seemed certain to make the trip a nail-biter.

The seas did turn rough, and swells were running at ten to twelve feet. Waves crashed against the passenger-lounge windows, and several passengers looked a bit queasy before dashing off for the bathrooms. I felt fine, however, and even drank a little tea without spilling any. I chatted with a couple from London who said they travel every year. Last year they went to Cambodia for three weeks, and now they're returning from a week they spent the Orkneys. They said the Cambodia trip cost less. As for me, I never stopped regretting my departure; I wanted much more time to have savored the Orkneys. I regretted once again that Boswell and Johnson couldn't have visited here. Bozzy surely would have loved reading those bawdy Viking inscriptions.

14

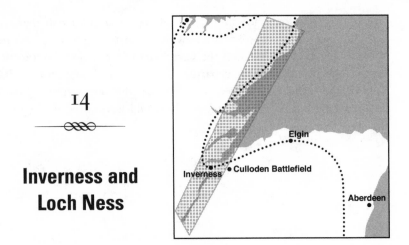

Inverness and Loch Ness

Back on the Scottish mainland for the first time in a week, I welcomed the sun, and though I didn't realize it at the time, I was heading into one of the seasonally warmest and longest rainless periods in recent Scottish meteorological history. It would rain exactly once over the next fifteen days (and that was only a passing shower), and high temperatures would climb into the upper sixties and low seventies for the rest of April. I celebrated by taking off my sweater for the first time since I drove through Mull.

I was now trekking down the northeast coast of Scotland, a landscape that seemed gentler and more inhabited than the lonely, barren west coast. I drove on the A99 south through Wick, originally a Viking settlement and looking as if it hadn't been spiffed up much since then. I picked up the A9 heading farther down the peninsula, and I was struck not only by the milder weather off the North Sea, but the increasing signs of civilization as well. Not only was this road the main avenue from the Lowlands to the Orkneys, but it showed evidence of growing settlements along the way. I spent the night in the former coal-mining community of Brora which now boasts a fancy hotel with an indoor swimming pool (rarer than a Royal Bank of Scotland that doesn't charge fees).

On the road out of Brora after a fine breakfast, I stopped at a small convenience store to buy a Sunday paper, hoping I could find at least one while so far away from any urban area. To my astonishment I had a choice of eight including several from England. I was so pleased I bought a copy of each, and it was the elderly proprietor's turn to look astonished.

"I like to read," I said.

"Like the comics, do ya?" he replied.

"I just like to know what's going on," I said.

"That's the last place you'll learn anything," he said, pointing to my mountainous stack of newsprint.

As it turns out I never got around to reading all of them because when I was preparing to turn in the rental car at the end of the trip I found two of those papers on the floor in the rear, unopened and never read.

A few miles down the road, a sign pointed out a major tourist attraction ahead, and I realized I had not nearly begun to exhaust my castle addiction. I pulled into Dunrobin Castle, driving a few yards on a driveway that expanded into a parking lot at the castle entrance. From where I sat, Dunrobin looked like the perfect fairytale castle with turrets and pointed roofs, built to a giant scale with nearly two hundred rooms inside. It was the ancestral home of the dukes of Sutherland, who were extremely wealthy landowners, influential over the centuries and responsible for destroying the lives of thousands of Scots—their dependents—in the nineteenth-century Clearances. The castle proved fascinating: expensive, tasteful furnishings, a sumptuous drawing room (part of the space where Queen Victoria stayed on a visit here), knowledgeable staff, gorgeous views out to sea and overlooking the handsome landscaped gardens. There was a wonderful demonstration of falconry in the gardens featuring a skilled trainer with a falcon and an owl.

It was all most intriguing. I took a sit-down break to read over the castle's self-published book about its accouterments and history. The book didn't exactly dwell on the clearances, and I was finding it increasingly difficult to reconcile the obvious attractiveness and appeal of the castle with the cataclysmic events associated with it. Between 1807 and 1821 thousands of tenants were forcibly removed in a carefully planned capitalist blitzkrieg, their lands turned over to pasture for sheep with the aim of adding wealth to the already substantial coffers of the duke of Sutherland (an Englishman, by the way).

"The dislocation for the people was great and the psychic wounds inflicted did not heal; a sense of wrong was carried from generation to generation. Hence the Sutherland Clearances were the most dramatic and sensational of all the Clearances," wrote historian Eric Richards in 2005. The duke's well-coordinated removals provoked resistance, violence, communal responses, and a deep-seated challenge to authority. Those persist to the current generation, where a one-hundred-foot-high monument to the duke of Sutherland has been the target of protesters for years. The monument has an inscription from 1834, after the duke's death, that reads, unbelievably, that it was erected "by a mourning and grateful tenantry to a judicious, kind and liberal landlord [who would] open his hands to the distress of the widow, the sick and the traveller." Right. And Hitler was a saint. Actually that's not a far-fetched parallel; historians have compared the actions of the Nazis and those of the duke in eliminating "undesirables." For now the monument remains, in dark, grimly compelling contrast to the lovely castle only a short distance away. I wondered what Boswell and Johnson would have written. Both men, I suspect, would have been angry.

Speaking of those two gentlemen, I was finally on the verge of reconnecting my journey with theirs as I headed into Inverness. "We got safely to Inverness, and put up at Mackenzie's at the Horns," Boswell wrote in his journal on August 28 at the most northerly point of their trip. "Mr. Keith, the Collector of Excise here, my old acquaintance at Ayr, who had seen us at the Fort, called in the evening and engaged us to dine with him the next day, and promised to breakfast with us and take us to the English Chapel; so that we were at once commodiously arranged."

Johnson was, of course, a bit more formal since Boswell had the relationships with people they visited, focusing in his writings especially on their manners. Of Inverness he wrote, "We came late to . . . the town which may properly be called the capital of the Highlands. Hither the inhabitants of the inland parts come to be supplied with what they cannot make for themselves; hither the young nymphs of the mountains and valleys are sent for education, and as far as my observation has reached, are not sent in vain."

They stayed only two nights in Inverness, and Boswell spent some time by himself, presumably visiting acquaintances; he was unaccompanied, and since he didn't spell out just whom it was he visited, there is speculation he might have dropped in on some of the town's prostitutes. Regardless, one of the most vivid and bizarre stories of the journey occurred in Inverness, and, strangely, it did not make its way into Boswell's writing but has been preserved in an account by the travelers' host.

At dinner on one of their two nights in the city Johnson regaled those at the table with a story about a remarkable creature just discovered in New South Wales. He suddenly stood up and began to imitate a kangaroo, with his hands held out as paws and his brown coat bunched up in front to pass for a pouch as he began hopping around the room. How could Bozzy not have described this for us? It's funny enough trying to imagine the corpulent Johnson bouncing up and down all over the room imitating an animal the guests surely would never have been able to imagine. He must have appeared as if he had lost his mind. Along with Boswell's dance on top of Dun Caan, Johnson as kangaroo provides one of the most memorable images of this memorable journey.

By the way, I read in Frank Delaney's *A Walk on the Wild Side* a delightful story I had never heard about the derivation of the name *kangaroo,* an animal discovered too late for inclusion in Johnson's *Dictionary.* The name, so legend has it, was bestowed by an English explorer (Captain Cook?) who observed the animal and asked an Aboriginal, "What in heaven's name is that?" The reply was "Kangaroo"—native tongue for "I don't understand what you're saying."

With a population of eighty thousand and serving as a hub of transportation in and through the region, Inverness is the relatively prosperous capital of the Highlands. It has a busy and not-very-pretty commercial center on the banks of the River Ness, and it is easily accessed and conveniently close to a lot of places I found more interesting. It was the last "city" of any import that Boswell and Johnson passed through on their journey into the Highlands and Islands, and the first "city" I had been to since Stirling at the start of my trip. It was also useful: I was able to load up a new selection of books (as Johnson did), buy some cooler shirts to replace my now too-warm sweaters, purchase a new phone card at a store whose employees spoke perfectly understandable English, and walk right past the Royal Bank of Scotland to cash my travelers checks elsewhere.

I did need to take a bathroom break and slipped into the public library. Big mistake; for some reason the library didn't have any restrooms, and a woman at the circulation desk directed me across the street to the bus station. They had a restroom, but it was closed. Frantic, I raced down the street until I found a bookstore, whose clerk mercifully allowed me to use their facilities—another reason to spend time in bookstores, as if I needed one. My investment in books so far had exceeded the money I had spent on petrol, one of those quirks of the ledger sheet that still puzzles most people.

While in Inverness Boswell wrote his wife and lamented the absence of a note from her. It was an occasion for him to compliment himself on his affection for her: "I value myself on having as constant a regard—nay, love—for her as any man ever had for a woman, and yet never troubling anybody else with it." He could overlook easily those falls from grace with lower-class women because, I suspect, they were not affairs of the heart and did nothing to dilute his evident and continuing affection and devotion and support to his family. Or, he was just really good at compartmentalization.

The two men did visit what they believed to be Macbeth's castle; unfortunately, that castle had been destroyed in the eleventh century. The structure they actually saw was Inverness Castle, which had been mostly destroyed by Bonnie Prince Charlie's soldiers in 1746 and was razed in 1834. The travelers did not stay long in Inverness; they were eager to press forward toward Skye and eventually Iona, little aware, of course, of the wonderful and sometimes frightening circumstances that would envelop them on the way.

Johnson, meanwhile, wrote in his *Journey* of the nature of Highlanders, comparing the English and the Scots and seldom in favor of the latter: "Yet men thus ingenious and inquisitive were content to live in total ignorance of the trades by which human wants are supplied, and to supply them by the grossest means." Until the Treaty of 1707 made them familiar with English ways, he continued, "the culture of their lands was unskilful, and their domestick life unformed; their tables were coarse as the feasts of Eskimeaux, and their houses filthy as the cottages of Hottentots." Such observations (even though Johnson's firsthand knowledge of Eskimos could scarcely fill one sentence in a one-page book) would bring down scorn upon Johnson from Scots who read his words in his published book. And even though Johnson qualified his judgments by finding improvements in living and manners, he couldn't resist adding, "What remains to be done they will quickly do, and then wonder, like me, why that which was so necessary and so easy was so long delayed. But they must be for ever content to owe the English that elegance and culture, which, if they had been vigilant and active, perhaps the English might have owed to them" Had some of the Highlanders the pair would soon visit know of Johnson's words, their greetings likely would have been much chillier.

With mounting excitement—"We were now to bid farewell to the luxury of travelling, and to enter a country upon which no wheel has never rolled," Johnson wrote joyfully and expectantly—the two travelers departed Inverness. They headed southwest along the banks of Loch Ness on a gorgeous fall day, heading ultimately to the Isle of Skye, where we have already met. Just over twenty-three miles in length, no more than two miles in width, Loch Ness lies between Inverness to the north and Fort Augustus at its southwestern tip and is framed by mountains and lovely glens on both sides of its high banks. Loch Ness is Scotland's best-known waterway, even more so than Loch Lomond. And yes, that's entirely because of the sea monster said to inhabit its dark, cold, deep waters.

Neither Boswell nor Johnson apparently ever mentioned rumors of the monster, but in the years since it has become something of an epic industry almost rivaling Mel Gibson's Braveheart, who will be making a surprise appearance in this story in a moment. Johnson thought the loch beautiful and full of exaggerated tales, none of which had to do with Nessie. First he realized that geographic reports placing the loch's width at a dozen miles suggested that the compilers had never visited the area. Then he discounted stories that a loch so far north had never frozen. (It really has never frozen.) And finally he discredited stories that the loch could be 140 fathoms deep. (It is that deep, maybe more.) Boswell thought the whole scene "as remote and agreeably wild as could be desired." Mercifully both were spared what has become of this place today.

The legend of Nessie has spawned the worst of tourist entrepreneurs catering to the worst instincts of modern travelers. Here's how bad it has gotten: there are now *two* competing Loch Ness Visitor Centres built within a few yards of each other near the village of Drumnadrochit. It's not enough to have one tacky, contrived, laughable establishment to separate visitors from their cash, but there are two! I, of course, visited both, beginning with the Loch Ness 2000 Exhibition, housed in a castlelike structure. It boasted seven themed walk-through areas complete with sound and visual effects documenting the monster with something of a scientific veneer. But it ended up, oddly enough, slightly pooh-poohing those who have claimed a sighting of Nessie. As I walked out I regretted wasting my money, but then again I have to admit I've always been a sucker for the too-tacky. I was obviously in the right place.

That Loch Ness attraction was separated from its competitor by a whisky shop (always a good idea), a shop selling tartans, shortbread, postcards, and local crafts (local if your neighborhood is Beijing), a restaurant and a hotel, which seemed to be doing steady business only in its restroom. I tried to see Loch Ness from the car park, but it was blocked by shrubbery and cars. The rival Nessie attraction around the corner was the Loch Ness Monster Visitor Centre.

Now that was more like it—if you've got something to sell, sell it up front. This attraction featured a thirty-minute film narrated by a gentleman who didn't seem to believe a word he was saying, but the presentation was sort of entertaining and definitely more oriented to the notion that there really is something huge (and not just another visitor centre) hiding in those great depths. There was also a statue of Nessie in the car park for the kiddies to climb on. The monster looked something like a Disney character as interpreted by a fifth grader.

The Loch Ness Monster Visitor Centre also had a little house in the rear that was labeled the Braveheart Museum. And having come this far through Mel Gibson, Braveheart, kilts, bagpipes, Mary, queen of Scots, Bonnie Prince Charlie, and Sean Connery, there's no way I could possibly resist this. The house turned out to be a cabin with lots of small rooms, each with paintings depicting colorful moments in Scotland's colorful history, all painted in color. The paintings consisted of crudely drawn figures, everyone wearing kilts, and most of them getting killed in one way or other. It was as if the fifth grader who created the Nessie monster outdoors had apprenticed on these paintings as a third grader. It was hilariously amateurish if not embarrassingly foolish, absolutely the worst museum I had ever stepped into, surpassing even that museum of string I saw once somewhere in Iowa, I think. I forgot all about Scottish history—a good thing, since I recall the painting captions were occasionally misconceived nuggets of history. There was another painting out front that apparently depicted Mel Gibson; I don't think he would be flattered.

I assumed, by the way, that admission to the Braveheart Museum came with admission to the Monster Centre. A clerk informed me otherwise, but perhaps taking pity on someone who had already been to the museum, she didn't make me pay extra. She did, however, confide that she'd always wanted to visit the United States, especially some place in the West with wide-open spaces, like Montana or Wyoming. She loved cowboys and Indians, and was eager to see both up close.

Before leaving the area, I drove south along the loch a few miles to Urquhart Castle, a once mighty, impossibly picturesque ruin on the western shore of the loch that Boswell and Johnson passed near but did not see. It has played host to some famous people including St. Colomba, who stopped by around 580 A.D. The decidedly unpleasant King Edward I of England—whose bitter adversary was William Wallace (will Mel Gibson never go away?)—seized it in 1296, and later the lords and henchmen of the Macdonald Clan ruled from here before the Grant Clan took over. When the last blood was shed here in 1692 English soldiers blew up most of the castle to ensure it would not be garrisoned by Jacobite-leaning Scots, and the castle was indeed never repaired or occupied. Natural decay and plundering of the stones by locals reduced it to what we see today: picturesque ruins which allow a romantic view into Scotland's past. It is much more interesting—and real—than any prospect of viewing Nessie.

Boswell and Johnson continued down the loch, stopping for an over-the-top, hilarious encounter with an old Highlands woman. Let's allow Boswell to tell the story:

> I perceived a little hut with an oldish woman at the door of it. I knew it would be a scene for Mr. Johnson. So I spoke it. "Let's go in," said he. So we dismounted, and we and our guides went in. It was a wretched little hovel, of earth only, I think; and for a window had just a hole which was stopped with a piece of turf which could be taken out to let in light. In the middle of the room (or space which

could be entered) was a fire of peat, the smoke going out at a hole in the roof. She had a pot upon it with a goat's flesh boiling. She had at one end, under the same roof but divided with a kind of partition made of wands, a pen or fold in which we saw a great many kids.

Johnson inquired of her where she slept. The old woman, apparently misunderstanding, announced that she was afraid the group wanted to assault her.

This coquetry, or whatever it may be called, of so wretched a like being was truly ludicrous. Mr. Johnson and I later made merry upon it. I said it was he who alarmed the poor woman's virtue. "No sir," said he. "She'll say, 'There came a wicked young fellow, a wild dog, who, I believe would have ravished me had there not been with him a grave old gentleman who repressed him. But when he gets out of sight of his tutor, I'll warrant you he'll spare no woman he meets, young or old.'

"No," said I. "She'll say, 'There was a terrible ruffian who would have forced me, had it not been for a gentle, mild-looking youth, who, I take it, was an angel.'"

Between the wild dog and the terrible ruffian, the two men had clearly enjoyed a great laugh at the old woman's expense. Their bantering does seem a tad cruel in retrospect, but taken in these writings it conjures up images of a bizarrely amusing nature, the corpulent Johnson and the randy Boswell behaving rather like two giggly teenage girls. Once those matters were resolved, Boswell recounted fascinating aspects of the woman's life with her eighty-year-old husband, perhaps even being intrusive in the process. With typical Highland hospitality, however, their host offered her guests a dram of whisky, and then asked for snuff, her sole "luxury." Not having any, Boswell and Johnson offered a sixpence each. In return she brought out the entire bottle of whisky and collected another sixpence. It must have been a good bargain all the way around.

Johnson offered more details on the hut, obviously similar to the previously described blackhouses of the Hebrides, and also of the woman, who was the mother of five children, "of which none have yet gone from her." (Further evidence that getting the birds to leave the nest is hardly a new problem for parents.) But Johnson made no mention in his published *Journey* of the lengthy conversation about bedding the woman with which Boswell so delighted us, a reminder for modern readers of why it is best to follow these two accounts side by side.

Without tossing cold water on the accounts above, I should advise readers of what Boswell and Johnson were not aware of at the time, and that is the very good reason why the old woman, whom we know now as Mrs. Fraser, was so fearful of her visitors. She had acquired the small property under her care in 1747, just a year after some of her relatives had been forced to leave it. The ouster came when officers and soldiers of the English duke of Cumberland passed by following the battle at Culloden and found only a small girl and her grandmother present. An officer raped the girl with the help of his soldiers and strangled the old woman in order to silence her. His behavior was later uncovered, and he was said to have been punished in some way. But the inhabitants of the home could no longer live at the scene of the horrible crime and left it to Mrs. Fraser. She would unquestionably have known of the story, and as Moray McLaren writes, "The Celtic people have long memories, and it may not have been only pathetic ageing female vanity that had made the woman fearful of two English-speaking travellers who wanted to see her bedroom." In everyone's defense let us recall that Boswell and Johnson departed from her on happy terms and with her prayerful blessings.

The travelers soon headed west across the Highlands toward Skye, stopping at a house in the village of Anoch (no traces of this site remain). Johnson encountered an attractive young woman, educated in Inverness and daughter of their host, and presented her the gift of a book he was carrying. He said nothing further of the brief incident. Boswell, however, enlightens us considerably with some wonderful details in a footnote that helps make this stop in the journey unforgettable:

> This book has given rise to much inquiry, which has ended in ludicrous surprise. Several ladies, wishing to learn the kind of reading which the great and good Dr. Johnson esteemed most fit for a young woman, desired to know what book he had selected for this Highland nymph. "They never adverted," said he, "that I had no *choice* in the matter. I have said that I presented her with a book which I *happened* to have about me." And what was his book? My readers, prepare your features for merriment. It was *Cocker's Arithmetic!* Wherever this was mentioned, there was a loud laugh, at which Dr. Johnson, when present, used sometimes to be a little angry. One day, when we were dining at General Oglethorpe's, where we had many a valuable day, I ventured to interrogate him, "But, sir, is it not somewhat singular that you should happen to have *Cocker's Arithmetic* about you on your journey? What made you buy such a

book at Inverness?" He gave me a very sufficient answer. "Why, sir, if you are to have but one book with you upon a journey, let it be a book of science. When you have read through a book of entertainment, you know it, and it can do no more for you; but a book of science is inexhaustible."

Legions of novelists and poets have disliked Johnson ever since then.

The rest of the journey toward Skye continued without the same high level of entertainment. Johnson provided some valuable descriptions of the rugged countryside, and Boswell supplied some interesting details of their encounters. There was a point just before they reached the boat to take them to Skye, as they proceeded through the woods, when Boswell rode ahead, leaving Johnson in his wake. His companion, however, shouted after him angrily. "He was really in a passion with me for leaving him," Boswell wrote contritely. Johnson apparently was genuinely frightened to find himself alone; he was, after all, an old man with a variety of ailments in an unfamiliar country, and he was tired after a strenuous trip on horses through the afternoon. The discomfort was not resolved until the next morning when Johnson relieved Boswell's uneasy night by telling him, "Let's think no more on't." It was now September 2; Skye awaited.

For me it was back to Inverness. At my B&B the next morning my hostess asked if I would like some fresh salmon for breakfast. I of course said yes, and added that I would enjoy some sausage, too. There was a moment of dead air while my hostess inhaled. With a kind of tone of voice that suggested she was asking a pederast if he wanted to play with her child, she inquired, "Did you want sausage *with* your salmon?" It occurred to me that perhaps that just isn't done in Scotland, that I had committed a gross culinary faux pas. I hastily replied that no, absolutely not, of course I didn't actually want the sausage with the fish—who would do that? Ha-ha—I meant only that at some point in my stay I would love to eat some sausage. She backed away, still looking rather pale, and slipped into the kitchen, no doubt to whisper to her befuddled husband what peculiar people Americans really are. When I left the next morning after a breakfast of eggs, tomatoes, mushrooms, and sausage—no fish, of course—I suspect both of them breathed a sigh of relief and vowed not to take in weirdos again.

Having made sure that I wouldn't need to make any bathroom stops, I parked in Inverness to take care of a few bits of business including paying a visit to a nifty, well-stocked used-book store occupying an old downtown church. Over a cup of tea I read in the newspaper that Loch Ruthven, a small freshwater loch a dozen or so miles south of Inverness, had become the most important site in the United Kingdom for breeding Slavonian grebes. I almost choked on my tea. I had no idea Slavonian grebes could be found so far north. Or south. Or anywhere away from Slavonia. And where is Slavonia, and what the heck are grebes, anyway? Later, having resolved the most burning question (grebes are birds), I was back in the car for an eastward jaunt, back on the trail of Boswell and Johnson.

15

Culloden

It was now the middle of April, and it felt like mid-spring in the Highlands. The sun shone brightly in a cloudless sky, and by early afternoon the temperature was hovering near seventy. If anyone in the Highlands actually owned a swim suit, I'm sure they would have had it on, soaking up some rays. I was sweltering when I got to the Culloden battlefield, scene of the most |pivotal clash in Scottish Highland history and arguably the bloodiest in a lengthy history stained by bloodshed.

It has always seemed strange to me that Boswell and Johnson didn't stop at Drummossie Moor, the site of the clash between the Jacobite army of Prince Charles and the duke of Cumberland's troops in 1746, a mere twenty-seven years earlier. Neither man mentioned it, though it is impossible that they did not know that the site was nearby and unthinkable that they were unaware of its significance. Johnson, in fact, was receiving a pension from King George, the brother of Cumberland. So both must have ignored it on purpose, and it is worth a moment to consider why. According to Boswell, Johnson was not unsympathetic to the Jacobite cause; he certainly professed much interest on Skye when he visited with Flora Macdonald and had at least been an earlier-in-life supporter of the Jacobite cause. He had little affection for the Hanoverians currently on the throne, and some years before had actually spoken aloud of the right of the Stuarts to claim the English crown. Boswell clearly had both sympathy and sentiment for the Jacobites. Perhaps the reason neither man wanted to venture there lies in the raw passions that the Jacobite Rising still inflamed. Were Johnson to walk the moor and put his feelings into words, he surely would have provoked anger from one side or the other. Given his receipt of money from the king, he could hardly appear so ungrateful as to belittle his royal benefactor. Boswell also had a family and professional associates in Scotland and England and could scarcely afford to risk alienating them with bold declarations of his thoughts about the battlefield. So it seems likely that neither man pressed the other to go to Culloden; and at the least since Johnson didn't go there or say anything about it, Boswell chose not to write anything himself. Discretion is the most likely and logical winner here.

The story of what led up to the battle and the aftermath of the conflict have been told thoroughly and dramatically in several books, but because of its centrality to so much of Highland life and legend, it merits recounting here. Bonnie Prince Charlie arrived in Scotland aboard a French frigate on July 25, 1745, at what is now Arsaig village on the west coast, some thirty miles west of Fort William. It took nearly a month for enough Highlanders—actually scarcely more than a thousand—to come to his support, enabling Charlie to raise his standard formally at Glenfinnian at the head of Loch Shiel (commemorated by a monument erected there in 1815) and to declare the beginning of the Stuart's efforts to reclaim the throne of England. His ragtag army managed to secure Edinburgh, then moved south toward London where Charles expected to have the crown placed on his swelled head.

Whatever inspiration Charles was in figure, in the flesh he must have been lacking a bit. "Charles no longer displayed any semblance of leadership, preferring to sulk, seemingly indifferent to the welfare of his men, with whom his stock plummeted. This is perhaps the real cause of failure: Charles ultimately lacked the quality of leadership necessary to retain the unquestioning loyalty of his men," writes historian John Sadler. The army got as close to London as Derby (which is actually a lot closer to Birmingham than London), but close enough to start a panic in the capital, described by Chevalier de Johnstone, an aide-de-camp in the prince's command:

> Our arrival at Derby was known at London on the 5 of December, and the following Monday, called by the English Black Monday, the intelligence was known throughout the whole city, which was filled with terror and consternation. Many of the inhabitants fled to the country with their most precious effects, and all of the shops were shut. People thronged to the Bank [of England] to obtain payments of its notes, and it only escaped bankruptcy by a stratagem. . . . They dreaded to see our army enter London in triumph in two or three days. King George ordered his yachts, in which he had embarked all his most precious effects, to remain at the Tower Quay, in readiness to sail at a moment's warning.

The prince wanted to press on to London, but his commanders insisted that would not work. A large English army was massing to his front; his army was weary and underfed; no additional recruits had come forward in England; and the rumors of significant French intervention, spread mostly by the prince, simply weren't true. So the lengthy, morale-lowering retreat began back into Scotland as winter set in. Pursued by Cumberland's army, Prince Charles's army ended up on the bleak moor near Inverness on the evening of April 15, 1746 (almost exactly 261 years before my arrival at the battlefield). The prince, still sulking, and his advisors came up with a highly risky proposal: a night march with a tired army, a dozen miles through unfamiliar terrain in rain and sleet, to take the Redcoat encampment by surprise at dawn. It couldn't work, and it didn't. Some forty-five hundred men began the march, but hundreds fell out from hunger and exhaustion, and others got lost. As dawn began to break, the army was forced to concede failure, turn around, and march back to the moor whence it started. The duke's men—some twice their number, well rested, and eager for battle—followed on their heels.

The responsibility for the choice of ill-suited Drummossie Moor for the army is generally placed squarely on the head of the twenty-five-year-old prince, whose behavior was increasingly removed from reality and who had thoroughly alienated his officers. His field commander, Lord George Murray, thought it poor ground with all advantage to the duke; the prince believed Cumberland's horse and artillery would find it treacherous for movement. This time the prince's decision was followed, however reluctantly, and the Jacobite Rising would soon end with his decision.

Thus it was a weary, wet, cold, and dispirited Highlander army that set up for a climactic battle on Drummossie Moor, some 3,800 men spread thinly without reinforcements in their rear. The English, with all the advantage of artillery and horse on the field, were ready for the slaughter when the action began at midday. It didn't take long: from start to finish the Battle of Culloden lasted only forty minutes. Artillery shells shredded the Highlander line, negating their advantage of the "Highland Charge," the wild rush into personal combat that had so alarmed their opponents. When the charge finally began across open field—the analogy to General George Pickett's ill-fated charge by brave Confederate soldiers on the final, conclusive day at Gettysburg is inevitable—it was a massacre. And when the sides collided hand-to-hand, bravery succumbed to firepower and numbers.

The dead and dying bodies of the prince's army lay on the field; Cumberland's men advanced, on his orders bayoneting and clubbing anyone who still breathed, earning the duke his sobriquet of "butcher" though whether the killings were justified remains in doubt. The duke estimated his army losses at some three hundred men; the number of Highlanders killed was said to be close to two thousand, though the historian Sadler says we will never know exactly because so many were missing, either having slipped away or been carried off the field. Whatever the number, it was horrendous. Prince Charles, some say in tears, made his getaway and struggled through the next year to return safely to his home in France.

Some Scots have adopted a strong view of all this. The prince's name generates something less than rapture in a few quarters. A man I engaged in conversation in Pitlochry said he was sick of the entire story, adding, "Charles was an ass." The novelist and poet Ian Crichton Smith wrote a novel, *The Dream,* in which one of his characters professed a cold, bitter view of the Young Pretender: "He was an evil ghost who had drifted into the Highlands, like some kind of vaporous poison, with his powdered hair and his boyish rapacity for adventure, intoxicated by the new air, the mountains, the lochs, the heather, and by his selfish opportunism he had brought tragedy on the Highlands. And later he was cruel, a wife-beating drunkard, after he had destroyed the Highlands in a storm of hailstones and fire."

By way of contrast the romantic view of Culloden has spawned the tourist industry that revels in the cult of the Bonnie Prince and everything to do with him, including the loyalty of Jacobite supporters among the Highlanders. That romance has brought millions of dollars into Scotland, and it has been encouraged ever since the nineteenth century. Boswell and Johnson were really the first to give the tourist industry a boost; until their books were published the notion of taking a trip to the Highlands, much less of finding anything romantic or interesting about the region, was just a lunatic, impractical idea.

The man who gave tourism its biggest shot in the arm was Sir Walter Scott, the creator of the Scottish Romantic Movement. His novels *Waverly* (1814) and *Rob Roy* (1817) and poems such as "The Lord of the Isles" (which the cynical English writer Charles Jennings says now are "unreadable unless you're in prison or fantastically old") spread the image of the swashbuckling Highlander (plantation owners in the American South were eager to appropriate and abuse some of these chivalric images for their own cultural reasons) and inspired generations of visitors. It was Scott who helped arrange a visit by King George IV to Edinburgh in 1822, which led to a terrific photo op (or more accurately a portrait op) of the king wearing a kilt. Queen Victoria, then a mere babe at twenty-nine, followed in 1847 with her husband, Albert, both huge admirers of Scott. They took a lengthy journey to the Highlands and wrote of their beauty, to which Jennings added his own deliciously sour note: "Victoria and Albert . . . responded immediately to the Romantic landscape in front of them. They could afford to: minus the violence and crushing deprivations which Highlanders had to endure for centuries, and with plenty of food, drink and attendants to make things comfy, they could have fun, apart from the rain and the midges." Victoria, incidentally, apparently under the Highland spell, recalled more fondly than might be expected of the English crown the trekking of the Young Pretender over this same ground. It's almost laughable to imagine Victoria speaking with pleasure of the Stuart who, if he had been successful in his quest, would have ensured that Victoria would never have ascended the throne of England.

Ah well, the Jacobite movement "had thus succeeded in popular romance where it had so signally failed in historical reality," wrote one clear-eyed historian recently. "Whether any of those who shivered in the morning showers on the cold Culloden Moor, so many years before, would have appreciated the irony has to remain questionable." It's also hard for me to avoid thinking of the American Civil War, where the South lost on the battlefield but won decisively in the pages of history books for decades after the fighting ended.

There's a magnificent new visitor center at Culloden now. It's a mammoth, multimedia tribute to what some have called the Scots' "glorious loser mentality." Of course, in the American South Civil War memorials to the losers abound at such places as Vicksburg, Atlanta, and Columbia. Charles Jennings, the English author, put it a bit more harshly several years ago. The visitor centre—the scene of pilgrimages by lots of Jacobite-remembering Scots each year—made him feel like a "Nazi" so antagonistic was its portrayal of the English at the battlefield. A life-size mannequin of Cumberland at the entrance depicted a man "fat as a sumo wrestler" with something of a sneer on his face. Prince Charlie's mannequin, however, cut a rather svelte, dashing figure, so there was no doubt about who to pull for here.

That was the "old" interpretation. The new center had just opened, however, and it addressed a lot of concerns about the balance of the Scots versus the English, including the fact that there were Scots on both sides. There was a bagpipe on display that is said to have been removed from the field, but no one knows exactly which side it belonged to. That's because—though not everyone wants to admit to it—the Highlanders had their pipers, but so did the English, whose army included Lowland Scots and even a scattering of Highlanders. (The Scottish courts of justice once ruled that a man carrying bagpipes was a man carrying a weapon, so inspiring was the music of the pipers to the clans in battle.) There also was an electronic display that illuminated the movements of the armies across the field and which made it abundantly clear just how easily the English accomplished their victory. Their triumph was decisive; it very effectively put an end to the dreams of rebellion.

The battlefield was open and atmospherically quiet. Other than the sound of cars passing in the distance, the moor catches only the wind and the occasional words of visitors, like me. I walked freely around the site (not all the original battlefield is open, only that portion, about one-third, overseen by the National Trust for Scotland) and found a mass grave where some of the English soldiers are buried. A twenty-foot-high stone monument from 1858 nearby carries an inscription honoring "gallant Highlanders who fought for Scotland and Prince Charlie." The Leanach Cottage on the site is where Jacobite soldiers lay wounded and where as many as thirty were killed by the duke's men. The original structure no longer exists; the cottage has been reconstructed, though there is a sense of gloom about it. There are stones scattered about the field that marked where men fell, and another on which the duke of Cumberland is said to have stood while directing the battle. The stones are sad memorials. Everything about Culloden seemed sad to me. I spent many hours there, being unable to pull myself away, and I regretted leaving. But I also was grateful to depart; this is not a place where hearts are at ease. I wondered again what Boswell and Johnson would have made of it.

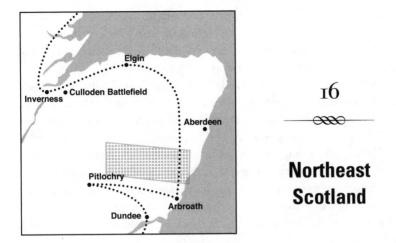

16

Northeast Scotland

After a comfortable overnight stay nearby, I ventured out on yet another sunny morning to see something else Boswell and Johnson missed: Clava Cairn, prehistoric burial chambers that date from about 2000 B.C. The site is reached by a narrow road flanked by farmland along the River Nairn. Only one other car was there when I arrived and its occupants left soon after I got there. There was no on-site staff, so I was alone as I walked through the standing stones, some with low covered entranceways and large, open central chambers. I was amazed once again to be so close and unrestricted around these ancient cairns. Interestingly, as far as I could tell, there were no evidences of recent vandalism.

My real target was Cawdor Castle, however, for Boswell and Johnson visited there, and it has, of course, the association with Shakespeare's *Macbeth;* the witches' prediction that Macbeth will become thane of Cawdor fuels his ultimately tragic desire to be king. History doesn't mix well with legend once again, however, for the castle dates from the early fourteenth century, long after the real events occurred upon which Shakespeare based his play. Nonetheless, I wanted to see for myself if being thane of Cawdor amounted to a suitable reward for Macbeth in the play.

I spotted a sign which said the castle was only one mile away; I drove three miles and never saw the entrance. I did, however, find another sign while coming from the opposite direction that said the same thing: one mile to go. I did a back-and-forth maneuver for about fifteen minutes before giving up and driving into the fairytalelike, almost precious, village of Cawdor with its stone cottages and every other building apparently a tearoom. I found out that the castle wasn't open for the season yet, and the entranceway signs had been taken down so as not to encourage people like me. No one invited me in for tea, so I left, not wanting to part with any money in a place that obviously didn't want me around. And besides, *Macbeth* isn't my favorite of Shakespeare's plays anyway.

Boswell and Dr. Johnson had their own conflicts during their visit, though Boswell's description made the castle sound exactly the way most Americans expect a castle to appear. "The old tower must be of great antiquity," he wrote. "There is a drawbridge, what has been a moat, and a court. There is a hawthorn tree in one of the rooms, still undecayed, that is to say, the stock still remains. The tower has been built round it by a strange conceit. The thickness of the walls, the small slanting windows, and a great iron door at the entrance on the second storey, coming up the stairs, all indicate the rude times in which this building has been erected. There is a great deal of additional building 250 years old."

The minister at Cawdor, Kenneth Macaulay, got on Johnson's nerves when he spoke disparagingly of the English clergy. "This is a day of novelties," Johnson told Boswell. "I have seen trees in Scotland, etc., and I have heard the English clergy treated with disrespect." Johnson couldn't let the subject rest, either; at another point on the journey he called Macaulay "ignorant as a bull" and later even labeled him a "bastard." Macaulay did a service for the travelers, however, by providing them with instructions to assist in navigating their route from Inverness to Skye. I heard later that the castle has been well kept; the Campbells of Cawdor live there, and its rooms, dungeons, and turrets are open to the public, if you get there at the right time of year. I've heard tell a visit is most enjoyable.

One thing I saw was that the women in this particular area appeared perfectly normal. That was a point of some interest because of what I had read about them from William Thomson, who visited this neighborhood in 1785, just twelve years after Boswell and Johnson dropped by. Thomson had observed the approximate location of Shakespeare's scene between Macbeth and the witches, and found it "judiciously chosen, for all the women in this part of the country have the appearance of midnight hags. They only want the cauldron and the broom-stick to complete them for the stage." I'm going to venture a guess here that Thomson never attempted a second trip to this area.

The real Macbeth, something less than the villainous character depicted by Shakespeare, became king in 1040, when he killed Duncan, the sort of thing that royal Scots did quite a bit of in those times. Boswell and Johnson went to the heath where Macbeth is said to have met with the witches, and Johnson began quoting from the play (don't you just hate show-offs?).

Boswell, of course, was dazzled and delighted. "He [Johnson] then parodied the 'all-Hail' of the witches to Macbeth, addressing himself to me. I had purchased some land called Dalblair; and, as in Scotland, it is customary to distinguished landed men by the name of their estates, I had thus two titles, Dalblair and Young Auchinleck. So my friend, in imitation of 'All hail Macbeth! hail to three, Thane of Cawdor!' condescended to amuse himself with uttering: 'All hail Dalblair! hail to thee, Laird of Auchinleck'!" Boswell, as we've seen, could be quite easily amused by Johnson.

Later that same day Boswell encountered a grisly sight, though one he never grew tired of: a dead body. This one was hanging from a tree just off the road. The body was that of Kenneth Leal—who surely would never have anticipated such literary notoriety—found guilty of mail robbery and hanged on July 7. "As he had not hung but about two months, the body was quite entire. It was still a *man* hanging. The sight impressed me with a degree of gloom." Johnson was quiet about this incident. He had no liking for scenes of death, indeed, they provoked fears of his own passing.

About eight miles from Cawdor Castle the two men visited Fort George, constructed over a twenty-year period beginning in 1747 as a bastion for the Hanoverian troops stationed in the Highlands in the wake of the battle at Culloden. Once again it was puzzling that Boswell and Johnson would have inspected the fort so thoroughly with the help of several officers, being fully aware of why it was built and garrisoned, and yet made no mention of Culloden and what transpired there. They were wined and dined, treated to a concert, and toured all areas of the fortress.

Fort George sits on a spit of land that juts out into Moray Firth a few miles to the east of Inverness. It makes an imposing sight, and it must have been so when it was built to keep the Highlanders at bay. But, of course, the rebellion was thoroughly crushed at Culloden, and by the time the fort was completed around 1769, there was virtually no reason for its existence. The Highlanders had been subdued and their only threat to the magnificent fort would have been to hurl stale haggis at it. The army converted it into a barracks and a training facility for recruits, which appeared to be what it is used for these days. So if any twenty-first-century Jacobites decided to reorganize, their biggest obstacle in retaking the fort would probably be what to do with all of those tourists now crawling over the place. Johnson, by the way, chose not to leave us any details abut his visit, writing, "Of Fort George, I shall not attempt to give any account. I cannot delineate it scientifically, and a loose and popular description of it is of use only when the imagination is to be amused." For most of us latter-day writers a modest stirring of the imagination is about the best to be hoped for.

The travelers spent a night in Elgin, a market town that grew up in the thirteenth century around the River Lossie. The inn they found disappointing and the meal inedible, according to Johnson. It was one of only two times on their long journey—the other was during a stop in Glenelg as they approached Skye—that Johnson complained about the quality of the food: "Such disappointments, I suppose, must be expected in every country, where there is no great frequency of travellers," he declared.

It seems there may have been a little more to this story than either man knew of at the time. One of the great Johnson scholars, G. B. Hill, relates the anecdote, possibly apocryphal, but now widely known. It seems that Johnson dined at the Red Lion Inn, where a penurious commercial traveler by the name of Thomas Paufer was accustomed to dining and drinking with regularity. Really he preferred drinking to eating, and he tended to order a sparse dinner so that he would have more money to spend on drink. Unfortunately for Dr. Johnson, he bore an uncanny resemblance to Paufer, and when Johnson arrived at the inn the waiter mistook him for Paufer "and such a dinner was prepared as Paufer as wont to receive." In other words the tavern owner figured he could get away with serving a second-class meal to Paufer, who would be too plastered to know the difference. Johnson, of course, was criticized for many things he said about Scotland when his book was published, and it may be that the proud denizens of Elgin, stung by his complaint about the food, searched diligently for an exculpatory story. Offering another perspective, the Irish-born writer Frank Delaney, who followed Boswell and Johnson's trail in the early 1990s, engaged a local man in conversation about Johnson's remark:

"Dr. Johnson had a meal here that was so bad he couldn't eat it," Delaney said.

"When was that?" he asked.

"In August 1773."

"Ach," he said. "He could have had the same yesterday."

My experience was much better, perhaps because Elgin is no longer infrequently visited. It seemed a rather lively, busy town of twenty-four thousand that was buzzing with delight at the uncommon appearance of the sun at this time of year. The temperatures reached into the mid-seventies this afternoon, and when I drove to the pond green, there were literally hundreds of people sunbathing, walking their children and dogs, or lining up at the ice cream stand, all in various stages of undress. (I hasten to add that undress in this case means shedding sweaters, not removing all clothing; Scotland is not a clothing-optional country, at least not in the Highlands.) The sight seemed a tad incongruous after hours spent reading Boswell and

Johnson. Then Elgin was an outpost, as Johnson observed, a place few visited. Now it appeared more of a sun-washed resort. No rain, no wind; could this really be the Scotland I had been journeying through?

At breakfast I encountered a pair of singers on tour with the Scottish National Opera giving performances of Johann Strauss's *Der Fledermaus* in the city. We were intrigued with our differing missions. They knew of Boswell and Johnson and were eager to inquire into my adventures following their journey. "Boswell was such a tell-all, I laughed at a lot of what I read about him," said the tenor. "And Johnson seemed rather a stick-in-the-mud by comparison. I know he was very intelligent and very respected, but he seemed to distant to me." I reminded them of the story of Johnson imitating a kangaroo in Inverness, and they both laughed loudly, the baritone choking just a bit on his cereal. The tenor added, "I've never read of their journey to the Highlands, but I imagine they were probably just right for each other because of being such different personalities. People like that can travel well together." He looked at his opera companion, and they both smiled. We enjoyed a little more conversation over tea, and they discussed their careers. Both were from Birmingham (England) and had been singing for nearly ten years; they expected to have long careers in Europe, though both would like to experience the stage at the Metropolitan Opera in New York. I suggested that they undertake a Boswell-and-Johnson-type journey to New York and the States, maybe even keep a journal, and we all toasted the possibility with our cups before heading out to our respective duties.

My duties, of course, weren't quite so strenuous as their rehearsing. I walked to the site that had most interested Boswell and Johnson when they arrived in Elgin: the fourteenth-century ruins of the famous cathedral, once regarded as the most beautiful in Scotland. Boswell called them "noble ruins" And Johnson observed that "there was enough yet remaining to shew, that it was once magnificent." The cathedral suffered a dreadful history, which both men commented upon. Built in the early thirteenth century, it survived a major fire in 1270, but it would face far worse dangers, namely Alexander Stewart, the earl of Buchan and better known as the Wolf of Badenoch (and that's not a complimentary nickname). He was powerful and imperious, the illegitimate son of King Robert II, and when the bishop at Elgin excommunicated him for leaving his wife, he sought revenge. In 1390 he and a group of thugs burned the cathedral to the ground along with the homes of all of the bishops and chaplains. Some rebuilding was accomplished. In the post-Reformation period (the second half of the sixteenth century), the cathedral was stripped of its lead roofing and bells, and without a roof overhead usage declined. Vandals and storms destroyed more of the structure over the next two centuries, and the central tower collapsed on Easter Day in 1711, not exactly a good omen.

Johnson raged at the mistreatment of the once majestic building:

> The church of Elgin had, in the intestine tumults of the barbarous ages, been laid waste by the irruption of a Highland chief, whom the bishop had offended; but it was gradually restored to the state, of which the traces may be now discerned, and was at least not destroyed by the tumultuous violence of Knox, but more shamefully suffered to dilapidate by deliberate robbery and frigid indifference. There is still extant . . . an order . . . directing that the lead, which covers the two cathedrals of Elgin and Aberdeen, shall be taken away, and converted into money for the support of the army. A Scotch army in those times was very cheaply kept; yet the lead of two churches must have born so small a proportion to any military expence, that it is hard not to believe the reason alleged to be merely popular, and the money intended for some private purse. The order however was obeyed; the two churches were stripped, and the lead was shipped to be sold in Holland. I hope every reader will rejoice that this cargo of sacrilege was lost at sea.

He was correct. The ship carrying the lead was so overweighted that it sank, its cargo lost. Johnson went on to add a note about historic preservation: "Let us not however make too much haste to despise our neighbours. Our own cathedrals are mouldering by unregarded dilapidation. It seems to be part of the despicable philosophy of the time to despise monuments of sacred magnificence, and we are in danger of doing that deliberately, which the Scots did not do but in the unsettled state of an imperfect constitution."

Efforts to stabilize the Elgin ruins began in the nineteenth century and have permitted visitors today to see much of what Boswell and Johnson saw then. The sandstone ruins do indeed evoke a grand structure. And the site is still in use. In fact a wedding was in progress when I arrived, some of the male guests attired in Highland kilts. I watched the bride and groom ascend several stories on the steps inside one of the remaining towers and smile down at the guests for a series of photographs. It was quite picturesque and frankly rather bracing to find this old edifice hosting a contemporary service. There were cracked gravestones scattered around the site; the oldest I found dated back to 1644, but there were others that looked older whose inscriptions I could not read. The finest intact tomb is that of Bishop John of Winchester, who died in 1460. Little remains of the original nave, but the west front tower, through which ceremonial processions entered the cathedral, is largely intact and majestic, affording even to the unimaginative a vision of how magnificent this structure was before its destruction began. The choir and the presbytery are the most complete parts of the cathedral to survive, though they date from the rebuilding after the damage caused by the Wolfman. History is hardly dead here; it is raw and etched into the surrounding ruins, and after all these centuries it still weighs heavily.

Elgin was near to a number of castles of some historic distinction, and my addiction was beginning to act up for the first time since I passed through Dunrobin. I gave way to that irresistible tug of drawbridges, moats, turrets, dungeons, and an assortment of peculiar lords, dukes, and earls, and I set off for the closest. It turned out to be Spynie Palace, technically not a castle at all, I discovered, but important—and close.

Spynie—the name reeks of intrigue, doesn't it?—was the residence of the powerful bishops of Moray for five centuries. Those bishops included Bishop Bur, whose excommunication so infuriated the bastard Wolf of Badenoch. The palace was abandoned and fell into disrepair in 1689. The medieval ruins now include a six-story tower built in the late fifteenth century. Visitors are encouraged to walk over the site without restriction, even though some areas pose dangers for the careless. There's not even an "at your own risk" sign. I liked the absence of overprotectiveness here, so opposite to what is found at most American sites. For instance access to one of my favorite waterfalls in North Carolina has become more and more restricted over the years because several people have jumped from waterfalls and died. My belief is that dumb, careless people deserve what they get and shouldn't be permitted to prevent the rest of us from being able to move around such wonderful sites. Yes, caution is assumed, but so is no lawyer showing up waving a suit based on negligence. People need to be responsible for themselves. I will now climb down from the tower, carefully, and also abandon my soapbox.

When I got back to the attendant's office I was delighted to find the young man there, Harold, to be an unabashed fan of Boswell and Johnson. He regretted that the travelers didn't get to see Spynie Palace, but he knew they felt the tragedy of the cathedral. "Boswell was always empathetic, sometimes more than he should have been, but when they got to Elgin, it was really Johnson who was outraged at the destruction that took place there over the centuries. I rather liked the old man for that. There were things he said about Scotland I didn't like. A number of them, really. But he got that part right." He laughed remembering their unhappiness with their lodging in Elgin, which "has gotten a lot better since then, I think." Harold said he envied my experience following Boswell and Johnson, and smiled at my doing it backwards. "Oh I wouldn't worry a bit about that. I think Bozzy would rather enjoy the idea, turning things on their head, as it were. Maybe you get a very different look at what they did and said, a different perspective. I'd like to read it when you're done." I put Harold down on my list; I'll certainly send him a copy. Before I left he suggested I make a visit to Duffus Castle near his home, a little to the north of Elgin. "There's a lot of history there," he added, though he really didn't have to. At the mention of another castle, I was ready to go.

Duffus—the *u* is a short *u*, not a long one the way you'd pronounce it if you were calling someone a bit daft or slow of mind—was a fortress and residence from 1150 until 1705. Originally made of earth and timber, it was rebuilt with stone atop the original foundations sometime during the fourteenth century, and a two-story stone tower, perched high on a sloping green hill, now towers over the surrounding countryside. One wall of the rebuilt structure has stayed intact and solid, slanted outward at about a twenty-five-degree angle. Getting to the castle was arduous; I walked up the grassy hill, which was quite steep. I was out of breath and leaned against the leaning wall until I caught my breath a couple of minutes later. The view was 360-degree spectacular; the placement of the castle must have indeed been formidable to enemies when it was occupied.

My Victorian-era inn in Elgin proved a wonderful home for several days while I hit the castle road. And the sun stayed out, keeping temperatures up and making my travel easier than I had anticipated. My first castle of the next day was Brodie, off to the west toward Inverness. The castle's setting was lovely—175 acres of woodland and water—and the castle itself quite handsome. It has showed up in several films, including *Rob Roy*. For an amazing eight hundred years, until the National Trust for Scotland acquired it in 1980, it was the home of the Brodies. Originally a Celtic tribe loyal to King Malcolm IV, the Brodies were rewarded with land somewhere around 1160. One of them was an outstanding golfer about 1640 after learning the game at St. Andrews.

After the Treaty of 1707 the Brodies threw their support behind the English king, and government troops were garrisoned at their castle in 1715. In the Jacobite Rising of 1745 Alexander, the nineteenth Brodie of Brodie, allowed the duke of Cumberland's troops to camp on the grounds on the eve of Culloden. The family persevered in spite of crushing debts at several periods, and it was the expensive upkeep of the castle that led the family to turn it over to the National Trust. I fortunately had a wise and witty tour guide who brought the castle's occupants and history to life. Rarely have structures as vast as this, he said, been inhabited so late into the twentieth century. The furnishings were those of a modern family's residence, and all the more personal and intimately rewarding to observe. Outside, a couple of miles to the east, is an area where King Duncan was said to have been killed by Macbeth in 1040; I was never able to locate it.

Next up in this castle-rich area was Ballindalloch Castle, located in the heart of Speyside region near numerous whisky distilleries, which turned out to be among my favorites in all of my travels. That's unquestionably because of the opportunity to meet and chat with the owners of this gorgeous lived-in and working estate. The castle is an extraordinary enterprise, and an expensive one to keep up, which perhaps explains why the occupants are so down-to-earth. Ballindalloch is no secret. Set in the beautiful Spey Valley, it has been the subject of a BBC documentary, featured on travel programs from as far away as Canada, Japan, and Germany, and CNN has called it one of the United Kingdom's "hot spots" (whatever that might mean). From the outside it has all the things visitors want in a castle: soaring turrets and towers, gracefully landscaped grounds and a garden, a look of permanence and great history. But inside is where I was surprised.

When I approached for an interior tour I was met not by a guide but by the smiling face and extended hand of the first female laird of Ballindalloch, Clare Macpherson-Grant Russell, a charming middle-aged woman who exuded energy and a casual elegance. She welcomed me and two other visitors, and instead of then turning away proceeded to invite us to follow her around the first-floor rooms as she talked about the family history and the furnishings. She has spent her life at Ballindalloch, and as an only child she inherited the estate. She married Oliver Russell of London and settled in to "tackle the challenge of modernizing a traditional Highland estate."

I met her husband on the second floor; he had been sipping tea and had the morning newspaper clutched in his hand. Tall and chatty, his informality matching that of his wife, he asked about my background and was pleased to hear I was pursuing my journey with Boswell and Johnson through Scotland's Highland history. He knew Atlanta well from a number of visits there as well as to Augusta for the Masters golf tournament and to the Sea Islands for vacations. He also has done research at the Library of Congress and knew the librarian, Dr. Ray Billington, whom I had met on one occasion.

He explained how the estate functioned to provide the necessary money to sustain its operation, maintaining everything from a golf course on the banks of the River Avon to a herd of Aberdeen Angus cows, said to be the oldest in the world, descended from black, hornless cattle whose presence goes back to the twelfth century. "With a banking background," the lady laird wrote in *Ballindalloch Castle* of her husband, "he realised that substantial growth in income stream was needed to pay the salary and maintenance bills at a time when farm rents were falling behind. . . . Twenty-five years later there is no doubt that the strategy has worked, with the cherished family home also functioning as a successful business. . . . None of this is change for its own sake. It is the sympathetic development of a Highland estate in tune with modern times."

The castle interior reflected the presence of a family whose ancestors had lived there since the sixteenth century. It also included some important modernization, like the addition of five bathrooms, completed in the 1970s, where only one had existed previously. The walls showcased portraits of the Macpherson and Grant ancestors. One in the drawing room especially stood out: James Grant, the Revolutionary War governor of Florida. Actually there were two portraits. The first, commissioned in 1770, showed Grant has a young boy in military uniform. In later life Grant was known as a gourmet who traveled with his own cook charged with tasting his food before he ate to ensure its high quality. The other portrait of Grant on the wall was a caricature made in 1798 that shows a distinguished, older and incredibly corpulent man; next to him Dr. Johnson would appear more like Richard Simmons. Mr. Russell told me the portrait has been labeled "The fattest man in Scotland." How refreshing that they have such an appealing sense of humor.

I had a delicious lunch in the castle's public tea room, looked over the gift shop, and decided to purchase a baseball cap with the Ballindalloch logo as a souvenir. It's still one of the most prized possessions from my trip, and I have memories of the lady laird and her husband that I wish I could share with Boswell and Johnson to reassure them of the continuing hospitality of Highlanders. The sun was going down, but it was still warm when I arrived back in Elgin for a fine dinner of fresh salmon and single malt from the nearby Glenfiddich distillery in one of Scotland's most whiskified regions. Apparently the waiter didn't think that I looked much like anyone to mistrust or that I bore any resemblance to the cheap Mr. Paufer.

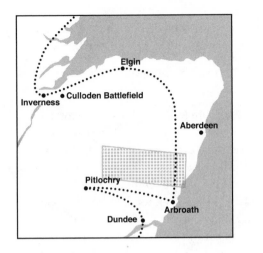

17

Down the East Coast

Boswell and Johnson came to Elgin after a trip along the coast, through the small towns of Banff and Cullen, as they had pursued a path up the east coast of Scotland from Edinburgh to Dundee, to St. Andrews, Arbroath, and Aberdeen. At breakfast one morning in Cullen they encountered "dried haddocks, broiled," the famous "smokies" of the Scottish coast. Boswell ate just one, and Johnson "disliked their presence, so they were removed." The best-known dish of this region is the Cullen skink which, no matter what you might think it is, is a soup made from milk or cream, potatoes, and smoked haddock. It shows up on many menus around Scotland, and I found it a simple preparation and invariably delicious.

The night before at Banff—which I did not visit—Johnson was unhappy with the windows in his room at the inn and launched into a small tirade. The doctor loved fresh air and was always opening windows at night, even in cold weather. This time he was frustrated, and Boswell recorded his annoyed remarks:

> Here unluckily the windows had no pulleys; and Dr. Johnson, who was constantly eager for fresh air, had much struggling to get one of them kept open. Thus he had a notion impressed upon him, that this wretched defect was general in Scotland; in consequence of which he erroneously enlarged upon in his *Journey*. I regretted that he did now allow me to read over his book before it was printed. I should have changed very little, but I should have suggested an alteration in a few places where he has laid himself open to be attacked. I hope I should have prevailed with him to omit or soften his assertion that

"a Scotsman must be a sturdy moralist, who does not prefer Scotland to truth"—for I really think it is not founded; and it is harshly said.

And what did Johnson say that provoked outrage from the Scots? Here, with a bit of editing, it is:

> The art of joining squares of glass with lead is little used in Scotland, and in some places is totally forgotten. The frames of their windows are all of wood. They are more frugal of their glass than the English, and will often, in houses not otherwise mean, compose a square of two pieces, not joining like cracked glass, but with one edge laid perhaps half an inch over the other. Their windows do not move upon hinges, but are pushed up and drawn down in grooves, yet they are seldom accommodated with weights and pullies. He that would have his window open must hold it with his hand, unless what may be sometimes found among good contrivers, there be a nail which he may stick into a hole, to keep it from falling.
>
> What cannot be done without some uncommon trouble or particular expedient, will not often be done at all. The incommodiousness of the Scotch windows keeps them very closely shut. The necessity of ventilating human habitations has not yet been found by our northern neighbours: and even in houses well built and elegantly furnished, a stranger may be sometimes forgiven, if he allows himself to wish for fresher air.

Alas that does not conclude the good doctor's thoughts on the subject, though you might be forgiven for hoping otherwise. He continued with a rant, admitting that, while that such moments are petty, "it must be remembered that life consists not of a series of illustrious actions, or elegant enjoyments; the greater part of our time passes in compliance with necessities, in the performance of daily duties, in the removal of small inconveniences, in the procurement of petty pleasures." In other words, if they couldn't even get the windows right, then there's not a lot to be said for the Scots as nation. Boswell was right in this instance, though as usual it's fun to read about all sides of the journey.

Johnson and Boswell did get into a rather frolicsome discussion on the way to Banff that survives in Boswell's account and which surely would have offended any educated Scot who might have overheard it. Boswell proposed, as something of an amusing mental entertainment, that he and Johnson and the members of their famous literary club in London should take over the highly regarded St. Andrews University (which they had just visited) and rebuild it in their own way. "Mr. Johnson entered fully into the spirit of this idea," Boswell wrote, and the two engaged in a lengthy discussion of assigning the club members to various educational departments. Boswell would teach "Civil and Scotch law," and Johnson—who initially said he would trust "Theology to nobody but myself"—eventually agreed to devote himself to "Logic, Metaphysics and Scholastic Divinity." It was obviously a high old time for both. (The Club was the brainchild of the painter Sir Joshua Reynolds and was founded in 1764 in London. Its esteemed members, thirty-three initially, included an assortment of writers, religious people, debaters, actors, and others whose strong opinions would make for lively conversation and penetrating thought.)

Bozzy and Dr. Johnson had done a little castleling on their own just before Banff, when they accepted an invitation to stop at Slains Castle, then an elegant cliff-top residence between Aberdeen and Peterhead on the east coast and now an abandoned ruin. The writer Bram Stoker used to spend some vacation time there, and it is said that the castle's dark, stark setting served as the inspiration for the castle in *Dracula*. Boswell and Johnson visited several natural sites nearby including the Bullers of Buchan, still a striking 250-foot-deep chasm through which the ocean crashes. Johnson was impressed: "No man can see with indifference, who has either sense of danger or delight in rarity. . . . The edge of the Buller is not wide, and to those that walk round, appears very narrow. He that ventures to look downward sees, that if his foot should slip, he must fall from his dreadful elevation upon stones on one side, or into the water on the other. We however went round and were glad when the circuit was completed." Boswell found it "somewhat horrid to move along" and thought it "alarming to see Mr. Johnson poking his way." Later the two at their most adventuresome were rowed into the cave, an amphitheater of natural rock. Boswell seemed much happier when he returned to the castle and could relax and sip warm tea.

I managed enough time to get to a few more castles in the continuing glorious, unseasonably warm early spring weather. Some thirty miles southeast of Elgin I came across Huntly Castle, a baronial residence for five centuries with a few remaining sections dating back to the twelfth century. Like other ruins, it had no roof but a grand tower still stood and below was a passageway where five-centuries-old graffiti was scrawled on the plastered walls. Nothing about Kilroy or Thorni bedded Helga (only because Helga never got this far south of the Orkneys, I'm sure), but rather drawings of a clock face, a bull, and men and women in sixteenth-century dress. Quite fascinating.

About an hour farther south I pulled the car into the crowded car park at Crathes Castle, my thirst for castleling not yet slaked in this incredibly castle-rich nation. The castle was spectacular and so were the six-hundred-acre, gracefully landscaped grounds surrounding it. The grounds were filled with people lying about in the grass, picnicking and sunning, enjoying the temperatures that had now reached into the low eighties. I was hardly the only one talking about the weather; one man was telling his wife he couldn't remember a spring "so bloody hot." And on the television, I heard later, the weather forecaster said northern Scotland was having a record heat wave and that most places had gone a couple of weeks without rain. And no one mentioned wind.

Crathes, dating from the sixteenth century, was the seat of the Burnett family for centuries before the National Trust took over its care in 1951. It has been attractively preserved. It must have been a tough place for enemies to penetrate; the walls at ground level are five feet thick. I met a guide who said that rooms in the castle are not hosted and that, while photography is prohibited, there was no reason I couldn't make photos as long as I didn't use a flash and disturb anyone. I thought that was exceedingly generous counsel, and I took him up on it.

I skipped the grounds to get to my third castle of the day while it was still daylight. It was Drum Castle, only about ten miles west of Aberdeen, which was a stop for Boswell and Johnson (neither of whom saw any of the castles I previously visited on this day). Drum turned out to be my first castle disappointment in spite of its rich history. Given by Robert the Bruce to his armor-bearer William de Irvine, the castle remained in Irvine family hands for twenty-four generations until the National Trust acquired it in 1976. It's a bit of a hodgepodge, combining a thirteenth-century tower with a Jacobean mansion and a Victorian-era extension. It has been furnished with a variety of items that don't really go with anything, and most definitely not with the castle itself. My guide, who was rather smug about everything, continually pointed out chairs and tables that didn't match the rooms.

I decided I had become castled-out for the day and needed to take a break. So I slipped away from my guide and headed for exit. Outside I suddenly was overcome by weariness and the heat. I was getting cranky, too, which might have accounted for my displeasure with the tour. I definitely wasn't in the mood to deal with a busy city like Aberdeen that evening—even though Boswell and Johnson had been there—and I made a last-minute decision to skip it and find a closer, quieter stop. I would make up for this slight by rereading my companions' entries for Aberdeen before going to sleep.

"We came somewhat late to Aberdeen, and found the inn so full, that we had some difficulty in obtaining admission, till Mr. Boswell made himself known; his name overpowered all objection, and we found a very good house and civil treatment," Johnson wrote. Boswell supplied the details of their meal: "broiled chicken, some tarts, and crab's claws." I knew the inn where they stayed had been destroyed many years ago, so I didn't miss staying in their wake. Aberdeen was their home for three nights during which ensued a variety of social engagements and conversations with the gentry of the city. They spoke of religion and education and literature, and Johnson—who was slowly edging toward ill humor—delivered himself of a few more opinions that would not endear him to the Scots when his book appeared. Johnson's spirits did lift the morning of their departure, however, when the landlady at their inn asked Boswell, "Is this not the great Doctor that is going through the country?" When Boswell replied that indeed he was, she said,

"We heard of him. I made an errand into the room on purpose to see him. There's something great in his appearance. It is a pleasure to have such a man in one's house; a man who does so much good. If I had thought, I would have shown him a child of mine who has had a lump on his throat for some time."

"But," said I, "he's not a Doctor of Physic."

"Is he an oculist?" said the landlord.

"No," said I, "he's just a very learned man."

Said the landlord, "They say he's the greatest man in England except [Lord Chief Justice] Lord Mansfield."

Boswell wrote that Johnson "was highly entertained with this," and he later wrote that Johnson observed with pride that, "To have called me the greatest man in England would have been an unmeaning compliment; but the exception marked that the praise was in earnest."

All things considered, I didn't feel I was missing too much when I awoke and abandoned any lingering notions of a stop in Aberdeen. The novelist Lewis Gibbon said of it, "One detests Aberdeen with the detestation of a thwarted lover. It is the one hauntingly and exasperatingly lovable city of Scotland." I was never quite sure whether he liked it or hated it, but I had gotten quite tired of reading about it. Yes, Aberdeen is the third largest city in Scotland after Glasgow and Edinburgh, and yes it is a busy industrial city, but there is a lot of traffic and there are no castles there, and I had recovered from my burnout the day before. I had in mind a stop at Dunnottar, which my breakfast companion had strongly advised visiting, before picking up the trail of Boswell and Johnson in Arbroath.

The eighteenth-century travelers passed near Dunnottar as they approached Aberdeen but didn't stop. I don't know how they could have resisted. (Well, actually, given that the castle was largely in ruins, and in private hands apparently unknown to Boswell, there was no likelihood of a visit there.) I couldn't imagine not stopping here: the castle ruins were utterly breathtaking; even the least militarily strategic wizard among us could take one quick look and see instantly that the castle was perched at a powerfully defensible site but also on a most beautiful one: an enormous, flat-topped rock with sheer cliffs on three sides jutting out into the North Sea and attached to the mainland only by a very narrow neck of land.

On this bright and sunny day it was both rugged and picture-book pretty; some may remember it as the backdrop for Franco Zeffirelli's film version of *Hamlet*. Its history is amazing, filled with many of the most famous names in Scottish history and awash in their blood. Not only that, but it was also at Dunnottar that a small garrison of troops withstood an eight-month siege by Oliver Cromwell's army and assured the safety of "The Honours of Scotland," that is, the Scottish crown and other coronation regalia.

The castle is reached these days only by walking first down then up a narrow, steep staircase of maybe eighty to ninety steps each way; signs advised accurately that anyone out of shape would experience difficulties in reaching the interior. It was a challenge well worth meeting. There was a lot of walking required once inside, too, but the remaining structures were fascinating and well described in my guidebook, and the views out to sea and the waves crashing against the cliffs below were nothing less than awe-inspiring. Alastair Cunningham's guidebook *Dunnottar Castle* proved a valuable companion for my visit, packed with interesting details yet not neglecting the full scope of the castle's role in Scottish history.

Briefly, Scotland's first saint, Ninian, brought Christianity to this part of the country in the fifth century, founding a fortified church at this site. The Vikings invaded in the ninth century, but Dunnottar remained a religious site for several more centuries until it became a prized possession in the ceaseless wars between Scotland and England. King Edward I's English troops occupied the castle in the late thirteenth century, when William Wallace attacked. Many of the English garrison hid in the chapel; Wallace burned it down (suggesting the English had some reason for torturing him to death when he fell into their hands a few years later.) Wallace's exploits here were later celebrated in a poem by Blind Hary as part of his truthful/fanciful accounting of Wallace's life. The castle continued to be occupied first by the Scots, then the English, and there was no want of fighting. Mary, queen of

Scots, visited here several times before Cromwell claimed the structure a century later. And it was Cromwell's siege guns that demolished much of the castle, leaving the rest for the storms and winds that normally blast the castle as they roar off the North Sea.

The existing chapel ruins at Dunnottar date back to the sixteenth century, since Wallace burned down the first chapel in 1297. The vaulted cellar that constitutes the prison is the most striking of the remaining structures; it was there, in a semi-derelict castle, that 167 men and women were kept for nine weeks in the mid-seventeenth century with little food and no sanitation. There were few breathing holes. Walking through the prison and imagining 167 people in it, each starving, struggling for breath in a fetid, squeezed atmosphere, was incomprehensible. I had had enough; I took the long walk back to the car, and, exhausted mentally and physically, turned south to Arbroath.

18

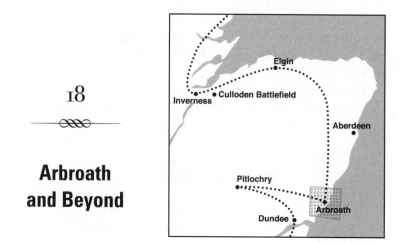

Arbroath
and Beyond

Boswell and Johnson were in only the third day of their journey out of Edinburgh when they stopped briefly at Aberbrothock (Boswell) or Aberbrothick (Johnson), now known as Arbroath. They didn't spend the night—I would stay there for four nights—and their visit was beset with rain and confined to the ruins of the cathedral, once among the finest and most sacred sites in all of Scotland.

"Its ruins afford ample testimony of its ancient magnificence," wrote Johnson, who was clearly impressed with what he saw. "I should scarcely have regretted my journey had it afforded nothing more than the sight of Aberbrothick." He wrote, "The two corner towers particularly attracted our attention. Mr. Boswell, whose inquisitiveness is seconded by great activity, scrambled in at a high window, but then found the stairs within broken, and could not reach the top." And so, in the gathering dusk, the travelers moved on to Montrose, about which more in a moment.

Nearly two and a half centuries later, the ruins of the Arbroath Abbey still offer a quiet reflection of a much earlier time. The abbey occupies a special place in Scotland's national consciousness, one that Boswell and Johnson knew of. The Declaration of Arbroath—the nation's Declaration of Independence—was written in 1320 and issued from here; it was the document that first spoke to the right of the Scottish people to freedom from English interference. Signed by forty nobles, barons, and freemen, it eloquently and courageously asked Pope John XXII to reverse his excommunication of Robert the Bruce and to recognize him as the king of an independent nation. The words still resonate: "For so long as one hundred of us remain alive, we will never in any degree be subject to the dominion of the English, since it is not for glory, riches, or honour that we do fight, but for freedom alone, which no honest man loses but with his life." The pope agreed four years later. I've been particularly surprised that Boswell did not acknowledge this signal document; he wrote only a few lines about their visit. Perhaps the presence of Johnson inhibited him and he thought better of beginning their trip with a pointed reference to England that might stir Johnson's voice.

I walked past the tower Boswell attempted to climb in the rain and paused. I rubbed my hand over the smooth stone, leveled by weather and the years. I could imagine him, full of life, hauling himself up through one of the windows—an impossible task now—and scrambling over the stones before realizing the stairway could not be walked upon. I could imagine his disappointment as he returned to Johnson, prowling through the weedy, roofless nave (the ground is well tended today), probably using his favorite stick. I had another one of my Bozzy moments, telling him out loud that I couldn't get up the stairs either and asking why didn't he write me a little more about all of this remarkable site. There was no answer. But it was quiet over the grounds, so maybe he heard me.

I spent several hours walking around the imposing abbey ruins. King William I ("The Lion") founded the monastery here in 1178 in memory of his boyhood buddy, Thomas Becket, who had been murdered in Canterbury Cathedral only eight years earlier. The abbey fell into general disuse after the Scottish Reformation of 1560, and an engraving from 1693 shows the abbey church in ruins, not much better off than Boswell and Johnson found it in 1773 and others since them.

There was a fine visitor center at the abbey with a computer simulation that allowed me to see how it might have looked in the thirteenth century and what happened to the structures over succeeding centuries. The attendant behind the desk assured me that, with Iona, the abbey was one of the two sites of greatest religious importance in Scotland. We fell into conversation about my Boswell and Johnson; he knew their writings well and thought that Boswell was being "circumspect" in not writing more about Arbroath. "I wish he had stayed here a little longer. He had a very good eye, you know, and he would have caught details that others missed." He wished me well on my book and urged me to contact him with any questions about Arbroath. "I rather like the idea of an American following Dr. Johnson and Boswell; we don't see very much of that at all." That was encouraging, to be sure.

Overnight the temperatures fell, and in Arbroath for the first time in several weeks I faced an overcast, chilly morning. It felt more like Scotland, to tell the truth. My bed and breakfast was a warm and inviting home just off a busy street. My hostess couldn't have been more agreeable; when she wasn't serving a delicious breakfast—smoked fish was always an option—she even ironed my shirts! And I did put away a few of the famous Arbroath "smokies," the dried and smoked haddock that are so well known they are shipped from here to connoisseurs all over the world.

Arbroath served well as my jumping-off spot for a series of visits through the area, including Montrose, where Boswell and Johnson spent an evening. Their accommodation was awful, and Boswell gleefully pointed out to Johnson that it was run by an Englishman. "We dined on haddock, veal cutlets and fowl, and I myself saw another waiter put a lump of sugar with his fingers into Dr. Johnson's lemonade, for which he called him: 'Rascal'!" Johnson was a lover of lemonade, to be sure. A few lines later in his *Journal* Boswell writes that Johnson became angry when he proposed to carry lemons to Skye so that the good doctor could enjoy his lemonade. "Sir, I do not wish to be thought that feeble man who cannot do without anything," Johnson said. "Sir, it is very bad manners to carry provisions to any man's house, as if he could not entertain you. To an inferior it is oppressive; to a superior it is insolent."

Most surprising, I think, is Johnson's equanimity at this scene. As Boswell sees him, we have one of the most famous men in all of England, a man renowned for his sharp wit and temper, recognized wherever he goes and fawned over by many, sitting quietly in a dirty, dingy tavern where no one knows his name, And rather than behaving with outrage, umbrage, and anger as well he might in the face of blatant rudeness, shabby food, and downright unsanitary antics, Johnson merely utters "rascal" and behaves with a quietly gracious manner and surpassing calmness. There is no bellowing of temper. This is a very different side of Johnson, and it adds to the complexity of his character as it shows us again why Boswell is unrivaled as a keen observer of men. This, to me, is one of the most telling of passages on the entire journey. And finally, to no one's loss, I suppose, the inn where the two men stayed and were so insulted has long since disappeared. No one seems to know exactly where it stood—or care, for that matter.

This incident led to one of the more curious engagements of the trip. Boswell wrote a short note to Lord Monboddo who lived nearby, suggesting a visit and adding that Johnson "says he would go two miles out of his way" to see Monboddo. That is an odd phrase any way you look at it. Does it mean Johnson is so eager that he is willing to go two miles out of his way? Or is he saying that he cares so little that he would go no more than two miles? It could have been either given the fractious relationship that existed between Johnson and Monboddo. While Johnson wrote in his

Journey that "the magnetism of his [Monboddo's] conversation drew us out of our way," Boswell reminds us that he was well aware the two men "did not love each other, yet I was unwilling not to visit his lordship, and was also curious to see them together." Boswell was usually eager to push the envelope a bit.

Lord Monboddo (James Burnett) was a judge, a landowner, and an early anthropologist who would seem to have been one of Scotland's premier eccentrics. He was a man of learning, and possessed an "eminent legal mind," according to the *Oxford Companion to Scottish History*. His neighbors thought him "peculiar." His neighbors were right, too. He held some ideas about the evolution of human beings, preceding the more thoughtful Darwin by a century. One of the nuttier ideas, author Frank Delaney neatly summarized, held that "monkeys became men when the practice of sitting down eroded their tails." There were some other equally bizarre concepts that other scholars and Johnson, too, thought to be . . . well, without thought. One of them concerned the notion that orangutans could be taught to speak. In Edinburgh a week before this Johnson had disposed of that idea quite cleverly: "It is as possible that the orang-outang does not speak as that he speaks. However, I shall not contest the point. I should have thought it not possible to find a Monboddo, yet *he* exists." Monboddo would produce a series of volumes in which he dismissed Johnson's grand accomplishment with his *Dictionary,* describing it as a compilation of "barbarous language." That was yet to come, however, and Johnson did not know of his lordship's disparaging thoughts when they met at Monboddo's residence.

Johnson had little to say of this meeting, only that "the entertainment which we received would have been a sufficient recompense for a much greater deviation." Apparently he might have been willing to go more than two miles. It is Boswell once again who gives us the details. The visit started off badly when Monboddo greeted them and observed that "in such houses . . . our ancestors lived, who were better than we." Not so, Johnson said, adding with a mild slap at Monboddo's evolutionary theories, "We are as strong as they, and a great deal wiser." Boswell feared an altercation, but Monboddo took no offense. Inside the conversation flowed with Boswell fueling the topics, from emigration to farming, from manners to learning. Monboddo was most hospitable, and Johnson proved agreeable. At one point Boswell found the two "agreeing like brothers," which satisfied him; he devoted several pages in his *Journal* to this encounter. After a few hours Johnson and Boswell left in good spirits to continue their journey toward Aberdeen.

I mentioned that Monboddo was regarded as "peculiar" by many who knew him. Lest anyone think that I made that up, consider the evidence provided by Elizabeth Stucley in *A Hebridean Journey,* where she wrote that his lordship was a believer in the good health produced from cold baths and fresh air "and his neighbors said that his hardy treatment had killed two of his children." As for his belief in evolution she said he was certain that "every baby was born with a vestigial tail that was privily snipped off by the midwife" and that Monboddo tried to get into the cottages of his tenants whenever a baby was expected in order to confirm his theories. If so, it's a wonder someone didn't whack off his prying lordship's privates.

Having surveyed Arbroath and Montrose, polished off more Arbroath smokies than anyone should, and found an fee-agreeable bank (not the one-whose-name-shall-not-be-mentioned) to get much-needed cash, it was time for me to get out of town and head to some of the castles in the vicinity. One of them, regrettably, is associated with the most awful and embarrassing of my memories of Scotland, so I'll delay my account of that part of the trip as long as possible.

On a positive note I drove east into the charming twin villages of Dunkeld and Birnam, linked by a two-hundred-year-old arched bridge at the southern end of the Grampian Mountains. Dunkeld, on the east side of the River Tay, featured an array of whitewashed houses and pleasant tourist shops, though graying skies and a chilly wind had sprung up and kept me from lingering outside very long. Instead I stepped into a hotel for a bite and a cup of hot tea. The bar was empty and the windows were open, and the temperature was as chilling inside as out. I asked if the windows could be shut, and the young woman behind the bar couldn't have looked at me with more surprise had I turned into a grasshopper before her eyes.

"Yew want the winder shut?" she said in a strange accent I hadn't heard before.

"Yes, please," I said, and she moved gracelessly to comply.

"Where are you from?" I asked.

"Carlyyyyle," I think she replied.

"Where is that?" I asked.

"Do yew know where England is?"

I asked for a pot of tea and went to the loo. Incredibly the window was open there, too, so I shut it and did my business with much haste. The place never warmed up. But to my amazement the tea was delicious and my sandwich the same. I left a bigger tip than I ever would have thought possible a half hour before.

Birnam, the sister village, is home to Dunsinane Hill, just a wee bit to the southeast, about where Macbeth confidently declared, "I will not be afraid of death and bane. / Till Birnam Forest come to Dunsinane." Not too many lines later in Shakespeare's play Macbeth learns that the woods can and did move. Things go downhill quickly for the king, you may recall. I hate to ruin anyone's lingering hope to tear a souvenir from one of those movable trees, but the famous forest doesn't exist any more.

Birnam was hosting an exhibition of drawings by another well-known author when I happened by. The focus of this show was Beatrix Potter, the creator of the much-loved Peter Rabbit series. The exhibit showcased her watercolors—most enchanting—and a small outdoor garden populated by charming miniature figures of her memorable characters. Potter vacationed in this area as a young woman, and it provided the inspiration for her first stories.

19

Pitlochry

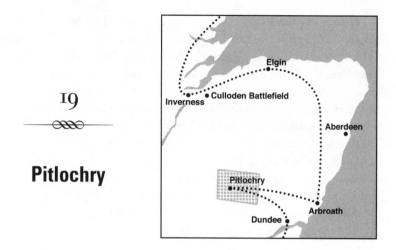

My base for the next few days before rejoining Boswell and Johnson was the tourist town of Pitlochry with the attractive River Tummel winding through it. The town, however, isn't especially attractive. It is filled with stores catering to visitors, and unless you drive well off the main road into the residential area, you would have no idea that Pitlochry has any permanent population.

The town advertises itself as the "Gateway to the Highlands" and even if it isn't quite that it was good enough for my needs. I stayed just off the very busy main road in a large, rambling guest house built in 1881 and hosted by an easy-going, quick-to-laugh Irishman named Jim. Jim's breakfasts were delightful: fresh juice (I kept looking for the orange trees in the backyard), tasty sausage, well-cooked eggs, and opera. The last was a pleasant surprise: a background of Mozart, Bellini, Rossini, and Verdi, most of which I could identify, to Jim's surprise. "You Yanks think you know a bit of opera, eh?" he said with a challenge one morning. Moments later Jim walked out of his kitchen, chef's hat in place, singing at full voice an unfamiliar Irish song. I conceded.

Before succumbing to yet another castle, I drove three miles into the Grampian Mountains to the Pass of Killiecrankie, another memorable battle site. It is spectacularly situated in a steep, heavily wooded gorge through which runs the fast-moving River Garry. The explorer Thomas Pennant described it as "a scene of horrible grandeur." It's part of a natural corridor linking the Scottish Highlands and the Lowlands, therefore a likely place for a battle. The one here took place on July 27, 1689, and if you guessed that it somehow involved the Jacobites you would be correct.

In fact the first of the Jacobite rebellions occurred at this time, shortly after the Stuart King James VI (of Scotland) and II (of England) was chased off the throne and fled to France. The rebellious clans were led by John Graham of Claverhouse, viscount Dundee, while the government opposition—mostly Lowland Scots—was led by another Scot, the Highlander General Hugh Mackay. His army was making its way through the narrow pass headed to Jacobite-held Blair Castle when Dundee's soldiers attacked; they charged forward into Mackay's line. Swords swung, heads rolled, and the blood flowed. Within a matter of minutes the outcome was decided: Mackay's men could not advance and were pinned down, and they fled in a rout. Mackay joined them, leaving behind nearly two thousand men dead, wounded, or captured—nearly half of his army. Dundee was mortally wounded, however, and the attempts by others to follow up the victory failed, as, ultimately, did the Jacobite cause.

There is an amazing story about one moment in the battle that has become a part of the lore of Killiecrankie. It has to do with one of the government's soldiers, one Donald MacBean. During his retreat MacBean found himself on a rocky ledge with his enemy in hot pursuit and seemingly only one avenue of escape: jumping hundreds of feet below into the River Garry. Instead MacBean made a prodigious and still-hard-to-believe eighteen-foot leap across the gorge to the rocks on the other side. MacBean left a colorful memoir in 1728 that detailed his narrow escape. Visitors to Killiecrankie can see the site of this dramatic incident as they walk over the area.

So much for battles, though; it was time for more castles. First up: Glamis, a castle associated with royalty since 1034 when King Malcolm II was wounded and brought here to die. Not a good omen, perhaps, but things worked out fine for the king. Work on the castle as it survives today—and it is quite handsome inside—was begun in 1400; it has prospered over the years because of its royal associations. Queen Elizabeth's mother, the Queen Mum, was born here, and so was Princess Margaret.

Not too far away is Menzies Castle, built in the sixteenth century and occupied until 1918. Its condition had declined precipitously until Clan Menzies acquired the dilapidated structure in 1972 and began a restoration, which is still under way. The restorers have done a splendid job, leaving the interior mostly empty and using occasional pieces of period furniture to suggest how the rooms might have looked. One of them is known as "Prince Charlie's Room" because the Young Pretender slept there in February 1746 when he was retreating with his army toward Inverness. There is also a death mask of Charlie on the wall, not at all grisly. The castle seemed truly medieval, and the tour was very instructive and appealing.

Finally, because I was so close to the town of Kirriemuir I couldn't resist seeing the home of another well-known Scottish writer: J. M. Barrie, the creator of *Peter Pan*. It took a bit of wandering around the small town before I located the unpretentious two-story cottage where he was born in 1860. Barrie recounted in a memoir written in 1896 that "On the day I was born we bought six hair-bottomed chairs, and in our little house it was an event." Presumably so was his birth, although Barrie was one of ten children, so perhaps it really wasn't as big a deal as getting the chairs after all. Two of those chairs survive and are still in the house. Outside was a small wash house with a communal pump where the young Barrie and his friends acted out his first play, written when he was seven. There was also an exhibit showcasing costumes and the program from the first production of *Peter Pan* in London in 1904. Barrie left Kirriemuir at the age of eight to attend Glasgow Academy; he died in 1937 at the age of seventy-seven.

I knew I had put things off long enough. Leaving Kirriemuir and the celebration of Barrie's achievements, I headed to Blair Castle in spite of the "horrible grandeur" that I knew awaited me there. Blair Castle at Blair Atholl, some five miles from Pitlochry, was the scene, I hated to recall, of my great embarrassment years ago during my first visit to Scotland. It was there that I met the gracious Iain, tenth duke of Atholl, and greeted him with—my teeth are starting to itch as I write this—"Good morning, Duke." I've already described the scene, but arriving on the spot I could not delete the memories. I wondered as I approached Blair if the duke would still be there, a much older man to be sure, but still able to recognize the bald American who offered such a laughable insult many years before. I hoped to see him again and apologize.

Blair is a fascinating, eye-catching castle. It has the requisite turrets and high walls, but it also has lovely landscaped grounds with herds of cattle grazing peacefully and strutting peacocks picking their way through the car park. Bagpipers usually play at the front of the castle as visitors arrive; they are members of the Atholl Highlanders, a select group of men retained by the duke as his private army. It's the only private army in Scotland, and the privilege was granted to the Atholls by Queen Victoria in 1844.

The castle goes back to 1269 and has seen its share of winners and losers, Jacobites and royalists, adventurers and politicians. The family was badly split during the Jacobite Rising when the duke and his second son supported the government and the eldest and youngest sons were Jacobite enthusiasts. And yes, Bonnie Prince Charlie stayed here for a while on his march southward to capture Edinburgh. The effects of war and the economic depression forced the family to open the castle to the public for the first time in 1936; it has since become one of Scotland's most visited castles, thanks in large part to the efforts of the tenth duke, my friend Iain.

I took the tour of some thirty rooms, and they were as magnificent as I remembered from years before. But I saw no sign of the duke's presence. Back outside later I stood listening to the bagpiper, and when he took a break, I invited myself into conversation. I first told him an abbreviated version of my embarrassing story on meeting the duke, and he smiled. "He was indeed a very fine man, the duke was," he said, "but he died in 1996, I'm afraid." I knew the duke would have had to have been old, but I was surprised and deeply saddened when I heard that. "He passed away quietly. I miss him. I think we all do. A lot has changed here since his passing, and not for the better. The castle is now in the hands of a family charitable trust. It's not the same, my friend. I'm glad you met him when you did. You met a great man."

I discovered later that the tenth duke, who was childless, had placed the castle, its contents, and the surrounding estate into a trust in 1995, the year before his death. His action ensured that Blair would remain open to the public and be cared for by a private corporation. That was good. But I couldn't get over my regret that I never had the opportunity to apologize to the duke for my faux pas. I was sure he had forgotten it; he had far more important matters to deal with. But I really would have given a lot for the opportunity to thank him for his kindness. I drove back to my lodging in Pitlochry and drank a toast in his honor. I told Jim my little story the next morning. He was sympathetic: "If you'd called me, I'd have shared that drink with you," he said. I wish I had.

20

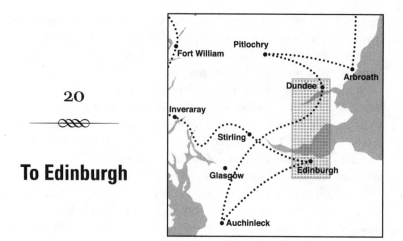

To Edinburgh

Now that my anticipated worst moments were over, I was eager to meet up again with Boswell and Johnson at the place where all this started: Edinburgh. I picked up their trail again along the east coast at St. Andrews and Dundee before driving into the Scottish capital. Actually Dundee got pretty short shrift from both men. Johnson wrote tersely, "We stopped at Dundee, where I remember nothing remarkable." He was being kind. To Mrs. Thrale he was blunter: "We came to Dundee, a dirty despicable town." Boswell was, by comparison, verbose and almost full of civic boosterism: "Came to Dundee about three. Good busy town, P. Murray the landlord. Fresh chaise there."

I fared better, though I was disappointed if hardly surprised to read that the building that housed Peter Murray's inn where the travelers stopped no longer exists. I got lost and wound up making several loops of the city including a crossing of the Tay River Bridge, which at two miles in length was the world's longest when it opened in 1878. The year after that, the wooden structure collapsed, killing seventy-five poor souls.

The scale of the disaster shocked all of Scotland, indeed all who heard of it. There were civic endeavors all over the country to honor the victims, none more wretchedly carried out than the commemorative poem written for the occasion by the Scottish poet William McGonagall called "The Tay Bridge Disaster." It has become famous among bad poems as arguably the worst because it was so seriously intended.

McGonagall was a curious fellow who has become more famous for being a bad poet than most writers are for being good. Born in Edinburgh in 1830 to an Irish immigrant family, he worked in Dundee's mills until he had an epiphany in 1877 and "discovered myself to be a poet." There was no stopping him; ignorance of technique and style were no bar to his ever-growing desire to compose verse for special occasions. Tragedies proved wonderfully fertile for his muse, and the collapse of the Tay Bridge just two years after his discovery of his poetic gifts gave him the opportunity to compose his masterpiece of pedestrian ineptitude. The poem is too long and too witless to quote in its entirety, but three stanzas should give you the idea, and if anyone wishes, it's easy to read the entire thing—and everything else he wrote—because it's all still in print and online. With apologies, here's the poem:

> Beautiful Railway Bridge of the Silv'ry Tay!
> Alas! I am very sorry to say
> That ninety lives have been taken away
> On the Sabbath day of 1879,
> Which would be remember'd for a very long time.
>
> The train sped on with all its might,
> And Bonnie Dundee soon hove into sight,
> And the passengers' hearts felt light,
> Thinking they would enjoy themselves on the New Year,
> With their friends at home they lov'd most dear,
> And wish them all a happy New Year.
>
> So the train mov'd slowly along the Bridge of Tay,
> Until it was about midway,
> Then the central girders with a crash gave way,
> And down went the train and passengers into the Tay!

McGonagall concluded his poem with a nice touch of advice for anyone concerned that this sort of thing might happen in the future: "For the stronger we our houses do build / the less chance we have of being killed." McGonagall died in 1902, and like a bad piece of pizza he just doesn't seem to go away.

I remembered seeing Dundee some thirty years earlier and finding it a rather dirty and dull city. Nothing remarkable, to echo Johnson. My guide at the time thought little better of it, and he was a native. In fact he had advised me not to stop there: "Nothing worth seeing for anyone who's got an education." But when I finally located a parking spot downtown in the City Center I saw a city that seemed to have changed, and for the better. It had a sense of dynamism about it. The streets were clean, the sidewalks were filled with professional-looking men, women, and lots of students, and the stores were busy. There was a good bookstore—always an indicator of quality in a city—and a sense of pride about the place. I asked directions from one neatly dressed middle-age man, and when I spoke to him of the city's attractiveness, he was obviously pleased. "It's a fine good place to live. And a very different place from what you saw before," he said when we conversed a bit.

I walked a few blocks over to Verdant Works, a series of impressive interactive exhibits housed in a converted jute mill that chronicle Dundee's grim, dingy history. In the nineteenth century Dundee was the busy, dirty processing heart of Great Britain's jute industry, jute being the world's most important vegetable fiber after cotton. Dundee was "Juteopolis," and for some fifty thousand people who labored there it meant long hours, poor health, and the lowest pay in Scotland (and that's really saying something in a nation that ranked among the poorest in the nineteenth century). The jute barons who ran the industry like fiefdoms wouldn't hire men to work because they could get women for half the wages, and there was never a lack of workers trying to find employment. It made for a system of terrible abuse, and the men of Dundee stayed home and drank, often to death. When World War I came along there was no need for conscription into the army: Dundee's male population volunteered in staggering numbers, no doubt partly for the pay, partly to escape. For many it was the first paycheck they had ever drawn. Such was Dundee's low reputation well into the first half of the twentieth century. Verdant Works offered a compelling educational look at this disturbing social history. Now there are few evidences of this history remaining outside the museum, and even fewer who would mourn for that past.

I returned to my car, or what I assumed was my car. It was parked in the same place, but it was buried beneath an avalanche of gull poop. My once-red automobile was now a more patriotic if messy red and white. And that wasn't all. Around back was a meter maid—an Amazonlike woman whose glowering face would unquestionably have scared the kilts off William Wallace. She was writing me a ticket for letting my meter expire. I considered several possibilities: telling her I was a writer and I could put her in my book or asking if she thought she could really track me down in the States. I settled on telling her I was really sorry, that I was an American, and could she please tell me how I would have to pay the fine? To my surprise the Amazon suddenly changed into Flora Macdonald and said she'd be happy to tear up the ticket. She wished me a good time in Scotland and walked across the street to nail the driver of some other gull-pooped car. Johnson was wrong; Dundee is a great city.

Before arriving in Dundee the two men had set out from Edinburgh and stopped in St. Andrews. On the way Johnson—who would soon find the Highland roads, or lack of roads, to be rough and challenging—was pleased with their passage. "The roads are neither rough nor dirty; and it affords a southern stranger a new kind of pleasure to travel so commodiously without the interruption of toll-gates. Where the bottom is rocky, as it seems commonly to be in Scotland, a smooth way is made indeed with great labour, but it never wants repairs." He also took note of something that would continue to appear in his notes: the absence of trees. "A tree might be a show in Scotland as a horse in Venice," he wrote. Boswell spotted one and pointed it out to Johnson; a nearby gentleman told the men that it was one of just two trees in the entire county. Boswell was chagrined by the falsehood, although amused by it; Johnson enjoyed it, but his entries about the subject of trees drew criticism from Scots when his book was published.

They arrived weary at St. Andrews, in the ancient kingdom of Fife, renowned then more for its fine university than for its very special golf course. Boswell was understandably upset by a daydream he had had on the trip in which he saw his child dead, her face eaten by worms, and then the image of a child's skull. He had been distracted by the images and failed to hear and join in Johnson's conversation. They both revived over a dinner of mutton and haddock and spent their first night out of Edinburgh at the home of a university professor, Robert Watson. The next morning they visited the ruins of St. Andrews Cathedral and its castle, had lunch with some academics (lunch included salmon, herrings, ham, chicken, mackerel, roast beef, and apple pie), did a little more sight-seeing and returned to their host for dinner.

Johnson was overwhelmingly negative about what he found in St. Andrews. He thought it "a city which only history shows to have once flourished, and surveyed the ruins of ancient magnificence, of which even the ruins cannot long be visible, unless some care be taken to preserve them." Johnson had little use for the ideals and practices of post-Reformation Scotland and John Knox. Johnson was a devout member of the Church of England, who composed hundreds of solemn prayers for himself and others. He seldom passed up an opportunity to offer his opinion about religion in Scotland.

Inspecting the castle—"built with more attention to security than pleasure"—he wrote that "Cardinal Beatoun is said to have had workmen employed in improving its fortifications at the time when he was murdered by the ruffians of reformation, in the manner of which Knox has given what he himself calls a merry narrative," which had nasty details about hanging the dead cardinal's body out the second floor window. Knox's actions followed in the wake of the death of Knox's close Protestant mentor, George Wishart, who was burned at the stake in 1546 outside the castle while the cardinal looked on approvingly. The cathedral at St. Andrews, Johnson wrote, "was demolished, as is well known, in the tumult and violence of Knox's reformation." If a cathedral wall required demolishing for safety's sake, Johnson would argue that it be left standing in the hope that "it may fall on some posterity of John Knox," When Boswell asked him where Knox was buried, Johnson replied, "I hope in the highway." You get the idea.

Johnson believed that after the Reformation the town had gradually decayed. In its streets he observed "the silence and solitude of inactive intelligence and gloomy depopulation." He thought St. Andrews to be a natural center for education, however, because it was removed "from the levity and dissoluteness of a capital city" (the kind of thinking that would have twenty-first-century educators get busy transplanting places like the University of Texas, the University of Wisconsin, and Georgia Tech from their respective capital cities). And then he added, "Seeing it [the university] pining in decay and struggling for life, fills the mind with mournful images and ineffectual wishes." It was a difficult period for the university, with only one hundred students enrolled, and some latter-day commentators have questioned Johnson's judgments. Johnson departed with yet another gloomy shot: "The kindness of professors did not contribute to abate the uneasy remembrance of a university declining, a college alienated, and a church profaned and hastening to the ground."

Boswell recorded snippets of Johnson's conversation on many topics, all a great deal more upbeat than Johnson's entries in his *Journey* (although Boswell himself was unhappy to see an overweight priest who was "strutting about . . . like a well-fed monk"). The doctor railed against writers accepting patronage, which then required them to honor their patrons at the expense of truth (never mind that Johnson got a small pension from King George), and explained that a national shift from ale to wine was causing a decline in drinking: "I remember when all the *decent* people in Litchfield got drunk every night, and were not the worse thought of. Ale was cheap, so you pressed strongly. When a man must bring a bottle of wine, he is not in such haste." Johnson added some more interesting observations about social habits in England at the time:

Smoking has gone out. To be sure, it is a shocking thing—blowing smoke out of our mouths into other people's mouths, eyes and noses, and having the same thing done to us. Yet I cannot account why a thing which requires so little exertion and yet preserves the mind from total vacuity, should have gone out [was Johnson punning?]. Every man has something by which he calms himself; beating with his feet or so. [Boswell's note: "Dr. Johnson used to practice this himself very much."] I remember when people in England changed a short only once a week; a pandour, when he gets a shirt, greases it to make it last. Formerly a good tradesman had no fire but in the kitchen; never in the parlour except on Sunday. My father, who was a magistrate of Litchfield, lived thus. They never began to have a fire in the parlour but on leaving off business or some great revolution of their life.

Boswell also recorded Johnson's words on the subject of writing, one of his favorite topics and one on which Johnson could get rather dull. "I would advise every young man beginning to compose, to do it as fast as he can, to get a habit of having his mind to start promptly. It is so much more difficult to improve in speed than accuracy." His host disagreed, saying one could get into "bad habits of doing it slovenly," which provoked Johnson further: "Why, sir, you are confounding *doing* inaccurately with the *necessity* of doing inaccurately." On the matter of producing sermons, which Johnson said he could do with much haste, the doctor added, "I would say to a young divine, 'Here is your text; let me see how soon you can make it a sermon.' Then I'd say, 'Let me see how much better you can make it.' Thus I should see both his powers and his judgment."

The ruins of the great cathedral and the castle fragments are still worthwhile stops for visitors to St. Andrews, and the university has become one of the great educational institutions in Great Britain, ranking with Oxford and Cambridge. England's Prince William, heir to the throne, attended college there. But what lures many visitors to St. Andrews is, of course, the famous Royal and Ancient Golf Club, which was founded in 1754, though the game was not new at that time. There is evidence that it was played as early as the fifteenth century; I was only slightly astonished to learn that no one has yet traced it back to William Wallace or Robert the Bruce. It is, at least officially, the home of golf and the international golfing authority, and the mecca for everyone who takes the game seriously. I am not a golfer, at least not that I'd admit, so I didn't play the course (and I belatedly discovered that you don't have to play it to enjoy it; you are allowed to take guided walks over the famous "Old Course"). But if you are so inclined and have a reservation and the money—the green fees are around two hundred dollars these days—you can play in the wake of golf's legends, from Bobby Jones to Jack Nicklaus and Tiger Woods.

I had one more detour to make before arriving in Edinburgh. And while Falkirk was the scene of yet another important Scottish battle—for American Civil War buffs, Scotland is sort of like driving through Virginia—it was the techno-marvel of the Falkirk Wheel I wanted to check out. Falkirk is about halfway between Edinburgh and Stirling and hosted not just one but two notable clashes between warring sides. And if you guessed that William Wallace and Bonnie Prince Charlie would be involved—at separate times, of course—then you win a free haggis dinner, my treat. The first conflict occurred in 1298 when Wallace, having previously defeated the army of King Edward at nearby Stirling Bridge, lost the rematch. The second took place in 1746 when the Young Pretender's army, in retreat from its failed incursion into England, scored an upset victory over the pursuing English. It would be almost their last victory. The finally tally for Falkirk, then: English 1, Scots 1. Not much to celebrate, really.

The more recent history at Falkirk is much more cheerful. The focal point is the Falkirk Wheel, an absolutely amazing, chin-dropping rotating boat lift that links the uneven waters of the Forth and Clyde canals, thereby opening shipping between the east and west coasts of Scotland. For years before boats had to negotiate their way through a very slow series of eleven locks, a process which could take an entire day to complete. Now the Falkirk Wheel, the key to the multimillion dollar Millennium Link project, scoops boats in two giant buckets the 115 feet between the two canals. I can't explain how this thing works, but I read that the concrete and steel lift is so incredibly efficient that the energy it consumes raising six hundred tons of water in one lift is equal to that used in eight toasters. It was very, very cool to climb into one of the passenger boats and be raised to the top canal, float around a bit, and then be lowered 115 feet back down to where I started from.

I had no idea what Bozzy and Johnson or Wallace or Prince Charlie would have thought, or indeed how they might possibly have conceived of such a thing. If it might have been imagined as something from another world to them, it seemed scarcely less to me.

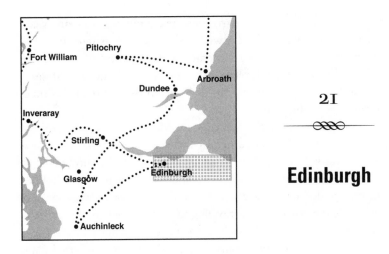

21

Edinburgh

On August 18, 1773, Samuel Johnson wrote in his *Journey*, "we left Edinburgh, a city too well known to admit description." Without Boswell—who thankfully wrote thousands of words on their time in Edinburgh—that is almost all we would know of the three days and four nights the two men spent in that ancient capital. And what a pity that would have been, for their time in Edinburgh—at what one writer called "the peak of its celebrated period of high thinking and high stinking"—produced a wealth of entertainment and enlightenment about both men as well as about the city and its inhabitants and their customs.

Edinburgh marked the site of their departure for the journey into the Highlands and Islands, and it would be the city that they returned to at journey's end. It was where Boswell was living with his family, and so we are given a wonderful glimpse into his home life as well as into his circle of acquaintants. In spite of his declaration that Edinburgh was too well known to be described, Johnson had never been there before—had never been out of England, in fact—and had never spoken with many of the people he would meet.

Boswell had carefully and thoughtfully orchestrated a series of engagements for Johnson, hoping that the great man would not find the company beneath him in any way. Boswell's plan was to introduce him and showcase him to a curious and mostly respectful Edinburgh society and to ensure that on their trip he would be greeted by as many notable figures as possible. To achieve those ends Boswell wheedled and begged favors from a number of dignitaries, asking them to ensure that Johnson enjoyed intellectual companionship and attention. The trip was the culmination of many years of planning and anticipation for Boswell, and, to a lesser extent, Johnson. It would thrust the two together intimately over a period of some three months and help to define the relationship so brilliantly delineated years later in Boswell's *Life of Johnson*. But that was in the future at this time. How did they get to this point?

Boswell met Johnson for the first time on May 16, 1763, in a London bookshop. Things didn't go smoothly for Boswell initially, but he pursued Johnson's interest vigorously, and the older man eventually succumbed to Boswell's undeniable charm, his close attention, and his incessant flow of ideas. During the decade of the 1760s Boswell and Johnson spoke on several occasions of the possibility of traveling to Scotland, where Boswell was born and was living. In 1771 Boswell wrote a specific proposal from Edinburgh: "I gave him an account of my comfortable life as a married man, and a lawyer in practice at the Scotch bar; invited him to Scotland, and promised to attend him to the Highlands, and Hebrides." Johnson, whose formidable intellectual curiosity could never permit him to abandon such ideas, wrote back optimistically: "Whether we climb the Highlands or are tost among the Hebrides . . . I hope the time will come when we may try our powers both with cliffs and waters."

The time did come, of course, and Johnson—then about to turn sixty-four—departed London on August 6 for the journey through northern England to Edinburgh to meet Boswell. His trip has been closely charted, almost by the mile. He rode in a post chaise and had company all the way. He was of mostly good humor on the trip through Lincolnshire, Stilton, Doncaster, York, Newcastle, Belford, and into the Scottish Lowlands. Johnson didn't complain much, though physically he would seem no comfortable match for such a journey, much less the one awaiting him. He was fat and slovenly and had breathing problems. His overall health was poor, and the physical impression he left—tall, stooped, a way-too-large nose, an ill-fitting wig, the markings of smallpox and scrofula on his face—could and did frighten small children. He seldom changed shirts, and on matters of hygiene, well, let's just say his hygiene left much to be desired (which would make him a perfect fit for the "stinking" part of Edinburgh). His temperament could be irritable, and he was often self-absorbed when he wasn't outright suffering depression. His movements were hardly graceful. Still, his eloquent expression and strong, searching mind harnessed to a sincere faith and belief in good manners endowed him with a tolerance beyond what could be expected. He arrived in Edinburgh after a nine-day journey in better spirits than most of us under similar circumstances.

In his *Journal* a profoundly excited Boswell—after a brilliant description of Johnson's person and personality, which everyone should read—chronicled the launch of their remarkable journey together: "On Saturday the fourteenth of August, 1773, late in the evening, I received a note from him that he was arrived at Boyd's Inn, at the head of the Canongate. I went to him directly. He embraced me cordially, and I exulted in the thought that I now had him actually in Caledonia."

It must have been a memorable moment for Bozzy. For more than a decade he had awaited this scene, scarcely daring to imagine it. And suddenly there was Johnson before him. It took only a moment for the greeting and to hear of Johnson's first experience with the sanitary problems besetting Edinburgh at this period. William Scott, who had ridden part of the way with Johnson, told Boswell in an aside that when the pair arrived in the city a little earlier they ordered lemonade at the inn. Johnson wanted his drink sweeter and then watched, appalled, as the waiter used his greasy fingers to lift a lump of sugar and drop it into his glass. Johnson was furious; he threw the lemonade out the window and almost struck the waiter. We already know, of course, that he reacted with considerable more calmness when the same thing happened to him a week later in Montrose. You may be cheered to know that the inn in Edinburgh where this nastiness occurred was demolished in 1868; a plaque now exists commemorating the spot where Boswell and Johnson had their encounter. Edinburgh today, of course, is much cleaner and considerably more expensive, at least for Americans, thanks to the decline of the dollar. A glass of lemonade in 2007 cost the equivalent of nearly six dollars, though I could add additional sugar with my own fingers.

Johnson's unforgettable first words to Boswell were, "I smell you in the dark." No kidding. Now Edinburgh wasn't all that different from other cities in the seventeenth century, and things had gotten better, but the testimony from everyone about that time is that it stank. And as the two men walked most agreeably arm in arm up the narrow Royal Mile to James's Court, where Boswell lived, they encountered the capital's "evening effluvia," as Boswell put it. Johnson may have been appalled, although he knew well the smells of London. And remember, this was a man who slopped food over himself while dining and was hardly a model of personal hygiene. No one, not even Boswell, ever recorded Johnson taking a bath. The good doctor did not have an orange with him, like the one he carried in London's streets to press against his nose to minimize the smells in that city. "A zealous Scotsman would have wished Mr. Johnson to be without one of his senses upon this occasion," Bozzy noted.

Fifty years before Johnson arrived Daniel Defoe visited Edinburgh and wondered if its citizens "delighted in Stench and Nastiness." He concluded that the city "stinks intolerably" and mentioned specifically the habit of residents tossing out their kitchen and toilet wastes onto the streets, no matter who might be walking by. Moray McLaren summarized the disgusting practice most vividly: "The 'slops' of each of the many-storied households were hurled out into the street at night time to dribble away down the hill if they were liquid, to await the later arrival of the scavengers if they were solid. And by 'slops,' it should be remembered, were not only the dregs of the kitchen but all the contents of the chamber-pot. When the warning bell for the nightly deluge and cascade sounded over the city, men in even the deepest taverns in the most secluded clubs would light brown-paper spills to fumigate the atmosphere against the all-pervading, the penetrating fetor." In Johnson's words, "Many a full-flowing perriwig moistened into flaccidity." The streets were so smelly and filthy that women in long dresses would seek a ride over the shortest of distances to avoid ruining their clothing. Public facilities were never cleaned. A fetid air hung over the overcrowded city day and night.

Boswell said the worst excesses of the practice had been curbed by the time Johnson arrived (which leaves a scary impression, doesn't it?). But in 1774, one year after Johnson's visit, another correspondent observed that little had changed, and that "many an elegant suit of clothes has been spoiled." As I walked up the Royal Mile in the wake of Boswell and Johnson, and particularly as I neared James's Court, the street narrowed to just about the width of a footpath, and multistory buildings—more than a few of eighteenth-century origin or even earlier—reached high on both sides. It would have been difficult for anyone to dump waste out the window and *not* hit me or anyone else strolling by. I mention this not as a warning to future visitors to Edinburgh, but only as an observation that while our sanitary practices have changed—mercifully—the physical circumstances that contributed to the "Stench and Nastiness" are still pretty evident. Curiously I saw a fruit stand nearby selling oranges; I wondered if anyone remembered how they were used a couple of centuries ago.

Perhaps the reason why Edinburgh was such a fascinating and contradictory city at the time of Boswell and Johnson has to do with the breathtaking (literally and figuratively) combination of stinking and thinking. This was the Enlightenment, the Golden Age for Edinburgh's intellectual life. David Hume, Adam Smith, Sir George Mackenzie, the poet Robert Fergusson, Lord Monboddo (wackiness and all), Sir Robert Forbes, and others were known throughout the western world and admired for their learning and scholarship in the fields of science, education, economics, religion, and literature. Matthew Bramble, the outwardly misanthropic central character of Tobias Smollett's *Humphry Clinker,* declared with awe in one of his letters home that "Edinburgh is a hot-bed of genius!" Walter Scott had been born in Edinburgh two years before Boswell and Johnson's trip; Robert Burns would find his fame there in a few years. The city's schools were acclaimed; students came from around the world for their education. Edinburgh was the commercial, educational, political, and cultural hub for Scotland.

Further, it boasted a dramatic setting, one of the most spectacular of any city, and a compelling history. Perched high atop a series of extinct volcanoes and rocky crags, seemingly higher than it is because the surrounding land is flat, Edinburgh is memorably striking to the eye. The writer Robert Louis Stevenson, who was born in the city in 1850, wrote a sterling appraisal of Edinburgh: "No situation could be more commanding for the head of a kingdom; none better chosen for noble prospects." Its past dates from the eleventh century and it was designated soon after as a "royal burgh," confirming its permanent association with the Scottish crown and government. The city played important roles in the wars between the Scots and the English, beginning with defeat of the Scots at the Battle of Flodden in the Lowlands in 1513, a calamity that led to the sacking of the city. The Treaty of 1707 changed Edinburgh's perception of itself; henceforth it would be seeking to define its role in a Great Britain whose capital would be London. In 1997 the Scottish people voted overwhelmingly to reestablish their own parliament in Edinburgh to deal with a domestic agenda, and there have been growing calls since for a vote on Scottish independence from England.

But I have gotten ahead of myself, and far ahead of Boswell and Johnson, holding their noses and walking up the Royal Mile to Boswell's home for the night. When told he would meet Boswell's wife, Johnson said he would change into a clean shirt, an admission of great meaning given the general state of cleanliness. "Tis needless," Boswell said. "Either don't see her tonight, or don't put on a clean shirt." Johnson replied, "I'll do both."

When they arrived at Boswell's apartments, his wife Margaret—Boswell's cousin, two years older, whom he had married in 1769—had anticipated Johnson's preferences and had tea ready. Johnson was delighted at the hospitality, "and as no man could be more polite when he chose to be, his address to her was most courteous and engaging, and his conversation soon charmed her into a forgetfulness of his external appearance." The delighted if not ecstatic Boswell said "I'm glad to see you under my roof," and Johnson replied, "And 'tis a very noble roof." To Mrs. Thrale later, he expanded on that, writing, "Boswell has very handsome and spacious rooms; level with the ground on one side of the house, and on the other four stories high."

James's Court—which was not, by the way, named for Boswell—is still there, at least the same high enclave that housed Boswell's accommodations. It fronts a small, modestly attractive square off the street with a tree in the center and a tiny fountain off to one side. The square is reached through a narrow, arched, stone-covered passageway connected to a building above it. Boswell's building was rebuilt after a fire in the mid-nineteenth century that damaged the exterior but left many of the apartments intact. Unfortunately Boswell's was not one of those. The apartments are all occupied now, so there was no admittance for me. Sadly and regrettably there is nothing to mark Boswell's presence so long ago nor the brilliant conversation and entertainment that occurred on one of Edinburgh's most memorable historical occasions.

Curiously there was nothing about him a few steps away at the Writers Museum, created to honor the life and work of three Scottish writers: Scott, Burns, and Stevenson. The museum acknowledged the existence of a dozen or so other Scottish writers, but its small store had no mention of Boswell and no copies of his books. I was stunned. I asked the attendant why the museum ignored Boswell and was told, "I really don't know. I'm sure he'll be added soon." I suggested that his museum was so much claptrap without Boswell and left. He appeared unconcerned, but I again found moral indignation—or high dudgeon, if you prefer—to be extremely satisfying.

Bozzy and Johnson stayed up until 2 A.M. chatting before they grew weary and went to bed. "My wife had insisted that, to show all respect to the sage, she would give up our own bedchamber to him and take a worse. This I cannot but gratefully mention, as one of a thousand obligations which I owe her, since the great obligation of her being pleased to accept me as her husband." He didn't mention, or was not aware, that when Johnson retreated to his room he discovered he could make the candles burn more brightly for reading by turning them upside down. The result was the dropping of fairly copious amounts of grease on Mrs. Boswell's carpet, a matter she did not appreciate. Yet Margaret Boswell could have been no more a gracious host and proud wife for Boswell during this time. She kept her complaints to herself; or, perhaps more realistically, she lacked the opportunity to preserve her thoughts in print as did her husband.

The period of Johnson's visit must have been a difficult time for her, for she was aware of Boswell's escapades with whores and associated most of that activity with his time spent in London, the time he was with Johnson.

She was, however, a practical woman who intended good for Bozzy. When he confessed his first marital infidelity to her, she forgave him and insisted that his surgeon treat him for possible sexual diseases. Johnson later wrote of her that she was "in a proper degree, inferior to her husband; she cannot rival him, nor can he ever be ashamed of her." Her affections for Boswell waxed and waned over the next few years; his behavior severely tested her, and she often became angry, which served only to provoke Boswell all the more. Margaret Boswell and Johnson, however, eventually enjoyed something of a rapprochement, the good doctor having become aware of her connecting him to her husband's dalliances. Margaret Boswell's health began a long decline in the 1780s; as death approached, Boswell sought to be near her, "awed by her courage and fortitude and overwhelmed with remorse and a sense of tragic injustice," wrote his biographer Peter Martin. She died in 1789; Boswell was a widower for the last six years of his life, fearing that his guilt would haunt him to the grave.

When Johnson awoke the next morning, he met Veronica, the Boswell's four-month-old daughter who charmed him completely. "She had the appearance of listening to him. His motions seemed to her to be intended for her amusement, and when he stopped, she fluttered and made a little infantine noise and a kind of signal for him to begin again. She would be held close to him, which was a proof from simple nature that his figure was not horrid." This is indeed a beguiling scene, and one that flatters Johnson, perhaps the greatest man in England, captivated by a baby, the two of them cooing and clucking and moving in response to one another. Though neither Boswell knew it at the time, Margaret—who had already miscarried twice—was or would very soon be pregnant with their second child, a girl named Euphemia.

Johnson met several of Boswell's acquaintances, had conversations about the law and emigration, and went to church services, though his hearing impairment prevented him from listening to what Boswell thought a fine sermon. Boswell dragged a number of important guests to his home to meet Johnson; all found fine hospitality and seemed to come away with the positive impressions of his guest that Boswell sought. And Johnson fulfilled the role Boswell sought for him no less: that of the mentor, sharing his beliefs and his words in increasingly intimate situations. Boswell's adulation, so obvious and so welcomed by Johnson.

Johnson spoke freely, certainly so in a lengthy conversation about Hume, whom Johnson detested for his atheism and his dislike for the English. Hume, for his part, was a likable, placid man until the subject got around to the English. A couple of sample comments: "Nothing but rebellion and bloodshed will open the eyes of that deluded people." And "An Englishman is a man (a bad animal too) corrupted by above a century of licentiousness." Hume made it clear he would have been delighted with the dissolution of England by whatever means and at whatever cost.

Johnson could match his ill humor, however, and the mention of his name provoked one of Johnson's most vitriolic attacks, in which he described Hume as "a man who has so much conceit as to tell all mankind that they have been bubbled for ages and he is the wise man who sees better than they, a man who has so little scrupulosity as to venture or oppose those principles which have been thought necessary to human happiness." Johnson then added something even stronger than anything Boswell wished to include in his published *Journal*. We learned later what that was; the remark was prompted by a comment from Boswell to Johnson, wondering why the doctor would be so serious as to attack Hume's heart. "Why sir, because his head has corrupted it. Or perhaps it has perverted his head. I know not indeed whether he has first been a blockhead and that has made him a rogue, or first been a rogue and that has made him a blockhead." Johnson rarely got blunter than that—unless he was talking about John Knox. Boswell discreetly held off telling Johnson that he was acquainted with Hume and that the philosopher had lived only a short distance away. Obviously it would be impossible for Boswell to bring these two combatants together. Edinburgh has one monument to Hume that I managed to locate; it is a statue of that noble native son in front of the High Court of Judiciary on High Street. He's wearing a toga, which I suspect would have sent Johnson into another rage.

Another well-known figure, Edmund Burke, the English statesman and writer who had strong political differences with Johnson, came up in discussion, and, according to Boswell's account, Johnson was a little easier in response. "Dr. Johnson said he had a variety of knowledge, store of imagery, copiousness of language," but when it was suggested that Burke also possessed wit, Johnson demurred. "No sir, he never succeeds there. 'Tis low; 'tis conceit. I used to say Burke never once made a good joke. What I most envy Burke for is his being constantly the same. He is never what we call humdrum; never unwilling to begin to talk, nor in haste to leave off. . . . So desirous is he to talk that if one is speaking at this end of the table, he'll speak to somebody at the other end."

A little later, Boswell remembered, Johnson offered a story about himself:

I remember I was once on a visit at the house of a lady for whom I had a high respect. There was a good deal of company in the room.

When they were gone, I said to this lady, "What foolish talking have we had!" "Yes," said she, "but while they talked, you said nothing." I was struck with the reproof. How much better is the man who does anything that is innocent than he who does nothing. Besides, I love anecdotes. I fancy mankind may come in time to write all aphoristically, except in narrative; grow weary of preparation and connexion and illustration and all those arts by which a big book is made. If a man is to wait till he weaves anecdotes into a system, we may be long in getting them, and get but few in comparison of what we might get.

In all things Boswell faithfully recorded the words—the anecdotes—and social encounters with a sharp ear and quick pen. He was affectionate and indebted to Johnson, but he was no toady, as some of his detractors have charged. In his voluminous entries for Edinburgh he affirmed the merit of Johnson's words and assured latter-day readers of precious, living insights into his character.

And so the visit continued, Boswell offering us a delicious share of Johnson as they toured some of the city's sights including the Kirk of St. Giles, Parliament, and Holyroodhouse Palace (more on that later). Some of the highlights of Johnson's opinions during these visits:

— On Boswell's plaint that the Treaty of 1707 had forever ruined Scottish independence: "Sir, never talk of your independency, who could let your queen [Mary, queen of Scots] remain twenty years in captivity and then be put to death without even a pretence of justice, without your ever attempting to rescue her; and such a Queen, too! As every man of any gallantry of spirit would have sacrificed his life for."

— At Edinburgh University, Boswell pointing out a wall in perilous condition, reminding Johnson that it was like those at Oxford that might fall upon some learned man: "Dr. Johnson, glad of an opportunity to have a pleasant hit at Scottish learning, said, 'They have been afraid it would never fall.'"

— On Jonathan Swift, of whom Johnson thought little and even suggested that Swift had plagiarized some of his work: "Swift is clear, but he is shallow."

— On witchcraft, which others found blasphemous in supposing evil spirits opposing the Deity: "If moral evil be consistent with the government of the Deity, why may not physical evil be also consistent with it? It is no more strange that there should be evil spirits than evil men; evil unembodied spirits than evil embodied spirits."

And then it was time to begin their journey. On Wednesday, August 18, Boswell and Johnson set off across the Firth of Forth north of Edinburgh and were soon on the road to Dundee, Arbroath, Montrose, and beyond. Johnson was persuaded to relieve himself of the load of weaponry he had brought along with him from London; we don't know whether he anticipated highway bandits along the way or perhaps some crazy bands of unreconstructed Jacobites. Boswell said they were brought "in erroneous apprehension of violence." Johnson left behind a pair of pistols, some gunpowder, and a quantity of bullets, which were stored at Boswell's home along with one of the most important literary treasures ever lost: Johnson's diary, which was later destroyed by some unknown means. Boswell wished his wife had used the three months they were gone to copy that document, and now many of us wish she had done so, too.

The trip that began in Edinburgh would end on November 9 when they returned to Edinburgh; Johnson would remain until November 22 when he began his final journey back home to London. My account will end when I rejoin them on what was their last stop on the trip as they made their way back to Edinburgh: at the Ayrshire village of Auchinleck. The village was the home of Boswell's father, a stern, dour Scottish judge, where Boswell nervously anticipated the outcome of a meeting between Johnson, a Church of England Tory, and the judge, a Presbyterian Whig. In the meantime, for the sake of togetherness and convenience I'm going to place the activities of the two men when they returned to Edinburgh at this point in my narrative. It fits more comfortably with my contemporary experiences in the capital, so my apologies to readers who would prefer a stricter chronology—even a backwards one.

"I cannot express how happy I was on finding myself at home," Boswell wrote when he arrived at his dwelling on the evening of November 9, and he unapologetically slept late the next morning. Visitors immediately showed up, desirous to learn all of the details and gossip about the tour, and both Boswell and Johnson were happy to oblige. (Who doesn't relish opportunities to talk about a just-completed travel experience? The problem has always been finding people who will listen and not want to tell you about *their* trip.) It must have been hard on poor Margaret Boswell, who served cup after cup of tea while nursing her grudges against Dr. Johnson. Boswell also got Johnson out to walk a few blocks uphill to Edinburgh Castle, which Johnson called "a great place" but then later added, "it would make a good *prison* in England." It was also at this point that Boswell corrected the location at which Johnson made one of his best-known sarcastic observations about Scotland. It had been alleged that from the castle

Johnson said, "the noblest prospect that a Scotchman ever sees is the high road that leads him to London." Not so, according to Boswell; those words were tossed out at a tavern in London back in 1763.

There was again lots of conversation as Johnson met more members of Edinburgh's intellectual community, and the topics ranged from dealing with rebels from the Jacobite Rising to law and literature. At one point a busy Johnson confessed to Boswell, "we have been harassed by invitations," adding quickly, "but how much worse would it have been if we had been neglected?" There were several times during this return to Edinburgh that Boswell admitted that he had not been keeping his notes as efficiently as before; I think he may be pardoned given what must have been great weariness following a long journey and an inevitable lassitude.

In his *Journey* Johnson had only a few things to say upon his return to Edinburgh and raised only two topics. One was the growing use of English rather than Scots English in communication. This had become the case after the signing of the Treaty of 1707 as more Scots mingled with the English in London, and English became the language of commerce, education, and politics. "The great, the learned, and the vain, all cultivate the *English* phrase, and the *English* pronunciation, and in splendid companies *Scotch* is not much heard," Johnson wrote with evident satisfaction.

The other topic, one which he described as "of philosophical curiosity," was a visit he paid to a school that provided learning to the deaf. The improvement of the twelve students at this Edinburgh school he found to be "wonderful," and he added, "It was pleasing to see one of the most desperate of human calamities capable of so much help; whatever enlarges hope, will exalt courage; after having seen the deaf taught arithmetick, who would be afraid to cultivate the *Hebrides?*" It seems hardly necessary to add that such condescension, commonplace in the eighteenth century and many decades beyond, scarcely represents twenty-first century attitudes toward education of the handicapped. Johnson's responses to his visit to the school, however, marked him in fact, among the more enlightened of his age.

Johnson left Edinburgh—with Boswell unexpectedly in his company—on November 22. I'll wrap that up a little later; for now, I return to more of my own exploring of Edinburgh. It seemed as if it had been a long time since I left Falkirk to drive into the capital in the pursuit of my companions.

Johnson and Boswell had Boswell's home to serve as lodging; I had a small hotel in New Town to the north of the Royal Mile. New Town, laid out in broad, symmetrical roadways, is not quite "new"—it was created more than two hundred years ago to alleviate some of the overcrowding and unsanitary conditions that made Old Town the mess that Boswell and others knew and wrote about. Edinburgh yields not much to London when it comes to pricey accommodations, and staying away from the Royal Mile and the busy thoroughfare of Princes Street helps to bring prices down for impecunious tourists (especially of the kind who have spent more than two months in Scotland). Fortunately Edinburgh has a good public transportation system, and getting around couldn't have been easier; by city bus I could travel from my hotel to the heart of Princes Street in less than fifteen minutes and only a few minutes more brought me to the Royal Mile.

I started my exploration on a beautifully sunny and warm day—"one of Edinburgh's best," a bookseller told me later that day—at the places where Boswell and Johnson visited or stayed. I've already discussed James's Court, where they stayed at the beginning and end of their journey, and as I passed James's Court again I spotted a plaque on a structure across the street identifying it as "Boswell's Court, number 352 Royal Mile." The building now hosts a tavern and an evening "Witching Tour." The plaque informed me that James Boswell and Samuel Johnson "are reputed to have met and dined in this building circa 1770." I was pleased to see Bozzy getting some notice along this street—since the Writers Museum didn't recognize him—but the key words on the plaque are *reputed* and *circa* because Johnson didn't get to Edinburgh until 1773, and it's unlikely that they dined there. I once ate in a restaurant in Virginia that claimed to have hosted George Washington. It was a grand experience that evoked a poignant historical moment; I didn't find out until years later that Washington never visited the area. The food wasn't all that good anyway.

Edinburgh Castle, on the top end of the Royal Mile, was crowded when I arrived; now that the calendar had reached May the number of visitors was picking up everywhere. I suppose I had been too long away from crowds; now there were long, slowly shuffling lines of people to eager see the opulent Scottish crown jewels. The history of Edinburgh and its castle are inextricably intertwined; one look at the castle's lofty, impregnable position makes clear why it was of such strategic importance. For nearly three thousand years there has been some kind of human presence recorded on the castle rock. The fortress itself probably dates back to the early seventh century and King Edwin of Northumberland, who allegedly called the structure "Edwin's Burgh." In the Middle Ages it became Edinburgh's chief royal castle, "enduring siege after siege during the long wars with England. By the time of King James VI's birth here in 1566, the castle was effectively little more than a garrison fortress," writes author Chris Tabraham. The Jacobite siege in 1745—Prince Charlie seized control of the city but never the castle—

was the last military encounter, and since that time the ancient fortress "has found new roles—as national symbol of Scotland, major visitor attraction and World Heritage Site—but still with its complement of soldiers."

The 360-degree views of Edinburgh and the countryside from the castle are spectacular, reinforcing the sense of dominion that unfolds here. The small chapel that dates from the twelfth century is the oldest surviving structure in the castle; other areas go back to the fourteenth and fifteenth centuries. Although Johnson said little about his visit, I believe it likely that the good doctor was a bit more impressed than he let on. I firmly suspect that if he had seen the castle lighted up at night, and I were the one having slop tossed on me while walking the streets, our opinions might have been reversed. Johnson had seen and stayed in many castles on the journey, and I had seen a few on mine as well. Only Stirling comes close to the grandeur of Edinburgh, though the wind-swept ruins of Dunnottar linger in my mind most memorably.

At the opposite, lower end of the Royal Mile is the Palace of Holyroodhouse, an attraction I found of more interest no doubt because of the romantic and bloody associations with the ever popular Mary, queen of Scots. For all of the beauty and history of Holyrood—and not minimizing the fact that Queen Elizabeth is in residence there at least one week each year—I'm convinced that it is the lure of Mary that packs this place with people like me.

When King James V died in 1542, his daughter Mary was only six days old. Sent to France as a child (the king's first wife had been French), she married the heir to the French throne who became king of France in 1559. There wasn't much time to celebrate; he died a year later, and the eighteen-year-old Catholic Queen returned to Holyroodhouse and a Scotland that was increasingly Protestant (think John Knox). She married Henry Stuart, Lord Darnley, in what turned out to be something less than a match made in heaven. In 1566 Darnley grew jealous of Mary's relationship with her Italian secretary (a man, not a piece of furniture), whose name was David Rizzio. One night Darnley and a group of coconspirators sneaked up a narrow spiral stairway from his apartment on the floor below the queen, burst in on a pregnant Mary and her attendants and the unfortunate Rizzio, who held tightly to the queen's skirts to protect himself. Darnley dragged Rizzio into a tiny room off his wife's chambers, stabbed him fifty-six times—I have no idea who was counting—and left him dying on the floor. This incredibly dramatic, unbelievably exciting, breathtaking moment in history was described by one historian this way—and I'm quoting him exactly, *every word* he wrote about the event—"Mary was greatly distressed by this." Really? Do you suppose? She was a mere twenty-three years old, six-months pregnant, enjoying tea with her ladies when her husband stormed into her room, grabbed her secretary, and began stabbing him while blood spurted everywhere and people ran and screamed. Hmmm, yes, I suppose one could become distressed at that if one were easily distressed. No wonder many readers get turned off by so many historians' bland treatment of real history.

Anyway, here's the cool part of this story: when you visit Holyrood and get to these rooms, there's the bedchamber, the spiral stairway, and the tiny stabbing room. There's even a brass plaque on the wall that points to Rizzio's bloodstains on the floor! Is history wonderful, or what?

Alas the scene is contrived. I hate to warn you off the tour because the palace is quite interesting in spite of this. But truth be told, the rooms have been changed and remodeled several times since Mary's time, and while the stairway is still around, the rest of the place isn't. Rizzio's alleged bloodstains are, well, whatever they are. The story and the sights have made Holyroodhouse a huge favorite for tourists for many years, and guidebooks used to toss around the facts rather cavalierly, apparently. When I was finishing my tour—which was entertaining and informative and accurate, as far as I could tell—I overheard two older American ladies discussing their visit.

"That was very exciting, wasn't it?" said the first.

"I could barely look at that blood," said the second. "That was horrible. Imagine poor Mary watching all of that in her bed."

"Don't you think she was scared?"

"Ooohh, I know, I know. All that blood. I just couldn't look at it. Why did they keep it all these years? Why didn't they just wash it off?"

"I don't know. Maybe it just won't come off. Do you think Elizabeth goes up there and looks at it?"

"I'd be frightened at night if I were her."

So much for guidebooks and facts. It seems a safe bet that Holyroodhouse will be attracting bloodthirsty tourists for many years to come. I thoroughly enjoyed my visit, though; Johnson's queen—whom "every man of spirit would have sacrificed his life for"—seemed very much alive, and her life's outcome all the more regrettable.

Before leaving the subject of Mary, I might add that both Mary and Darnley met unpleasant outcomes. Eleven months after Rizzio's murder Darnley was found strangled after a mysterious fire at the home in Edinburgh where he was staying. Exactly how the fire started and how he got choked to death have never been cleared up, but there was a lot of suspicion cast toward Mary, whose estrangement from her husband was quite obvious and understandable. Very soon thereafter Mary married the fourth earl of Bothwell, a marriage condemned by everyone, and in 1567 she was forced to abdicate in favor of her one-year-old son, James VI (of Scotland) and I (of England). A year later she fled to England, where cousin Elizabeth—with the assistance of the queen's clever secretary William Cecil—saw to it that she would never return to the throne. Those are pretty much the facts, but don't let them ruin any good stories you might have heard.

There were a couple of other sights to check out along the Royal Mile including the new Scottish Parliament structure across the street from Holyroodhouse. It's very modern, one of those love-it-or-hate-it structures, and it has led some Scots to wonder if the architect, Enric Miralles, had actually finished his drawings before construction began. Completed in 2004, it is one of the most expensive public buildings in Scotland; with cost overruns the final tab was something getting on to half a billion dollars. Admirers think it was worth it; it won the most prestigious architectural prize in Great Britain several years ago. If Scotland pursues its independence from England, that is where it will happen—right across the street from where Sean Connery—one of the most outspoken advocates for independence—was knighted by the woman who would then no longer preside over the Scottish kingdom, Queen Elizabeth II.

Farther up the Mile, heading toward the castle again, is the mighty St. Giles Cathedral, the original and sole parish church of medieval Edinburgh, where John Knox launched the Scottish Reformation and where Boswell and Johnson spent some time. Boswell was disappointed because the church had lost its "magnificence" by being partitioned. In an adjacent area (the partitions have since been removed) the two men found considerable dirt, which Johnson ignored at the time. Later, however, when they visited the Royal Infirmary and saw a sign reading "*Clean your feet!,*" Johnson slyly remarked, "There is no occasion for putting this at the doors of your churches." The cathedral was much cleaner on my visit and probably much brighter, too, than it must have been in the 1930s when the idiosyncratic, jocular travelers Hesketh Pearson and Hugh Kingsmill passed through on the trail of Boswell and Johnson.

"There's a monument somewhere here to Robert Louis Stevenson," Pearson said.

"Thank God, it's too dark to see it," muttered Kingsmill.

One of the joys of Edinburgh then and now are its bookstores, at least the ones that sell used books. There are a lot of them, widely scattered, unfortunately, and they offer evidence that Edinburgh has always been a city of books and learning. The chain stores have their offices on Princes Street and in the neighborhoods, and I found them well stocked with books by and about Boswell and Johnson. I bought a great many, in fact, and did the same at the used-book stores, delighted to help percolate the Scottish economy. The booksellers were invariably familiar with Boswell and Johnson; one of them told me he thought the Writers Museum, which pretends Boswell doesn't exist, "is run by crazies." Actually he said something quite a bit stronger, but take my word for it, he was in agreement with me. He seemed pleased with my objective and managed to come up with a book about Boswell that I had not heard of before. "It's not the best, you know? But if you want to know all about Bozzy, there are a few things in here for you."

I was tired by late afternoon and stopped off at one of the fancy bars/ brasseries that fill the area around Princes Street. I ordered a whisky, and the young male bartender served it with ice. I was appalled that Americans— does anyone else have such a fetish for ice?—have so infiltrated this part of the city that well-dressed barkeeps seemingly add ice to an order without asking. I drank it in a sulk; good whisky is good whisky after all. But I did make a point of asking for another glass at my inn; I was secretly pleased the bartender, an older man, didn't ask about ice, either, but offered me a straight shot with the option of a little water. My pleasure didn't last long, however, after I fell into conversation with a Scotsman who sat down beside me, He was neatly attired in a shirt with a slightly dirty tie and appeared to be in his seventies. The talk eventually got around to what I was doing in Scotland. We chatted a bit about my impressions of Scotland— very good, of course—and finally moved on to Boswell and Johnson. "He's the fellow who said so many bad things about us, isn't he?" asked my drinking buddy. I assured him that Johnson was both honest and outspoken and that he had both criticism and praise for the Scots after his journey. "No use for him, then," he said. "No use at all for that bastard." I smiled and waited. It appeared we had reached the sudden and unexpected end of our conversation. We sat silently for a few moments until I announced I needed to retire. My companion muttered something, and I left.

The experience reminded me of some passages I read in Moray McLaren's book *The Highland Jaunt*, written in the early 1950s. A fine, perceptive Scot born in Edinburgh in 1901, McLaren was on the trail of Boswell and Johnson when he reported a similar conversation with a man in one of the city's public houses. The man had little to say on behalf of Johnson for his slanders against the Scots and for Boswell because of his damaged reputation. McLaren, who knew something of the mind and temperament of the Scots, thought about those remarks, which came nearly two hundred years after Johnson's book was published. "The Scots are a highly sensitive people on a question of manners," McLaren wrote. And in spite of Johnson's good sense and generosity of observation "he was often, by modern standards pleasantly and crudely rude in Scotland, especially in Edinburgh. Traditions live long in the Northern kingdom and again particularly in Edinburgh."

As for Boswell, the apparent lingering distaste for him, McLaren suggested, might arise from tradition once again, for while Boswell was adept at "concealing his follies" in much larger London, he did not do well in Edinburgh, the city that was aware of his family, his background, and his circumstances. "Boswell was a supreme giver-away of himself. He never gave himself away with greater abandon than in London . . . and the Capital of Scotland has always, I regret to say, regarded this quality, whether as failing or virtue, with contempt."

I regretted the necessity of leaving Edinburgh, and, looking back over my notes, I saw that I regretted leaving almost everywhere I had been over the last ten or so weeks. I tried repeatedly but couldn't think of a proper homage to the capital. Nothing deserving came to mind until almost a year and a half after my return home when I came across the latest mystery novel from one of Edinburgh's finest contemporary writers, Ian Rankin. The book, *Final Exit,* was billed as the last bow for the retiring Inspector John Rebus, Rankin's memorable Edinburgh copper who first appeared in print in 1987 in *Knots and Crosses.* It is hard for readers of this enormously popular series to believe that Rebus is really departing, that Rankin doesn't have something else up his sleeve. And like Rebus, I couldn't believe I would be departing Edinburgh for the last time. Rankin himself has cautioned his fans that "there's no way he [Rebus] is going gentle into that dark retirement," adding that "I still like to spend time with him." Well, I still like to spend time with Edinburgh; Rebus and I will be back—of that I'm quite sure.

22

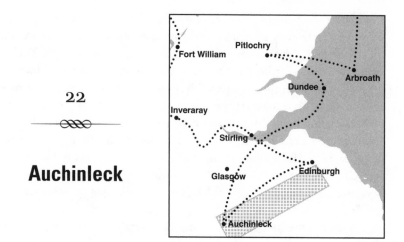

Auchinleck

The next morning dawned cool and overcast with light rain, perfect Scottish weather for a drive into the country. The road toward Auchinleck, south of Glasgow, passed lovely countryside, mostly well-tended farmlands occasionally interrupted by small, bland hamlets. Lanark was an exception; a very old town on hills above the River Clyde, it had an attractive main thoroughfare with interesting-looking shops and more restaurants than I would have imagined, suggesting it is a popular stop for visitors. I had a delicious early lunch of soup and salmon, again marveling at how the food on my trip consistently belied the expectations of Scotland as a land of edibles only slightly less tasteless than England. Truth be told, in recent years I've enjoyed many outstanding meals in England as well; I think there's a great deal of cultural bias at work when it comes to discussing food. London is one of the great food capitals of the world, and I believe its deserved reputation has been spreading into other parts of the United Kingdom, even the remote ones.

Back on the road I drove for about an hour to the village of Auchinleck in Ayrshire. There I would once again imagine that I was that lucky fly on the wall in that tense moment, packed with expectation, when Boswell introduced Johnson to his father. But first, I had to find the Auchinleck estate, a small matter that, of course, never concerned Bozzy.

He and Johnson passed through Glasgow as they made their way from Inveraray to the south and Auchinleck. Glasgow, with the largest population of any city in Scotland, was booming in 1773 when they arrived. Many a Glaswegian made a living off the trade with the American colonies, though it would soon dry up with the start of the Revolution. By the turn of the twentieth century Glasgow was known for one thing only: shipbuilding, everything from tugs to ocean liners. The economy of the 1930s sent that industry into a spiral from which it never recovered and left the city with a blight from which it has only recently recovered. Now a center of culture and commerce acclaimed throughout Europe, it is once again booming, its growth rapid and employment opportunities drawing Scots from throughout the job-deprived Highlands and Islands.

I earlier had designed a trip that bypassed Glasgow, I thought, but which really wound up going round and round through an endless suburb to the west called Airdrie. Something happened to Scotland's generally good road signage when I got to that point. I would have given my fish and chips for a sign of any sort, even one in Gaelic, but when I drove into Airdrie it was as if I had pulled into Mars. And so I circled and turned and found myself repeatedly back where I started. I struggled to find a place to pull over and ask someone for directions, and when I accomplished that at last I couldn't understand a word spoken by the man I stopped (please see the telephone purchase experience in Stirling on my second day in Scotland nine weeks previously for a fuller explanation). Traffic was building up, I was getting frustrated, imagining a life in which my grandchildren would hear stories of how their grandfather finally passed to the other side after sixteen years trying to get through Airdrie. To make an extremely long story bearably brief, I did make a right turn at some point and kept driving, figuring anywhere was better than where I was. Proof of my clean living came in the form of a road sign pointing me to my bed and breakfast for the night. When I arrived worn and bleary, my host greeted me cheerfully: "Still got your tires? Airdrie's a tough place. Glad you didn't stop." As if I could have.

But I digress. I leave it to Boswell and Johnson to negotiate Glasgow and will meet them on the other side, so to speak. As Bozzy and Johnson headed into Glasgow Johnson once again placed an entry in his *Journey* that reminded us that his prime interest in this almost-concluded expedition was the trip to the Highlands. As he had written off Edinburgh, he did the same with Glasgow, declaring, "To describe a city so much frequented as *Glasgow,* is unnecessary. The prosperity of its commerce appears by the greatness of many private houses, and a general appearance of wealth." Had he stopped there all might have been fine, but the doctor—who surely must have been very tired by this point in the journey—went on to disparage the educational system in Scotland, to the advantage of the English and to the irritation of the Scots when they later read his book. He did note that the university in Glasgow didn't seem to share in the town's overall magnificence and then opened fire with a broadside on the results of a Scottish education: "The students, for the most part, go thither boys, and depart before they are men; they carry with them little fundamental knowledge, and there the superstructure cannot be lofty. The grammar schools are not generally well supplied; for the character of a schoolmaster being there less honourable than in England, is seldom accepted by men who are capable to adorn it, and where the school has been deficient, the college can effect little." (Boswell scholar Ronald Black tells us that for university graduates "the teaching profession was generally regarded in Scotland as a step towards the ministry of the church. Those who remained in it were frequently ill-educated or frustrated—or both.")

Boswell was, as usual, more forthcoming about the pair's activities. In Glasgow he ordered a new post chaise for them to better enable the trip to Auchinleck, which today is about an hour's drive from Glasgow, if, that is, you don't drive through Airdrie. The two men stopped at Dumbarton Castle, making it, I hope, abundantly clear to readers of this book that I was not the only one addicted to castleling through Scotland. At Dumbarton, which rests high atop volcanic rock and dates to the Roman occupation, Boswell recorded Johnson scampering through the grounds and up the hills. In fact, Boswell wrote, through their entire journey together, Johnson "showed uncommon spirit, could not bear to be treated like an old or infirm man, and was very unwilling to accept of any assistance." As may be recalled from the Iona landing, Johnson did have a few moments when his temper grew short.

They stayed the night at the Saracen Inn in Glasgow—no longer in existence—where both men had letters awaiting them. For Johnson it was the first mail he had received in some two and a half months, and he eagerly fell to his correspondents (including the much-missed Mrs. Thrale). He relaxed and "seemed to be in high glee," Boswell wrote. At one point during the evening he kicked his heels up on either side of the grate and exclaimed with some light-hearted solemnity, "Here I am, an English man, sitting by a *coal* fire." At such moments we forget Johnson's age and infirmities and celebrate his energy, his good humor, and his patience.

The next day they were visited by some of the university professors, unaware of Johnson's earlier observations, who deferred to Johnson and thereby earned Boswell's gratitude. Johnson, he wrote, "was fully conscious of his own superior powers." That would seem to be the wrong attitude, almost guaranteeing a quarrel once the travelers reached their destination Auchinleck, where Boswell's father waited—menacingly?—for them.

On the way they visited yet another castle ruin—I understand this desire quite thoroughly—before Boswell persuaded Johnson to stop at a neighbor's residence, the home of the eighty-year-old countess of Eglinton. The conversation there proved most agreeable, and as they prepared to leave the countess noted that she had been married the year before Johnson was born and that she was of an age to have been his mother. With Johnson apparently smiling approvingly, she "adopted" the doctor on the spot and embraced him saying, "My dear son, farewell!" Johnson left "much pleased," in Bozzy's words.

And then it was Auchinleck, at that time pronounced *Affleck* but now, I have been advised, usually spoken as *Au-kin-leck;* my apologies to those who may know better. They arrived before dinnertime Tuesday. Boswell took note of a decline of his father's "strong mind and cheerful temper" (he was exaggerating a bit about the latter) which he attributed to the death of his mother some years before and his father's laborious duties as a law judge. What Boswell did not mention, now or at any time during this visit, was the presence of his stepmother, whom his father had married in 1769 after more than four years as a widower. She was there for this gathering and must have provided the hospitality, but Boswell carefully avoided any reference to her in his writings.

Part of the reason for the strained relationship between father and son had to do with their marriages. Lord Auchinleck was displeased when Boswell announced he would be marrying his penniless cousin Margaret; his father didn't care for her nor did he welcome her lack of money and connections. Perhaps to avenge himself on his son Lord Auchinleck arranged for his own second marriage—this to his cousin Elizabeth Boswell—to take place on the same day, November 25, 1769, that Boswell married Margaret. There was obviously no love lost between the two couples; when the Boswells had children they were never invited to Lord Auchinleck's estate, and when they were there previously Margaret Boswell was mistreated. Hence Boswell's failure to mention his stepmother was not to be considered a casual omission but rather one quite deliberate.

The wives were hardly the only issue between father and son. "My father," Boswell once complained, "cannot bear that his son should talk with him as a man." Lord Auchinleck was one of the most respected legal minds in Scotland, a classicist in his learning, and he had expected his son to follow in the legal profession. Boswell had other plans beginning with the hope of becoming a soldier (an ambition which would have served neither Boswell nor the army very well) and then a writer—anything to escape his father. Lord Auchinleck had no use for Boswell's pen; he either thought little of his son's writings or dismissed them. Bozzy, of course, liked his freedom, but he also desired the respectability conferred by his father and the estate, and he ultimately followed his father's wishes. Unable to tear himself away from the pleasures of London, he was dragged away by Lord Auchinleck who tutored him in the law. It took a few years for Boswell to pass all the examinations—he could never focus on one thing for too long a time—but he finally did become an advocate, something that did give his father at least a measure of satisfaction. It also set the stage for his marriage and reopened many old wounds with his father.

It's sad for Boswell—and Lord Auchinleck, I suppose—that he quarreled so with his father, for he was surely a man in need of a father in his life. His volatile personality, his shifting moods all craved the stability given by an older, wiser man. When his father failed him he set out to find someone who would fill the void; ultimately that man would be Johnson, and Johnson was only in Boswell's life for relatively brief periods. Sadly Boswell must have wavered constantly between his admiration of his idol and his awe of his father.

When he and Johnson arrived at Auchinleck for their visit, Boswell did, of course, invoke his father's low opinion of Johnson to give readers a reminder of why he anticipated trouble: "As he had not much leisure to be informed of Dr. Johnson's great merits by reading his works, he had a partial and favourable notion of him, founded on his supposed political tenets, which were so discordant to his own that, instead of speaking of him with that respect to which he was entitled, he used to call him 'a Jacobite fellow.'" Boswell knew he could be in for trouble, and he cautioned Johnson not to speak of topics certain to start a fight: Whigs, Presbyterians, and Sir John Pringle, physician to the king, Boswell's friend and a man for whom Johnson had a dislike. In other words be sure not to mention anything about anything to do with Boswell's father, who was both a Whig and a Presbyterian. Chatting about the weather might be nice.

On this first evening all went smoothly. It was rainy, and Boswell's father showed off his fine library; there were no disagreements recorded. On Wednesday it rained all day, giving Johnson an opportunity to talk about the weather. Actually, however, some neighbors arrived to talk with Johnson about his trip. When asked how he liked the Highlands Johnson was curt: "How, sir, can you ask me what obliges me to speak unfavourably of a country where I have been hospitably entertained? Who *can* like the Highlands? I like the inhabitants very well." After that rebuke the conversation understandably dried up.

On Thursday the weather improved and the two travelers spent time outside, prompting Boswell to talk with pride about the beauty of the landscaping and the gentility of his ancestors. He and Johnson walked the grounds, strolling to the west to the ruins of the former family seat, the "Old Place," built in 1612 to replace the castle that originally stood there. In a burst of enthusiasm he even proposed erecting a monument to Johnson on the grounds. The landscape was covered with trees planted by Lord Auchinleck and hedges, too, one possibly apocryphal story being that they were planted to grow thickly together and thereby block the view of nearby tenants.

Johnson admired the house, not only from inside but also the view of it from the green well-kept grounds. It had been built between 1755 and 1760 by Boswell's father, who is believed to have been largely responsible for its design, and it was the third house to be built on an estate granted to Boswell's forebears in the fourteenth century. The four wings that flank the house were put up in 1773 and 1774; Lord Auchinleck had tried to interest his son in their creation, but Boswell apparently had no hand in them.

On this day, after they returned from their walk outside, the local parish minister, the Rev. Dun, dined with the company. There was the potential for a heated discussion since the minister was Presbyterian, but Boswell did not record any tense conversations throughout the evening. On Friday they were invited to dine at the home of Mr. Dun, which provided another opportunity for Boswell and Johnson to get outside. The Presbyterian minister and Johnson predictably did not hit it off and after the reverend began attacking the Church of England, Johnson blasted him: "Sir, you know no more of our church than a Hottentot." End of conversation once again. The good reverend seems likely to have complained about the publication of his name in the first edition of Boswell's book because it disappeared in the second.

Saturday's weather was stormy, but it was nothing compared to what was about to happen inside—the collision between the two men that Boswell had feared. It all began innocently enough when Boswell's father showed his medal collection to Johnson; a coin with a depiction of Oliver Cromwell brought up the topics of Charles I and Toryism and set off Johnson. The two men "became exceedingly warm and violent." And then—as we brace for the fireworks, and to the dismay of Boswellians and Johnsonians everywhere ever since, Boswell wrote this:

> I was very much distressed by being present at such an altercation between two men, both of whom I reverenced; yet I durst not interfere. It would certainly be very unbecoming in me to exhibit my honoured father and my respected friend as intellectual gladiators, for the entertainment of the public; and therefore I suppress what would, I dare say, make an interesting scene in this dramatic sketch—this account of the transit of Johnson over the Caledonian Hemisphere.

How could Boswell have done this? Having given us Johnson fondling a "Highland wench," now all of a sudden, at the closing moment of the journey, he cannot find the words to describe the inevitable confrontation with his father? What got into Boswell? What demon of propriety grasped him after so long a time of impropriety? Boswell could spare nothing of himself, little of Johnson, but almost everything for his father, with whom he suffered a tempestuous and only occasionally respectful relationship? Well, he did it. Biographer Frank Brady calls this moment "the great unwritten scene in Boswell's journal." It would have made an extraordinary climax to his account of the tour, this confrontation between his spiritual and physical fathers, who embodied as well some of the deepest traits and most strongly held prejudices of the Englishman and Scot. But almost as if he had a second thought and was unable to resist, Boswell took up his pen once more to give us a teaser on their conversation. It is a little anticlimactic, perhaps, but still worth quoting in full:

> Yet I think I may without impropriety, mention one circumstance, as an instance of my father's address. Dr. Johnson challenged him, as he did us all at Talisker, to point out any theological works of merit written by Presbyterian ministers in Scotland. My father, whose studies did not much lie much in that way, owned to me afterwards that he was somewhat at a loss how to answer, but that luckily he recollected having read in catalogues the title of *Durham on the Galatians;* upon which he boldly said, "Pray, sir, have you read Mr. Durham's excellent commentary on the Galatians?"
>
> "No, sir," said Dr. Johnson.
>
> My father then had him before the wind, and went on, "How came you, then, to speak with such contempt of the writings of our church? You may buy it at any time for half a crown or three shillings."
>
> By this lucky thought my father kept him at bay, and for some time enjoyed his triumph; but his antagonist soon made a retort: "Sir, it must be better recommended before I give half the money for it."
>
> In the course of their altercation, Whiggism and Presbyterianism, Toryism and Episcopacy, were terribly buffeted. My worthy hereditary friend, Sir John Pringle, never having been mentioned, happily escaped without a bruise.
>
> My father's opinion of Dr. Johnson may be conjectured from the name he afterwards gave him, which was "Ursa Major." But it is not true, as has been reported, that it was in consequence of my saying that he was a *constellation* of genius and literature. It was a sly abrupt

expression to one of his brethren on the bench of the Court of Session, in which Dr. Johnson was then standing, but it was not said in his hearing.

(Ronald Black writes that Boswell told his father that Johnson was a "constellation of virtues," to which his father replied that yes, Johnson was Ursa Major and "you are Ursa Minor.")

The next morning was Sunday, and Boswell and his father went to church; Johnson, to no one's surprise, stayed home, not wishing to engage in Presbyterian worship. Nothing untoward occurred, and on Monday morning the travelers departed. Boswell's father was civil and wished them well. The weather was decent as they headed back to Edinburgh. Johnson had been expected to leave the capital soon for his return journey to London, but, as we have seen, he stayed in Edinburgh for nearly two additional weeks. In his *Journey* Johnson had little to say about his experience at Auchinleck beyond a few notes about the scenery and a pleasant reference to Boswell's father: "He has built a house of hewn stone, very stately, and durable, and has advanced the value of his lands with great tenderness to his tenants." Of Cromwell, Presbyterianism, Whiggery and the like, nothing.

The weather was unremarkable when I finally pulled into Auchinleck. The rain was coming down lightly, and the winds were brisk and chilly. There was a sign at the village limits that read "Auchinleck: Home of James Boswell"; some graffiti had been scribbled on it. The village was unpretentious and looked a bit decayed. The main street ran past a building that had the sign "Boswell Arms," with the *r* missing. I'm not sure what the building might have been—it looked empty now. Boswell's name also appeared on the Masons' building, and there was a small housing development called Boswell Park.

It was nice to see Bozzy remembered, I suppose, but nothing I saw suggested anything but passing, offhand memories. I had an early afternoon appointment with the housekeeper at the Auchinleck estate who was going to show me around, but I had no idea how to get there. Remembering my experiences in Airdrie, I determined to be careful in selecting someone to ask for directions. Choice wasn't really a problem, however, since I didn't see anyone outside on the streets. It was raining, and there simply was no one there. I parked the car at a convenience store and went inside. An elderly couple looked like a good prospect, and I asked if they knew where the Boswell estate was. No, they didn't. Then I asked about Auchinleck estate, and they brightened. "Aye, go doune the road t' the gate and keep goin.'" Seemed easy enough, so I got back in the car, drove off, and stayed straight for about four or five miles. I saw lots of gates, but nothing that looked like Auchinleck.

I turned around and drove back into town and stopped at the Railway Hotel, a solid-looking institution that appeared to have received an attractive renovation recently. It was there nearly 120 years ago when the scholar G. B. Hill visited the village and stayed in what he called "a curious old house, which boasted of two sitting-rooms and one bed-room." The hotel was larger now, though there were still two sitting rooms. A young man in his twenties with an armful of tattoos behind the hotel front desk looked up pleasantly when I walked in. "Very easy to get there from here," he replied to my request for directions. "I'm sure you'll like it. A big fan of Boswell are you?" I said yes, and we chatted a moment about how people in Auchinleck react to him these days. "There's a group of men who were organized and keep things up a bit, you know. At least they used to. And we get some people coming in to look the place over. Not too many, but sometimes we have a group of five or six." I mentioned my book project, and he laughed: "Never heard of an American writing about old Boswell! Have a good time with it." I recalled the scholar Hill likewise encountered a bright and sprightly employee, a landlady, during his stay at the hotel. I left with a very cheery feeling.

The rain had stopped, and a few minutes later I arrived at a point where the paved two-lane road ended and a single-lane road picked up, flanked by closely planted trees and rhododendrons. There was a small open metal gate with a sign on one side announcing "Auchinleck House," although no house was in sight. I kept driving and made several turns past some attractive older homes until I came to a narrower, rather muddy road that led to Boswell's home. There was no sign identifying it as such, but I could recognize it from photographs, and so I parked the car and stepped out. Maureen, the housekeeper, hadn't yet arrived, so I had a few minutes alone to walk around the grounds of the building. It was clear this had been a fine country home when Boswell and his father lived in it; it was still beautiful, symmetrical and surprisingly kept up, thanks to the Landmark Trust of Scotland. Frederick Pottle, the father of Boswellian studies, described it as "an exquisite piece of Neo-classicism in the Adams style."

Above the main entrance was (and is) a motto Lord Auchinleck chose. It reads (in Latin), "What you seek is here in this remote place, if you can only keep a balanced disposition." Seriously. That's what it says. It's not exactly inspiring these days, and it certainly didn't fit Boswell's personality, no matter how hard he tried. Lord Auchinleck lived to the ripe age of seventy-five, growing increasingly cranky and garrulous and never repenting his falling-out with his son; their disputes continued up to his last days. Boswell was forty-one when he inherited the estate at his father's death in 1782; he and Margaret and their children arrived to take possession of Auchinleck on September 18, 1782, a day that was also Johnson's birthday. Both men believed it a good omen. Boswell kept the estate until his own passing in 1795, and it then descended through the family for nearly another hundred years.

I walked to each of the four tall wing structures topped by baroque pavilions that Lord Auchinleck had tried unsuccessfully to interest his son in, examined them, and snapped pictures of the house from the four viewpoints. I had read earlier there were no traces of the "old castle" ruins remaining, so I didn't try to locate them. When Boswell was living there were actually three structures that made up Auchinleck. One was the ruins of the thirteenth- or fourteenth-century keep, known as the "old castle." The second was a Renaissance mansion, erected about 1530 by a Boswell ancestor, which stood in large fragments by Boswell's era and was not spotted by me at all, and the third was the current house, the one I was viewing. The ground was soggy, and several deep ravines made walking a little treacherous. I had stopped to snap some pictures when two walkers surprised me; they lived nearby and were curious about my business. I told them I was waiting for Maureen and they slipped off into the countryside with their walking sticks, oblivious to the bog.

Just about two minutes later Maureen and her husband, William, drove up, apologizing for their tardiness. Maureen was a treasure trove of information about the house and its history, and it was immediately evident that she did more than look after the structure; she cared for it and about it in a very personal way. The ground-floor rooms are used by the Landmark Trust, which acquired the house in 1999 and spent some ten million dollars restoring it. Now visitors can rent it at most times of the year (it's about two thousand dollars for four or five nights). We walked up the staircase in the middle of the house—the only staircase, by the way—to the first floor. The furnishings were simple and period-appropriate, and there were just enough of them to make it comfortable for visitors without trying fully to re-create Boswell's age. I walked into the library where Lord Auchinleck and Johnson had argued; we don't know exactly how it looked that evening in 1773, so the trust's restoration evokes the style of an eighteenth-century library in general terms.

There is nothing original to Boswell in the house that is also connected to Auchinleck, not surprising given how the family did their best to get rid of most things that belonged to him. What remains suggests the atmosphere of the eighteenth century. There are, however, several deep display cabinets that hold a variety of items from the Boswell Museum, all of which used to be kept in the chapel in Auchinleck village. There was one original painting on the walls (the rest were copies), and there was a lovely wood cabinet Maureen pointed out proudly to me that Boswell had kept in his London apartment. Of course I touched it, then rubbed it slightly, just to establish my own link to Boswell. Maureen nodded approvingly, I should add.

I had been told by the Landmark Trust that I would have only a thirty-minute tour and see just part of the house, but Maureen would hear of no such thing. We spent nearly three hours together, going through every room in the house including those in the attic, where I saw the original stone walls and wood beams. Maureen's enthusiasm for Boswell matched my own, and we were both happy that the house had been saved, but we regretted that care for it came so late. The views out the windows were wonderful, and Maureen said that on exceptionally clear days she could see from the upper rooms all the way to the Isle of Arran across the Firth of Clyde—a long way away. We sat and talked with her husband for what seemed a short time, but as the rain began to fall again I realized I had taken up nearly all afternoon with her. I apologized, and as we walked back to our cars I shook her hand and slipped some pound notes in it, then sped off before she could object. I wasn't sure a tip was appropriate, but she had been very generous with her time and her knowledge, and it seemed the very least I could do.

As I took to the road again I thought back to Boswell's time as laird of Auchinleck, those thirteen years from the time he inherited the estate until his death. Initially Boswell wrote of his expectation of settling down there: "The occupations of the estate, even in speculation content me." It didn't last, though; Bozzy needed the city life of London to stoke his inner fires. His wife—getting sicker and weaker from consumption—and the children spent much more time at Auchinleck than did Boswell in the 1780s. He kept a "Book of Company at Auchinleck" in which he recorded the names of his visitors and what they drank, partly to know how best to manage his cellar and perhaps partly to keep a control on his own drinking. In one entry in 1794, for instance, he observed the depletion of claret and ordered more even as he acknowledged that doing so would not be good for him after his excessive indulging in London. The situation was, pardon the pun, vintage Boswell. Before I left the house Maureen found a gorgeous recent facsimile copy of the "Book of Company," and I, of course, made certain that I took it with me.

I drove several miles away in the general direction of the village to the small church where Boswell and his family are buried. The Boswell Mausoleum was tightly locked, and it was too late in the day for me to inquire about getting inside. As I stood there in the off-and-on rainfall it did strike me as most ironic that there lay Boswell with his wife and his father, one on whom he occasionally cheated and the other whom he occasionally despised. Family ties are strong, however, and, for all of his misdeeds, regretted and otherwise, Boswell, I have found, was very, very hard to dislike. The better I have made his acquaintance, the better I have liked him. No wonder Dr. Johnson felt the same.

Back in Edinburgh after the conclusion of the stop at Auchinleck, Johnson remained for almost two weeks before leaving for London on November 22. This last chapter of the trip could have been dramatic or anticlimactic, but it turned out to be mostly amusing. An eccentric author by the name of Sir John Dalrymple had urged Johnson to visit him on the way out of Edinburgh, but Sir John had been rather outspoken in his low opinion of Johnson, so Boswell—anticipating a row between the two men—decided to accompany Johnson to see that things went smoothly. They dillydallied along the way—another castle, don't you know?—and arrived late for what had been promised as a "feast" on a seven-year-old sheep at Sir John's home. Johnson could have cared less; along the way he parodied Sir John's situation at the moment in the author's own highly mannered style:

> Dinner being ready, he wondered that his guests were not yet come. His wonder was soon succeeded by impatience. He walked about the room in anxious agitation; sometimes he looked at his watch, sometimes he looked out the window with an eager gaze of anticipation, and revolved in his mind the various accidents of human life. His family beheld him with mute concern. "Surely," said he, with a sigh, "they will not fail me." The mind of a man can bear a certain pressure, but there is a point when it can bear no more. A rope was in his view, and he died a Roman death.

When the guests finally showed up quite late, Sir John was most annoyed, dinner was brief, and conversation went poorly. At bedtime Boswell and Johnson settled into ancient, drafty rooms Boswell found "better suited the climate of Italy in summer than that of Scotland in the month of November." At breakfast matters went from the sublime to the ridiculous when Sir John—angered because a feast had prepared the night before by killing a sheep had gone uneaten by his guests—asked everyone whether they preferred the seven-year-old sheep's foreleg or hind leg for dinner. His wife favored the foreleg, and Johnson voted for the hind leg, leading to this scene: "He was certain of my vote, and Sir John, who could not in decency deny his guest what he liked best, was obliged to join. Poor Lady Dalrymple appeared much disconcerted, and was an innocent victim to the censure of Dr. Johnson, who supposed she was unwilling to give us what was best." Johnson said to Boswell later she was "an odious woman," adding, "Did you observe her when we voted leg? Sir, she looked as if we had voted for roasting one of her children." The truth, as Boswell discovered later, was that Sir John had never killed a sheep, and there was no leg in the house. The travelers, with no hint of regret, moved to a nearby inn for the evening—after stopping to see another castle, a decision I feel requires no additional comment. By the way, Boswell didn't seem to feel that Sir John's stature merited any concern about his response when he read the lines above once they had been published. Sir John was something of a weasel who had backed out of a duel, so Bozzy and Johnson could have cared less for his opinions.

The two men breakfasted together the next morning. Johnson climbed aboard a post chaise headed for London, and Boswell bade him good-bye. We don't know what their parting words were; neither wrote them down, so we are left to conjecture. Did they part with some emotion? That would have been more likely for Boswell than for Johnson, but I believe both had to have felt a measure of sadness as the carriage pulled away. They knew that they had experienced something unique and remarkable together. Perhaps there was a firm handshake or maybe an embrace? Maybe just a parting wave? When Boswell turned away, did he feel regret that the trip was over? He wrote later that Johnson had confided in him that "the time he spent in this tour was the pleasantest part of his life, and asked me if I would lose the recollection of it for five hundred pounds. I answered I would not; and he applauded my setting such a value on an accession of new images in my mind."

Boswell left us with these words, a tribute to Johnson to be sure, and an observation on the deep satisfaction he derived from the experience: "I have only to add that I shall ever reflect with great pleasure on a tour which has been the means of preserving so much of the enlightened and instructive conversation of one whose virtues will, I hope, ever be an object of imitation, and whose powers of mind were so extraordinary that ages may revolve before such a man shall appear." It will be ages as well, I know, before such a man as Boswell again appears to us. So let us celebrate the unforgettable lives of these two men, so different yet so forever intertwined, and whose history together has so illuminated a period of our past that would have been lost forever without their vivid recollections.

23

The Last Days

And so Johnson returned to London, and Boswell returned to his home in Edinburgh. This was hardly the end of their relationship, nor did it mark the final time they would be together. They would meet in London on other occasions; Boswell always needed an infusion of the city's exuberant life, and he wished to continue collecting material for his planned biography. After his father's death in 1782 and his ascension as laird, he invited Johnson to return to Auchinleck, and Johnson unquestionably would have liked to do so—he would write later of Boswell, "I love to travel with him." But Johnson's health was slipping away. He told Boswell, with obvious feeling, "I should like to totter about your place, and live mostly on milk, and be taken care of by Mrs. Boswell. . . . If I were in distress, there is no man I would come to so soon as you. I should come to you and have a cottage in your park."

Bozzy was stirred. His writing shows us the powerful feelings between the two men for all their shared experiences: "I got up to part from him. He took me in his arms, and said with a solemn fervour, 'GOD bless you for Jesus Christ's sake.' . . . I walked away from Dr. Johnson's door with agitation and a kind of fearful apprehension of what might happen before I returned." He wrote that in 1783, the year before Johnson's death.

Johnson suffered an assortment of maladies including worsening gout, asthma, dropsy (heart failure), and kidney stones. He kept a medical journal for a time in which he recorded his specific ailments and treatments. He knew he was failing—"God have mercy," he wrote despairingly at one point. Mrs. Thrale had remarried, and Johnson's spirits were low: "I could bear sickness better, if I were relieved from solitude." In May 1784 Boswell found Johnson somewhat improved, and he accompanied Johnson to Oxford with Johnson's lifelong friend William Adams, who shared anecdotes about the doctor. Those stories give us a sad picture of Johnson at the end, his melancholia overcoming him as he declared that he was "oppressed by the fear of death" and soon would join "the damned" in hell. When others sought to convince him otherwise Johnson declared that life was more miserable than happy: "I would not lead my life over again through an archangel should request it."

In June, hearing Johnson's wistful desire to escape London's cold winter for the Mediterranean warmth of Italy, Boswell and others hatched a plan to get him there. The centerpiece was a pitch to Lord Thurlow, the lord high chancellor, to speak to the king for an increase in Johnson's royal pension to enable him to afford the trip. Boswell's account of breaking the good news in his *Life of Johnson* sets the powerfully emotional scene quite affectingly:

> BOSWELL: "I am very anxious about you, Sir, and particularly that you should go to Italy for the winter, which I believe is your own wish." JOHNSON: "It is, Sir." BOSWELL: "You have no objection, I presume, but the money it would require." JOHNSON: "Why no, Sir!" Upon which I gave him a particular account of what had been done, and read to him the Lord Chancellor's letter.—He listened with much attention, and then warmly said, "This is taking prodigious pains about a man."—O!, Sir (said I, with most sincere affection,) your friends would do every thing for you. He paused,—grew more and more agitated,—till tears started into his eyes, and he exclaimed with fervent emotion, "GOD bless you all." I was so affected that I also shed tears. . . . We both remained for some time unable to speak.—He rose suddenly and quitted the room, quite melted in tenderness.

The next day Boswell met with Johnson and Sir Joshua Reynolds, who had helped put the Italy plan into motion, and they drove in Reynolds's coach for a meal. After dining, Johnson invited Boswell in, but "I declined it from apprehension that my spirits would sink," Boswell related. "We bade adieu to each other affectionately in the carriage. When he had got down upon the foot-pavement, he called out, 'Fare you well!' and without looking back sprung away with a kind of pathetic briskness (if I may use that expression), which seemed to indicate a struggle to conceal uneasiness, and it was to me a foreboding of our long, long separation." That was the end; Boswell and Johnson would never see each other again.

For Johnson the last few months were tragic. The journey to Italy did not happen; the king rejected an increase in the pension. Johnson's mental and physical suffering increased, and he knew his time was coming. He died on December 13, 1784. Boswell heard of it on December 17. He wrote, "I was stunned and in a kind of amaze. . . . I did not shed tears. I was not tenderly affected. My feeling was just one large expanse of stupour." He added that his mind's "great SUN," as he had once described Johnson, had set.

He made love to his wife that night and the next morning wrote in his journal a no-doubt heartfelt but typical Boswellian pledge, "My resolution was to honour his memory by doing as much as I could to fulfill his noble precepts of religion and morality." Boswell's morality and religion may have wavered here and there in the last years of his life, but he indeed honored Johnson's memory in two enduring ways: with his account of their journey to the Hebrides and in his *Life of Johnson.*

Of course not everyone felt kindly toward Johnson when the doctor's book about the Scottish journey was published, nor was there universal acclaim when Boswell's book appeared a few years later. Johnson's *A Journey to the Western Islands of Scotland* came off the press in 1775 and was met with what Boswell called "miserable cavillings" by the critics. In other words disdain for book critics is hardly a new thing, and even before the era of the Internet everybody was a critic. In general English reviewers liked it, and many Scots didn't. "Everybody finds some reason to be affronted," wrote Edward Topham in his *Letters from Edinburgh, 1774–1775.* "A thousand people, who know not a single creature in the Western Isles, interest themselves in their cause, and are offended at the accounts that are given of them."

While Topham said he preferred to stay above the storm, he couldn't resist some digs at Johnson, writing that in spite of warm, civil treatment afforded Johnson, the doctor repaid his hosts with "contempt," adding, "I look upon all his observations in regard to men and manners, to be those of a man totally unacquainted with mankind." In an effort to give some balance here, I should point out that in book after criticizing Johnson for criticizing the Scots, Topham proceeded to do exactly the same thing, finding "extreme ugliness" in the common people of the countryside, whom he believed worn down and "haggard" because of their hard labor and the terrible weather in their country.

What seems to have upset readers most about Johnson's *Journey* may come as a surprise: the author's passionate insistence that Macpherson's so-called discovery and translation of the work of the Gaelic bard Ossian was a fraud. Johnson believed the work *Fingal* was all Macpherson's, and, as we know, Johnson was correct. But in 1775 there were many believers in Scotland, and they were very unhappy with Johnson. After all, this was the great eminence, the most noted man of letters in England skewering not only the creator of this great work of Scottish literature but also pointing out that, incidentally, the work itself was no good. It was Scotland versus England all over again, and if King Edward had come riding in to slice up William Wallace one more time, a lot of Scots would hardly have wished less for Johnson.

We have already noted the pusillanimous Macpherson's threat to clobber Johnson, which we know from Johnson's reply since Macpherson's letter with the original insult has been lost, the doctor's strong-spined reply calling his bluff, and Macpherson's subsequent backing down. What gives this particular story an ironic twist is that, in death, the two men who had no use for each other lie close together, within a few feet of one another in Westminster Abbey. That seems incontrovertible proof that you don't have to be a king or a queen—or even be right—to get your remains into England's national cathedral. I think it was a Scotsman who told me that.

The most vituperative attack on Johnson's book came four years after its publication. It was in the form of a book from the fevered mind of the Rev. Donald MacNicol, an outraged Presbyterian minister on the island of Lismore in Loch Linhe not far from Oban. "The doctor hated Scotland; that was the *master-passion,* and it scorned all restraints," he wrote in *Remarks on Dr. Samuel Johnson's Journey to the Hebrides,* which turned out almost as long as Johnson's volume. MacNicol was something of a Gaelic scholar, and he found fault after fault with Johnson, but his incessant carping amounted to overkill, and he could never deny the fact that Johnson's conclusions about Ossian's authenticity were accurate. The preface to his book, quoted in Finlay Macdonald's *Journey to the Western Isles,* is almost comically ironic. MacNicol admits his reluctance to take on such a figure as Johnson without consulting "learned friends," but then he writes that "the distance of those friends made it difficult to procure their opinion; . . . besides, the Author was not so fond of his work as to be very anxious about its publication." Poor MacNicol. Finally, with unaccountable acumen he even admitted that it had been so long since Johnson's book appeared that his own would likely not be noticed. Contemporary scholars are reexamining MacNicol's book, and a reappraisal of his thoughts may be soon forthcoming.

Not all contemporary Scots disagreed with Johnson's conclusions, however. Thomas Knox, who completed a tour of Scotland years after Johnson returned, wrote that he had read Johnson's book many times but had "not been able to correct him in any matter of consequence." A distinguished Edinburgh educator concluded his review by saying, "It is plain he meant to speak well of Scotland; and he has, in my apprehension, done us great honour." And in 1927, a period when Scotland was more sensitive to criticism than these days, a Highland historian named W. C. Mackenzie concluded an address to the Gaelic Society of Inverness with the words: "Johnson's tour was a landmark in the history of the Hebrides which we would not willingly obliterate." In more recent times critics know Johnson's *Journey* as one of the great books of the eighteenth century, and its continued republication attests to its permanent place in English literature.

Boswell's *Journal of a Tour to the Hebrides* appeared in print for the first time in 1785, the year after Johnson's death. That was not a coincidence; Boswell did not wish it to be published while his dear friend and mentor was living and subject to questioning about Boswell's writings. He had gone to London in the spring of that year to complete the book with the help of his friend Edmond Malone. While there he witnessed several public hangings, drank a lot, got his pockets picked, and enjoyed intercourse with a variety of women including, apparently, a young, married Anglo-Italian miniaturist named Maria Cosway (who would soon have a love entanglement with Thomas Jefferson). And, oh by the way, he did finish writing the book.

It was published on October 1, and the first impression of 1,500 copies was sold out in less than three weeks. A second and third edition were published within the year; people found the book, in the words of one, "compulsively readable." Extracts appeared in newspapers and journals, and the book was received positively by many reviewers.

As noted earlier Sir Alexander Macdonald was one of the first to howl about what he read, annoyed by Boswell's mention of his shabby hospitality toward the travelers on Skye. The semicomic exchange of letters between the two somehow managed to uphold the honor of each. Macdonald was so insulting in his initial letter of complaint that Boswell anticipated a duel, and, desiring neither to shoot someone or be shot himself, he arranged with intermediaries to offer apologies and promise to eradicate some of the offending words from subsequent editions. When Macdonald hesitated to accept, Boswell summoned up the nerve to propose a duel, and Macdonald backed off. It all ended rather confusingly, but with no one injured and everyone's dignity sufficiently propped up.

In *Boswell: The Applause of the Jury, 1782–1785*, the scholars Irma Lustig and Frederick Pottle wrote that critics at the time were puzzled by the book's minutiae, its baffling pages of intimate detail: "Contemporaries of a great innovative work, they recoiled from its revolutionary feature: familiar and ignoble detail controlled by a presiding impression of magnanimity, goodness, and compassion."

Johnson's friends generally approved, though they were surprised by things Boswell recorded Johnson as saying about them. William Windham, a member of the club, believed Boswell had not been "sufficiently warm and hearty" to Johnson. Some shunned Boswell, but Sir Joshua Reynolds was said to be high in praise of the book.

Of course there was shock and laughter from many at Boswell's self-portrayal. Critics found the intrusions of Boswell's views upsetting because, in spite of the explicit title, they saw the book as a biography of Johnson. Nonetheless Boswell's coarseness and occasional behavioral antics generated not-always-good-hearted laughter—Malone had warned him about this and urged him to censor some of the passages—and hardly anyone noticed the travel aspects of the book. But if you accept the theory that as far as book sales go, any publicity is good publicity, Boswell definitely had a hit on his hands.

Eighteenth-century critics didn't write the way modern reviewers do. There are no references to the book as a "page-turner" or "the best book I've read this year"; nor are there statements that tout the author as the equivalent of "the new John Grisham." You have to peruse the reviews a little more carefully to extract the blurbs that modern publishers adore.

Here's one fairly typical note of praise for Boswell that appeared October 6, 1785, in the *Public Advertiser*: "I find in it, as I expected, all the qualities it was recommended to us for." (There's a dazzler of an endorsement that would sell a bunch of books today.) Here's another from October 25, in *St. James's Chronicle*: "It determined me to buy the book, and having read it, I am perfectly satisfied that my money was well bestowed." (A welcome guide for consumers, I suppose; your shillings won't be wasted.) And finally there is this comparatively generous observation that was printed in *Gentlemen's Magazine* in November 1785: "It would be not only uncandid but ungrateful to dwell on a few minute blemishes after the pleasure and profit we have received in the perusal of this work." (May critics be as kind to me.)

The book's success pleased Boswell, but the uproar over it in various places upset him. "I am now amidst narrow-minded prejudiced mortals," he complained as he contemplated revisions for future editions. The revisions improved the book, writes biographer Peter Martin, but they also set off a round of negative commentaries on it. Boswell's character was attacked, he was criticized for his vanity and impertinence, his history was belittled, and one reviewer even claimed that Johnson had told Boswell the book was not fit to be printed.

That was then. Now we may be forgiven for wondering what the fuss was all about. The anecdotes, even at their most revealing, seem decorous by current standards. The vivid prose pictures of moments on the tour are endearing, hardly shocking. The re-creation of a time long gone is magisterially accomplished, and the historical inaccuracies are wisely submerged into footnotes for the scholar's attention. Six years after Boswell's *Journal* appeared, an even greater book—his *Life of Johnson*—came to public light, again thanks to the immeasurably valuable and devoted assistance of Malone. It was warmly received and sold well. An author with a better sense of discretion and editorial insight—and what one writer has called "a less wayward and disconnected mind"—might have dodged some of the inevitable complaints by not passing along so many of Johnson's occasionally unconsidered thoughts on his contemporaries. But Boswell had his unquenchable curiosity about human nature and his "sacred love of truth." And at the bottom line he also had Johnson's consent, recalled in the doctor's words: "Sir, it is of so much more consequence that the truth should be told, than that individuals should not be made uneasy, that it is much better that the law does not restrain writing freely concerning the characters of the dead."

Boswell's last four years were spent as a "famous" man. Most friends, legal colleagues, and even strangers treated him with a newfound respect. Widowed, he enjoyed a sense of personal freedom that unfortunately included drinking, which would exact a toll on his health. He had literary acclaim, but as Martin tells it, he still most desired wealth, position, and social prestige. He moved restlessly from Auchinleck to Edinburgh to London, his public behavior occasionally appallingly embarrassing. His hypochondria worsened, and he quarreled with his daughters. A revised second edition of *The Life* appeared and was an immediate success.

His intellectual life now at a virtual end, Boswell took little pleasure at Auchinleck, where he became less and less involved. Even in London his spirits and both his mental and physical health declined. He was stricken with a fever at a meeting of the club in April 1795, and the pain from progressive kidney failure and uremia forced him to bed. He died there early on the morning of May 19. His death was mourned, and his stature—belatedly—has grown in death.

Afterword—Back to the Twenty-first Century

I hated to leave Boswell and Johnson and Scotland. If their journey to the Highlands and Islands represented the happiest days of their lives, I could with reasonableness claim the same. Immersed in the eighteenth century and alert to signs of its evidence, I could easily have fantasized my way around the country. And in some ways I suppose I did.

I had clocked 2,789 miles on my trip, enough to make the guy at the rental car check-in counter stare disbelievingly at me and ask if I "had driven the car to Iceland and back?" But the Scotland of the twenty-first century I saw and visited in March, April, and May bore little resemblance to that of the eighteenth century, in spite of some marvelously memorable scenes that popped into view along my journey. For all the tangibles—Inveraray Castle, the Abbey on Iona, and James's Court—where the footprints of Boswell and Johnson could be detected, the fact that the calendar had advanced by hundreds of years was unmistakable. For all the historical and personal imaginings about my own journey—the long-empty battlefields, the Bravehearts, the castles—the reality proved a constant corrective to the myths I believed or thought about.

Scotland as Myth is easy to recognize. Braveheart, kilts, tartans, Scottie dogs, Balmoral, Highland games, haggis, shortbread. You can find tokens of that mythical Scotland in shops all over the country, and there's really nothing wrong with that. Kitsch sells. Ask the folks who peddle lederhosen in Bavaria or Civil War bullets in Virginia. Facts and truth don't often have much to do with each other. What stores sell to visitors doesn't reflect the reality of Scotland today, a nation resurgent economically yet still struggling with unemployment, trying to find its place in the world, debating pros and cons of a long-considered goal of independence, with a strong national party advocating solidarity apart from England.

Among the most prominent supporters of Scottish independence has been the Academy Award-winning actor Sir Sean Connery, who said recently that he believes that his native country is "within touching distance" of making a final break with England. Connery was knighted by Queen Elizabeth II in 2000, but that hasn't mellowed him, apparently, since he also referred to the Scots who endorsed the Treaty of 1707 with England as "a parcel of rogues who sold their freedom." Connery has a tattoo on his forearm that reads "Scotland Forever," but he doesn't choose to live in the country. Instead he makes his home in the Bahamas, where the climate will never be confused with that of Scotland, although I know that it rains in the Bahamas, too.

I tried to resist the myths as much as possible. I did, however, buy into my share, literally and figuratively. That started with single malts, for which I offer no apology or explanation. But there were no bagpipes filling my return luggage nor was there a tartan kilt designed to reflect perfectly my own distinctive Highland heritage. Never mind that I don't have any discernible Highland heritage; there's surely a tartan pattern made just for my family, as there is for yours. Really. That's one of the myths promulgated most often in Scotland which few want to talk about because it undergirds a very profitable segment of the tourist industry. The whole business of "authentic" tartans for variously named clans is certainly open to question; a few serious skeptics call it an outright hoax.

There's an entertaining and controversial section in Hugh Trevor-Roper's 2008 book, *The Invention of Scotland: Myth and History*, titled "The Sartorial Myth." That acclaimed scholar took as his theme the history of "innocent ritualisation" in Scotland, "the process whereby the customs and costumes of the Scottish Highlanders, previously despised as barbarians, and at one time formally extinguished were resumed, elaborated and extended."

That process occurred over a period of about one hundred years that began with the Jacobite defeat at Culloden in 1746. Literary sources tell us that before then the idea of a kilt as we know it came into existence in the early years of the eighteenth century and there was not even a modest differentiation of tartan by clans until the same time; the kilt was the garb of the peasantry. After Culloden the Highland costume was banned, the censure was accepted passively, and those who had worn kilts got used to trousers. But toward the end of the eighteenth century the middle and upper classes took to the fashion. They did so because of the growing romantic movement in Scotland which relished the drama of the Jacobite period and the adventure of Ossian's poetry. From this grew the cult of supposedly ancient tribal dress, colorful and heroic. As Scotland eased into the early twentieth century, the revival of kilts and tartans mushroomed, aided and abetted by a pair of exceedingly clever entrepreneurs who fabricated a book connecting all the dots: kilts and tartans go back centuries, each clan has its own distinctive colors and patterns, and it was the stuff of royalty. Those entrepreneurs, according to Trevor-Roper, were the brothers John and Charles Allen, who deserve a special place in Scottish mythology. Little is known of their backgrounds; but in 1822 they suddenly appeared as poets of a glorious Scottish history with Scoticized names: John Hay Allan and Charles Stuart Allan. They acted the role of nobles and dressed in every imaginable Highland costume at least once. With evidence of a good education and the guile of skilled actors, they easily entered Scotland's high society and spent nights in castles as the guests of assorted dukes and the like.

Their antiquarian studies climaxed in 1829 when they disclosed the existence of an ancient document given to their family by none other than Bonnie Prince Charlie. This amazing document proved that not only did the Highland clans have tartan costumes by which each family distinguished itself but all the Lowland clans had them as well. Everybody had a tartan! In 1842 the brothers published the document as the *Vestiarium Scoticum,* complete with color illustrations. Two years later—for what was the high-water mark of tartan preposterousness—their editor joined with them to publish an even more sumptuous book aimed at a broader audience called *The Costume of the Clans,* which still is relied upon as the "bible" of tartanism. It has served as the foundation of the tartan industry.

Maybe, in spite of Trevor-Roper, it's a bit harsh to call the whole matter of tartans bunk, but it does seem reasonable to assume that there are some serious questions about the phenomenon and that it belongs, in some measure at least, to the realm of myth in a country that is rife with myths, from Nessie to Ossian to the image of the thrifty Scotsman. What works ultimately is what most people believe, so wear that tartan proudly.

I'm not trying to write off all the myths. I like most of them, frankly, and for every Braveheart Museum there's a Callanish Standing Stone. On an ironic note it's worth pointing out that while most of Scotland's population resides in the narrow east-west corridor linking Glasgow and Edinburgh, the country gets the largest slice of its identity from the virtually empty Highlands, a part of the country that few Scots visit or know much about. I read in a magazine recently abut a man living on the northwest Scottish mainland who called the National Health Service because he needed to get to a hospital and was told the nearest was only thirty miles away on Lewis. Right—that's thirty miles as the crow flies, entirely over the tempestuous waters of the Minch to the Outer Hebrides, a trip that would take hours in the best of conditions. Clearly someone at the National Health Service has little knowledge of Scottish geography; what might that suggest about others? While a lot of Scots talk about a need for independence from England, you can find islanders who talk about wanting independence from Scotland.

But how can you not appreciate a country that hosts a website bragging that it features "probably Scotland's dullest webcam?" Yes, that's the Neilston webcam, a camera focused on an extraordinarily quiet, unattractive street in the small burg of Neilston a few miles north of Glasgow. The camera's feed is updated several times during the day, giving viewers an opportunity to see whether or not it has started raining. Readers who find this compelling can check for themselves by visiting this url: http://homepage .ntlworld.com/neilstonwebcam/. I wouldn't kid about this.

And how could you not savor a nation whose favorite word is *numpty?* No typo there; it is the favorite word of Scotland's residents, according to a national poll taken in 2007. It's apparently derived from *numps*, an obsolete word for a stupid person (although it can be shaped into an endearment, as in *numpty-poo*). As used these days it also suggests a dose of windbaggery, which explains, I suppose, why it seems to pop up most often when describing members of the Scottish Parliament or in discussions about Prince Charles.

What other country would take one of its most celebrated areas—the gorgeous and popular tourist destination Isle of Skye—and decide to change its name to something unrecognizable to most Scots and everyone else? In 2008 the Highland Council decided to do just that. Never mind that Skye has been acclaimed in words and music for centuries; the council members decided to do away with its Anglicized "slave" name and substitute its Gaelic nickname, Eilean a' Cheo. That's pronounced something like *Eileen achoo,* which, if uttered out loud, would certainly be followed with someone's *gesundheit.* Ah, but it could have been worse: Eilean a' Cheo is a nickname—the full name of Skye would be An t-Eilean Sgitheanach, and I have no clue how that night be pronounced. It means winged isle, a lovely Gaelic name to be sure, but it is one that might turn many cash-totin' tourists back for home quickly.

Apparently others thought so, too. While everyone applauded the idea of preserving Gaelic names, many felt the idea was a radical and unnecessary. Maybe put up signs when people get there, but don't deter them from making the trip by calling the place something they can't even get out of their mouths. So the Highland Council in its collective wisdom rescinded the action and decided to keep calling the island Skye. For now at least.

That decision—or change of heart, perhaps—tells us something about Scotland both good and bad, a country trying to imagine its independence from England at the same time that it tries to cope with the prospect of staying in a dependent relationship with Westminster. It's a nation with a remarkable, distinctive history that isn't quite sure of what to do with itself these days. To lean on all that history—which is undeniably easy; it's been done effectively for hundreds of years—has given us all those silly caricatures and trinkets. That image seems to defy thoughts of Scotland as a serious global partner in anything but bagpipes. Yet presenting Scotland as an economically progressive nation that eschews all those trappings—which few seem to want to disappear entirely—would leave the country culturally impoverished.

Most public polls I've seen indicate that the idea of independence for Scotland from England appeals to a minority of Scots, not a small one, but a minority nonetheless. It's hardly a subject that has been sprung on anyone, however, as the nation's history attests. These days, if you go to Google and search using the term *Scottish independence* you'll come with up 431,000 entries. Use the term *Independent Scotland* and you'll get 844,000 hits. This is not a barren field for discussion. One of the websites promoting independence carries photos at the top of the home page of Robert Burns, Robert the Bruce, and—hold your breath—an American-born Australian named Mel Gibson. I swear I'm not making this stuff up.

Scotland's First Minister Alex Salmond, the leader of the Scottish National Party (SNP), says he sees independence for Scotland coming in the next decade. His party is obviously in the vanguard pushing for that goal. He wants Scotland to be part of an "arc of prosperity" by joining with other nations on the edge of Europe, such as Ireland, Norway, and Iceland. The party appears to have been making progress over the last decade, but its aggressiveness also seems to have angered some and made enemies of others. It has, however, unquestionably touched nationalist roots that run deep. "The sooner we're rid of the bloody bastards [the English], the better," said my companion at the bar in Edinburgh a few weeks earlier. "If we can't run ourselves better, then we should go to the devil, too." The more he talked and the less I said, the angrier he got. "They've milked us dry for centuries, and we won't have them sucking at our teat any more. Fuck 'em. Fuck 'em." I wasn't a participant in a conversation in which the other side was expressed, but I suspect those views are about as outspoken.

There is a lot of territory to be covered before independence arrives, surely. First there's the issue of the North Sea oil. The SNP says 90 percent of that belongs to Scotland and will be the backbone of the new nation's economy. England's lawmakers may charitably be said to feel differently. And then there's the matter of the U.K. national debt, so many billions of dollars; will an independent Scotland still share in that? What happens to English military bases that exist all over Scotland? And can the new Scottish Parliament prove capable of governing the country effectively? Can a small nation—the population is less than six million—with such extremes in culture and economy as exist between the Edinburgh-Glasgow axis and the Highlands and Islands ever be fiscally viable?

Three hundred years after the signing of the Act of Union in 1707, are most people still pissed off enough at England to want to break up? Or, as the Englishman Charles Jennings wondered in *Faintheart*, why does the Scots' "morgue-like grip on their past" demand that they characterize their neighbors always and forever "as predatory, hypocritical, self-obsessed bastards." Get over it, he argued: don't Canada and the United States get along, as do Germany and Denmark, albeit with some occasional misunderstandings and irritation? Well, yes, I suppose, but everywhere I went I found that a strong feeling about England definitely exists. Maybe it's not enough to demand independence, but there's clearly a deep reservoir of hard feelings about the long relationship between Scotland and England and to minimize that tension is to diminish the whole of Scottish history. That history may have given rise to some fanciful notions and myths over the centuries, and the opportunistic may have used them for their own profit. But there is powerful history in this nation. It hasn't been very pretty. It cannot be denied. And it will help to shape whatever is to happen.

Because I'm not a Scot it's not my cause. I just tripped through part of the nation on a short journey and can offer only an outsider's limited perspective. I can't imagine that anyone needs or wants my counsel on this issue. But I'm a passionate outsider; I care about this country and its past and its future. I'm going back to Scotland no matter what. I don't have a drop of Scottish blood in me, as far as I know, but there's surely something coursing in me that connects me to this very special place in a very special way.

Finally, I do take deep satisfaction from a headline that passed my way a year and a half after my journey ended. It had to do with the economic crisis that gripped so many nations in the fall of 2008, including England and Scotland. The effects were felt in many places, including at one institution that had invested so haphazardly, mismanaged its resources and mistreated the public that it had to be included in a near-$75-billion rescue by the government of Great Britain. What was that great institution? Well, do you remember a certain Scottish bank that kept trying to make someone pay a hefty fee to cash a travelers check written in English pounds?

That bank? That was the Royal Bank of Scotland. Those greedy little bastards. I could have told them.

Justice was mine. Finally.

I just love Scotland. Heck, I think I might even like Mel Gibson.

Selected Bibliography

As should be clear to readers, I have not attempted to write a scholarly book, although my hope is that I have produced one that scholars would not find distasteful. In the process of researching and writing the book, I made use of hundreds of materials in two countries. Some were much more useful than others; all helped in one way or another to give me a clearer sense of eighteenth-century Scotland and the lives and travels of James Boswell and Samuel Johnson. I have divided sources into the categories of nonfiction, poetry and fiction; neither section is meant to represent an exhaustive list. The nonfiction books are essential sources. The novels and stories indicated offer many pungent insights into Scotland in the eighteenth century and today. I recommend them highly.

Several books figured prominently in my research, and I want to acknowledge them even as I beg to absorb all blame that accrues from any misunderstanding of the work of their authors. Ronald Black's single-volume edition of Johnson's *Journey to the Western Isles of Scotland* and Boswell's *Journal of a Tour to the Hebrides,* published in 2007, proved indispensable. His editing is exemplary, and his notes, comprehensive and lucid, helped me over many a trouble spot. I urge anyone wanting to read Johnson and Boswell for the first time, or to reacquaint themselves with these wonderful journals, to acquire this book.

Peter Martin's splendid biographies of Boswell and Johnson, both published in the last decade, reflect the most recent scholarship on both men and offer readable, perceptive guides to the complex lives of my two companions. I envy Martin's skill at breathing life into Boswell and Johnson while capturing the remarkable fullness of their lives within single volumes. I warmly endorse both. Moray McLaren's *The Highland Jaunt* (1955) was a delight to read and helped me learn about Scottish landmarks visited by the two men. Frank Delaney's *A Walk to the Western Isles after Boswell and Johnson* (1993) offered contemporary views that were consistently edifying and perceptive. G. B. Hill's nineteenth-century *Footsteps of Dr. Johnson* remains a classic of knowledge about the places Boswell and Johnson visited.

And the legion of books about Boswell and Johnson and their works brilliantly edited and written by Frederick A. Pottle and his colleagues is no less inspiring now than those many books have been since they first appeared in print. Pottle's scholarship is deservedly recognized as a landmark in Boswellian studies, and I and everyone who write about these men owe him a huge debt.

Finally I should mention Charles Jennings's *Faintheart*, not because it provided a wealth of material on Boswell and Johnson but because reading its dark, cynical, laugh-out-loud humor helped me find a balance between the adulatory and the critical in my approach to writing this book. Jennings is an Englishman, and his view of Scotland is decidedly jaundiced; I hope my isn't, but I'm grateful to him regardless.

Nonfiction

Ballindalloch Castle. Derby: Heritage House, 2004.

Bate, W. Jackson. *Samuel Johnson*. Washington, D.C.: Counterpoint, 1998.

Black, Ronald, ed. *To the Hebrides: Samuel Johnson's* Journey to the Western Islands of Scotland *and James Boswell's* Journal of a Tour to the Hebrides. Edinburgh: Birlinn, 2007.

Blackden, Stephenie, and Christopher Hartley. *Brodie Castle*. Edinburgh: National Trust for Scotland, 2007.

Bold, Alan. *Scotland's Kings and Queens*. Norwich: Jarrold Publishing, 2004.

Boswell, James. *An Account of Corsica: The Journal of a Tour to That Island, and Memoirs of Pascal Paoli*. Edited by James T. Boulton and T. O. McLoughlin. New York: Oxford University Press, 2006.

Brady, Frank. *James Boswell: The Later Years, 1769–1795*. New York: McGraw-Hill, 1984.

Bray, Elizabeth. *The Discovery of the Hebrides: Voyages to the Western Isles 1745–1883*. Edinburgh: Birlinn, 1996.

Bryson, Bill. *Notes from a Small Island*. New York: William Morrow, 1996.

Buchanan, David. *The Treasure of Auchinleck: The Story of the Boswell Papers*. New York: McGraw-Hill, 1974.

Campbell, John Lorne. *A Very Civil People: Hebridean Folk, History and Tradition*. Edinburgh: Birlinn, 2004.

Chapman, R. W., ed. *A Tour to the Hebrides: Johnson & Boswell*. 1924. Reprint, London: Oxford University Press, 1957.

Clarje, David, and Patrick Maguire. *Skara Brae*. Edinburgh: Historic Scotland, 2004.

Clingham, Greg, ed. *The Cambridge Companion to Samuel Johnson*. Cambridge: Cambridge University Press, 1997.

Cowan, Edward J., ed. *The Wallace Book*. Edinburgh: John Donald / Birlinn, 2007.

Craik, Roger. *James Boswell 1740–1795: The Scottish Perspective*. Edinburgh: HMSO, 1994.

Cunningham, Alastair. *Dunnottar Castle*. Aberdeen: Gilcomston Press, 1998.

Dargie, Richard. *Scottish Castles & Fortifications*. Thatcham: GW Publishing, 2004.

Delaney, Frank. *A Walk to the Western Isles after Boswell and Johnson*. London: HarperCollins, 1993.

Fawcett, Richard. *Arbroath Abbey*. Edinburgh: Historic Scotland, 2006.

———. *Elgin Cathedral*. Edinburgh: Historic Scotland, 1999.

———. *Stirling Castle*. Edinburgh: Historic Scotland, 2005.

Finlayson, Iain. *The Moth and the Candle: A Life of James Boswell*. London: Constable, 1984.

Fenton, Alexander. *The Arnol Blackhouse: Isle of Lewis*. Edinburgh: Historic Scotland, 2005.

Foster, Sally. *Maeshowe and the Heart of Neolithic Orkney*. Edinburgh: Historic Scotland, 2006.

Fraser, Donald, Ben Notley, and Steve Townsend. *Killiecrankie*. Edinburgh: National Trust for Scotland, 2004.

Fry, Michael. *The Union: England, Scotland and the Treaty of 1707*. Edinburgh: Birlinn, 2006.

Gill, A. A. *This Angry Island: Hunting the English*. New York: Simon & Schuster, 2005.

Gow, Ian. *The Palace of Holyroodhouse*. London: Royal Collection, 2005.

Grove, Doreen. *Doune Castle*. Edinburgh: Historic Scotland, 2003.

Herman, Arthur. *How the Scots Invented the Modern World*. New York: Three Rivers Press, 2001.

Hewison, W. S. *The Great Harbour: Scapa Flow*. Edinburgh: Birlinn, 2005.

Hibbert, Christopher. *The Personal History of Samuel Johnson*. New York: Harper & Row, 1971.

Hill, G. B., ed. *Boswell's Life of Johnson, Together with Boswell's Journey of a Tour to the Hebrides and Johnson's Diary of a Journey Into North Wales*. London: Clarendon, revised and enlarged, L. F. Powell. ed., 6 volumes, 1934–50; reprint, revised, 1979.

Hill, G. B. *Footsteps of Dr. Johnson (Scotland)*. 1890. Facsimile edition, Menston: Scolar Press, [ca. 1980].

Humphreys, Rob, and Donald Reid. *The Rough Guide to Scotland*. 7th ed. New York: Rough Guides, 2006.

Hutchinson, Roger. *All the Sweets of Being: A Life of James Boswell*. Edinburgh: Mainstream, 1995.

———. *Calum's Road*. Edinburgh: Birlinn, 2006

———. *Polly: The True Story behind Whisky Galore*. Edinburgh and London: Mainstream, 1998.

Hyde, Mary. *The Impossible Friendship: Boswell and Mrs. Thrale*. Cambridge: Harvard University Press, 1972.

———, and Gordon Turnbull, eds. *James Boswell's "Book of Company at Auchinleck" 1782–1795*. N.p., 1995.

Innes-Smith, Robert. *Glamis Castle*. Derby: Pilgrim Press, 2000.

Jauncey, James. *Blair Castle*. Derby: Heritage House, 2004

Jennings, Charles. *Faintheart: An Englishman Ventures North of the Border*. London: Abacus, 2002.

Johnson, Alison. *A House by the Shore: Twelve Years in the Hebrides*. London: Gollancz, 1987.

Johnson, Paul, and George Gale. *The Highland Jaunt*. London: Collins, 1973.

Landmark Trust. *Auchinleck House*. Berkshire: Landmark Trust, 2001.

Lewis, D. B. Wyndham. *The Hooded Hawk, or, The Case of Mr. Boswell*. New York: Longmans, Green, 1947.

Lipking, Lawrence. *Samuel Johnson: The Life of an Author*. Cambridge: Harvard University Press, 1998.

Lustig, Irma S. and Frederick A. Pottle, eds. *Boswell: The Applause of the Jury, 1782–1785*. London: Heinemann, 1982.

Lynch, Jack, ed. *Samuel Johnson's Dictionary: Selections from the 1755 Work That Defined the English Language*. New York: Walker, 2003.

Lynch, Michael. *Scotland: A New History*. London: Pimlico, 2007.

———, ed. *Oxford Companion to Scottish History*. New York: Oxford University Press, 2007.

Macdonald, Finlay J. *A Journey to the Western Isles: Johnson's Scottish Journey*. London: Macdonald, 1983.

———. *Crowdie & Cream: Memoirs of a Hebridean Childhood*. London: Futura, 1988.

MacGregor, Alasdair Alpin. *The Western Isles*. London: Hale, 1949.

Maclean, Charles. *Island on the Edge of the World: The Story of St. Kilda*. Edinburgh: Canongate, 2006.

MacLeod, John. *Dunvegan Castle*. Isle of Skye: MacLeod Estate, 2005.

Magnusson, Magnus. *Scotland: The Story of a Nation*. New York: Atlantic Monthly Press, 2000.

———. *Vikings!* New York: Dutton, 1980.

Martin, Martin. *A Description of the Western Islands of Scotland circa 1695 / A Voyage to St. Kilda*. Edinburgh: Birlinn, 1999.

Martin, Peter. *A Life of James Boswell*. New Haven: Yale University Press, 2000.

———. *Samuel Johnson: A Biography*. London: Weidenfeld & Nicolson, 2008.

Massie, Allan. *The Thistle and the Rose*. London: Murray, 2006,

McLaren, Moray. *The Highland Jaunt: A Study of James Boswell and Samuel Johnson upon Their Highland and Hebridean Tour of 1773*. New York: Sloane, 1955.

~~McPhee, John. *The Crofter and the Laird*. New York: Farrar, Straus & Giroux, 1992.~~

Mitchell, Ian. *Isles of the North: A Voyage to the Realms of the Norse*. Edinburgh: Birlinn, 2004.

———. *Isles of the West: A Hebridean Voyage*. Edinburgh: Birlinn, 2004.

Mooney, Harald. *St. Magnus Cathedral Orkney*. Norwich: Jarrold Publishing, 1995.

Motion, Andrew. *Keats*. Chicago: University of Chicago Press, 1999.

Muir, Edwin. *Scottish Journey*. 1935. Reprint, Edinburgh: Mainstream, n.d.

Nicolson, Adam. *Sea Room: An Island Life in the Hebrides*. New York: Harper, 2007.

Nokes, David. *Samuel Johnson: A Life*. New York: Holt, 2009.

Pearson, Hesketh. *Johnson and Boswell: The Story of Their Lives*. New York: Harper, 1958.

———, and Hugh Kingsmill. *Skye High*. Pleasantville: Akadine Press, 2001.

Pennant, Thomas. *A Tour in Scotland and a Voyage to the Hebrides 1772*. Edinburgh: Birlinn, 1998.

Plant, Marjorie. *The Domestic Life of Scotland in the 18th Century*. Edinburgh: University Press, 1952.

Prebble, John. *Culloden*. London: Pimlico, 2002.

Pringle, Denys. *Spynie Palace*. Hawick: Historic Scotland, 2006.

Pottle, Frederick A. *Pride & Negligence: The History of the Boswell Papers*. New York: McGraw-Hill, 1982.

———, and Charles H. Bennett, eds. *Boswell's Journal of a Tour to the Hebrides with Samuel Johnson, LL.D 1773*. New York: McGraw-Hill, 1961.

Redford, Bruce, ed. *The Letters of Samuel Johnson: Volume II, 1773–1776*. Princeton: Princeton University Press, 1992.

Richards, Eric. *The Highland Clearances: People, Landlords and Rural Turmoil*. Edinburgh: Birlinn, 2005.

Ritchie, Anna, and Ian Fisher. *Iona Abbey and Nunnery*. Edinburgh: Historic Scotland, 2004.

Rixson, Denis. *The Hebridean Traveller*. Edinburgh: Birlinn, 2006.

Rogers, Pat. *Johnson and Boswell: The Transit of Caledonia*. New York: Oxford University Press, 1995.

Rogers, Pat, ed. *Johnson and Boswell in Scotland: A Journey to the Hebrides*. New Haven: Yale University Press, 1993.

Rosie, George. *Curious Scotland: Tales from a Hidden History*. New York: Thomas Dunne / St. Martin's, 2006.

Royle, Trevor. *Precipitous City: The Story of Literary Edinburgh*. New York: Taplinger, 1980.

Ruzicki, Gerald M., and Dorothy A. Ruzicki. *In Search of Ancient Scotland: A Guide for the Independent Traveler*. Mead: Aspen Grove, 2004.

Sadler, John. *Culloden*. Stroud: Tempus Publishing, 2006.

Scott, Paul Henderson. *Walter Scott and England*. Edinburgh: Saltire Society, 1994.

Shenker, Israel. *In the Footsteps of Johnson and Boswell: A Modern Day Journey through Scotland*. Boston: Houghton Mifflin, 1982.

Sked, Phil. *Culloden*. Edinburgh: National Trust for Scotland, 2006.

Smout, T. C. *A Century of the Scottish People, 1830–1950*. New Haven: Yale University Press, 1986.

Stevenson, David. *The Hunt for Rob Roy*. Edinburgh: John Donald / Birlinn, 2004.

Strathnaver, Lord. *Dunrobin Castle: Jewel in the Crown of the Highlands*. Derby: Heritage House, 2003.

Stucley, Elizabeth. *A Hebridean Journey with Johnson and Boswell*. London: Christopher Johnson, 1956.

Tabraham, Chris. *Edinburgh Castle*. Edinburgh: Historic Scotland, 2004.

———. *Huntly Castle*. Edinburgh: Historic Scotland, 2005

————. *Urquhart Castle: Loch Ness*. Edinburgh: Historic Scotland, 2005.

Thomson, Oliver. *Crathes Castle and Garden*. Edinburgh: National Trust for Scotland, 2006.

Thomson, William. *A Tour in England and Scotland in 1785*. N.p.: Kessinger Publishing, 2008.

Topham, Edward. *Letters from Edinburgh, 1774–1775*. Edinburgh: James Thin / Mercat Press, 1971.

Trevor-Roper, Hugh. *The Invention of Scotland: Myth and History*. New Haven: Yale University Press, 2008.

Wain, John. *Samuel Johnson: A Biography*. London: Macmillan, 1974.

Williams, Terry. "The Unraveling of a Noble Cloth." *Scottish Life* 13 (Autumn 2008).

Yeadon, David. *Seasons on Harris: A Year in Scotland's Outer Hebrides*. New York: HarperCollins, 2006.

Poetry

Brown, George Mackay. *The Collected Poems of George Mackay Brown*. Edinburgh: Murray, 2006.

Fiction

Beside the Ocean of Time. Edinburgh: Polygon/Birlinn, 2005.

Gibbon, Lewis. *Sunset Song*. Edinburgh: Canongate, 2006.

Gunn, Neil M. *Butchers Broom*. Edinburgh: Polygon/Birlinn, 2006.

————. *The Silver Darlings*. London: Faber & Faber, 1999.

Macintyre, Lorn. *Tobermory Days: Stories from an Island*. Glendaruel: Argyll Publishing, 2003.

Mackenzie, Compton. Reprint, *Whisky Galore*. London: Vintage, 2007.

Maclean, Alistair. *Night Falls on Ardnamurchan*. Edinburgh: Birlinn, 2001.

MacNeil, Kevin. *The Stornoway Way*. London: Penguin, 2006.

Munro, Neil. *Para Handy and Other Stories*. Reprint, Glasgow: Lomond, 1999.

————. *The Daft Days*. Reprint, Colonsay: House of Lochar, 2002.

Smith, Ian Crichton. *Consider the Lilies*. London: Phoenix, 1987.

————. *The Dream*. London: Macmillan, 1990.

Smollett, Tobias. *The Expedition of Humphry Clinker*. Reprint, London: Oxford, 1998.

Index

Macdonald, Allan, 70
Macdonald, Finlay, 87, 196
Macdonald, Flora, 69–70, 71, 73,
    76–77, 99, 123, 158
Macdonald, Sir Alexander, 58–59, 197
MacDonald, Coll, 44
Macdonald Clan, 54, 58, 118
MacFisheries, 89
MacGregor, Alasdair Alpin, 91–92
MacGregor Clan, 57
Mackay, Hugh, 153
Mackenzie, Compton, 92
Mackenzie, Mr. (Stornoway), 86–87
Mackenzie, Osgood, 95
Mackenzie, Sir George, 166–67
Mackenzie, W. C., 196–97
Mackenzies Clan, 85, 86
Mackinnon, Mrs. (Skye), 76–77
Maclean, Sir Allan, 41, 44
Maclean Clan, 41
MacLeod, Calum, 65
MacLeod, John, 62
MacLeod, Lady, 74
MacLeod, Malcolm, 62, 63, 69
MacLeod Clan, 51, 69, 71, 73–74,
    85
MacNicol, Donald, 196
Macpherson, James, 75–76, 195, 196
Macqueen, Donald, 62, 63
Maeshowe, 105–6
Magnus, 108
Malcolm II, king of Scotland, 153
Malcolm IV, king of Scotland, 136
Malone, Edmond, 9, 197, 198, 199
Manchester, 85
Mansfield, lord chief justice of En-
    gland, 143
Margaret, princess of England, 153
Margaret of Denmark, 102
Martin (Durness), 99
Martin, Martin, 10, 78, 81–82, 103
Martin, Peter, 6, 8, 169, 198, 199
Mary, Queen of Scots, 18, 19, 117,
    144–45, 171, 175–77
Matheson, Sir James, 93
Maureen (Auchinleck Estate), 189–90
McGonagall, William, 156

McLaren, Moray, 30, 41, 120, 166,
    178–79
McNabs Inn, 73
Mendelssohn, Felix, 49
Menzies Castle, 153
Menzies Clan, 153
Merkle, 101
Midden, 106
midges, 88–89, 104
Millennium Link Project, 162
Minch, 69, 79–80, 92, 94, 202
Miralles, Enric, 177
Mitchell, Ian, 89, 107
Monboddo, Lord, 148–50, 166–67
Montrose, 146, 148, 150, 165
Montrose, duke of, 57
Monty Python and the Holy Grail, 24,
    53
Moray Firth, 131
Morrison, Allan, 84
Muck, 50–51
Muir, Edwin, 108
Mull, 12, 38–42, 44, 47, 49, 50, 57,
    75, 96, 112
Munro, Donald, 78
Munro, Neil, 29–30
Murray, Lord George, 125
Murray, Peter, 156

National Health Service, 202, 203
National Trust for Scotland, 95, 128,
    136, 142
NATO, 95
Neeson, Liam, 56
Neilston, 203
Nelson, Ricky, 16
Nessie. *See* Loch Ness Monster
New Town, 173–74
New York Times, 98
Nicolson, Adam, 83
Ninian, 144
North Sea, 96, 112, 144, 145
Northlink, 102, 110–11
Norway, 103
Notes from a Small Island (Bryson), 7
"numpty," 203
nunnery, 45, 46

Sadler, John, 124, 126
Saint Andrews Castle, 159
Saint Andrews Cathedral, 159–60, 61
Saint Andrews University, 140–41
Saint Andrews, 12, 139, 156, 159
Saint Columba. *See* Columba
Saint Columbus. *See* Columba
Saint Conan's Kirk, 36
Saint Giles Cathedral, 177
St. James's Chronicles, 198
Saint Magnus Cathedral, 103, 108
Saint Magnus Festival, 103–4
Salmond, Alex, 204
Saracen Inn, 182
Scalpay, 84
Scapa Flow, 109–10
Sconser, 59, 74
"Scotch Symphony," 49
Scotichronicon (Bower), 20
Scotland: culinary practices, 97–98; drinking in, 98–99; education in, 182; emigration from, 67, 77; ferry service in, 38–39, 43–44, 49–50, 53, 80, 81, 102, 110–11; medicinal drinks, 98; nuclear power plant, 100; religion in, 45, 46, 62, 91, 103, 159; Stone Age sites, 103, 105, 106; tourism in, 3, 19, 36; war with England, 11, 18, 19, 20, 21, 32, 57, 65–67, 118, 123, 124–26, 127–28, 144, 152–53, 162, 167, 174–75; weather in, 1–2, 26, 36–37, 38, 80–81, 82, 94–95, 104–5, 112, 132, 142, 147, 150
Scott, Sir Walter, 57, 58, 74, 76, 126, 167, 168
Scott, William, 165
Scottish Journey (Muir), 108
Scottish Life, 87
Scottish National Party (SNP), 204–5
Scottish National Opera, 133
Scottish Parliament, 177, 203, 205
Scottish Reformation, 45, 147, 177
Scrabster, Port of, 101, 102
Sea Room (Nicolson), 83

Seasons on Harris (Yeadon), 83, 87
Shakespeare, William, 129, 130
Shenker, Israel, 33
Shetland Islands, 85, 96, 102, 103
Shiant Islands, 92
shipwrecks, 109
Skaill House, 106
Skara Brae, 106, 107
Skye, 12, 50, 52, 53, 56–60, 67, 68, 69–77, 80, 99, 116, 120, 123, 148, 197, 203–4
Skye Bridge, 57
Slains Castle, 141
Smith, Adam, 166–67
Smith, Ian Crichton, 126
Smollett, Tobias, 3, 167
SNP. *See* Scottish National Party
"Solitary Reaper, The" (Wordsworth), 83–84
Sound of Eriskay, 92
Sound of Harris, 91
Sound of Iona, 43–44
Sound of Mull, 39
Sound of Raasay, 60
Spey Valley, 137
Speyside, 137
Spynie Palace, 135
SS *Politican*, 92
Staffa. *See* Fingal's Cave
Stevenson, Robert Louis, 7, 167, 168, 177
Stewart, Alexander ("Wolf of Badenoc"), 133, 135
Stewart, Charles Edward. *See* "Bonnie Prince Charlie"
Stewart Clan, 53
Stirling, 15–22, 115, 162, 175, 181
Stirling Bridge, 162
Stirling Bridge, battle of, 20
Stirling Castle Rock, 16
Stirling Castle, 15, 17, 18–22, 24, 31
Stoker, Bram, 141
Stone Age, 103, 105, 106
Stonehenge, 85, 106
Stornoway, 79, 80, 84, 85, 86, 90, 93
Stromness, Port of, 104

About the Author

WILLIAM W. STARR has been executive director of the Georgia Center for the Book in Decatur since 2003. A native of Atlanta, he was an editor for United Press International and for thirty years a prize-winning writer and editor for the *Columbia (S.C.) State* newspaper. Starr is the author of *Southern Writers* and *A Guide to South Carolina Beaches,* an associate editor for *The South Carolina Encyclopedia,* and a contributing essayist for many newspapers and journals.

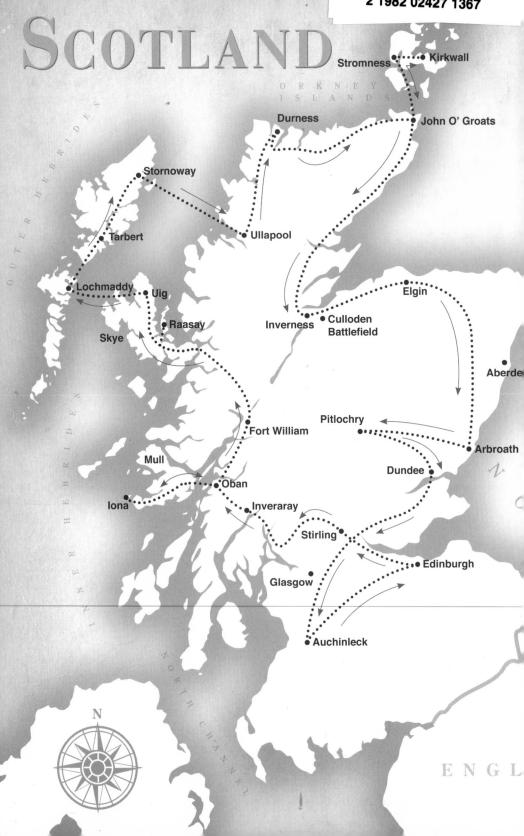

SCOTLAND

Kirkwall
Stromness

ORKNEY
ISLANDS

Durness

John O' Groats

Stornoway

OUTER HEBRIDES

Ullapool

Tarbert

Lochmaddy   Uig

Elgin

Inverness   Culloden
Battlefield

Raasay

Aberde

Skye

Pitlochry

Fort William

Arbroath

Mull

Dundee

Oban

Iona

Inveraray

Stirling

Glasgow

Edinburgh

Auchinleck

N

NORTH CHANNEL

INNER HEBRIDES

ENGL